WEiRD iLLiNOiS

WEiRD
iLLiNOiS

Your Travel Guide to Illinois' Local Legends and Best Kept Secrets

BY TROY TAYLOR

Mark Moran and Mark Sceurman, Executive Editors

STERLING

New York / London
www.sterlingpublishing.com

WEIRD ILLINOIS

STERLING and the distinctive Sterling logo are registered trademarks
of Sterling Publishing Co., Inc.

Library of Congress Catalog-in-Publishing Data Available

10 9 8 7 6 5 4

Published by Sterling Publishing Co., Inc.
387 Park Avenue South, New York, NY 10016

© 2005 Mark Sceurman and Mark Moran

Distributed in Canada by Sterling Publishing
C/o Canadian Manda Group, 165 Dufferin Street,
Toronto, Ontario, Canada M6K 3H6
Distributed in the United Kingdom by GMC Distribution Services,
Castle Place, 166 High Street, Lewes, East Sussex, England BN7 1XU
Distributed in Australia by Capricorn Link (Australia) Pty. Ltd.
P.O. Box 704, Windsor, NSW 2756, Australia

Sterling ISBN 978-0-7607-5943-1

Photography and illustration credits are found on page 254
and constitute an extension of this copyright page.

For information about custom editions, special sales, premium
and corporate purchases, please contact Sterling Special Sales
Department at 800-805-5489 or specialsales@sterlingpublishing.com.

Design: Richard J. Berenson
Berenson Design & Books, LLC, New York, NY

DEDICATION

The writing of this book would not have been
possible without the friendship and faith of
two "cohorts in crime": Mark Moran and Mark
Sceurman, who believed in the project and
believed in me enough to let me write it. They
are two great guys who became more than just
people I looked up to. They actually became
friends as well. In addition, I also have to thank
all of the friends, fellow weird travelers, and
often mysterious correspondents who helped
me along on this quest for the strange places of
Illinois. I don't have enough space here to
name you all but please know that this book
was possible only because of your help,
assistance, and belief. Thanks to Len and Kim,
Nancy, Bill, John, Tom, and Michelle to name
just a few. You're all the best!–*Troy Taylor*

CONTENTS

A Note from the Marks

Our weird journey began a long, long time ago in a far-off land called New Jersey. Once a year or so we'd compile a homespun newsletter called *Weird N.J.* to hand out to our friends. The pamphlet was a collection of odd news clippings, bizarre facts, little-known historical anecdotes, and anomalous encounters from our home state. The newsletter also focused on localized legends that were often whispered around a particular town, but seldom heard beyond the town line.

Weird N.J. soon became a full-fledged magazine, and we began doing our own investigating to see if we could track down any factual basis for all of these seemingly unbelievable stories. Armed with not much more than a camera and notepad, we set off on a mystical journey of discovery. To our amazement, much of what we had initially presumed to be nothing more than urban legend actually turned out to be real, or at least contained a grain of truth that had originally sparked the lore.

After about a dozen years of documenting the bizarre, we were asked to write a book about our adventures, and so *Weird N.J.: Your Travel Guide to New Jersey's Local Legends and Best Kept Secrets* was published in 2003. Soon people from all over the country began writing to us, telling us strange tales from their home states. As it turned out, what we had first perceived to be a very local interest genre was actually just a small part of a much larger and more universal phenomenon. So we decided to write *Weird U.S.*, in which we could document local legends and strange stories from all over the country.

Now, uncovering oddities in a little state like New Jersey is one thing, but unearthing these hidden mysteries in far-off states was a challenging task, to say the least. We decided that we needed to find like-minded fellow travelers in all of these far-flung localities who could fill us in on just what weirdness there was to explore in their own home states. One of the first writers we contacted was Troy Taylor.

When it comes to documenting the bizarre history, chilling tales, and weird sites of Illinois, Troy literally wrote the book—several of them actually. In addition to authoring books on the history and hauntings of the Midwest, Troy, like us, also publishes his own magazine, called *Ghosts of the Prairie*. Needless to say, when we discovered Troy's incredible body of work, we felt that we had found a true kindred spirit. We asked him if he wanted to help us in our quest to document the nation's weirdest tales, and, much to our delight, he jumped right on board. We soon came to realize that the hardest part

about collaborating with Troy on the *Weird U.S.* book was trying to decide which of his great stories we wanted to include. His work was so comprehensive and so well told that selecting just a few was nearly impossible.

In 2004, after *Weird U.S.* hit the bookstores, our publisher asked us where we wanted to go next. We said that we had come to the conclusion that this country had more great tales waiting to be told than could be contained in just one book. We wanted to document it ALL, and to do it in a series of books, each focusing on a particular state.

But where would we begin this state-by-state excursion into the weirdest territory ever explored? That choice was simple — with Troy Taylor telling the tales, breathing life into the legends, and recounting the histories and mysteries of the place we call *Weird Illinois*.

— Mark Moran and Mark Sceurman

Introduction

Greetings and welcome to the pages of strangeness that make up *Weird Illinois*. Talk about a book that happened by accident! As some readers know, I have had a lifelong interest in the history, mystery, and hauntings of Illinois, and I've spent almost two decades looking for our state's weird places and unusual people. But this book would have never come about without the guidance of my friends Mark Moran and Mark Sceurman from *Weird N.J.* As a big fan of their magazine, I started corresponding with them, and that led to an invitation to put together this book.

Mark and Mark must have tapped me because they recognized that I shared their love for the road and for unusual people and places. While this book is meant to be both a chronicle of my journeys and a guide for the reader's own travels, you will find the history of the places as well. As Mark and Mark say, "Where the line between history and legend begins to blur is the tightrope we like to tread."

Some readers are likely to ask why there are rarely directions given to the sites featured here. Although *Weird Illinois* is a travel guide, my goal is not to encourage people to trespass on private property or to go into a situation that might be dangerous. That being said, for sites that are accessible to visitors, you need to get out there and see them before they disappear. By the time you read this, perhaps many of them will have already vanished. I have faith, though, that many new oddities will pop up in the years to come to take their place.

While definitely a chronicle of the weird, *Weird Illinois* is not necessarily about the weirdest things or people in the state. In this book, we are concerned with things that are offbeat and to the left of the center. These are the kinds of things that may leave you chuckling, a little unnerved, or just scratching your head and wondering what it's all about. The idea of the book is to try to capture the best, and sometimes worst, parts of the state. Those things may be an abandoned mental asylum, a quirky roadside rock garden, or even a giant spaceman, but they are all part of things that make Illinois great — and a place that we are all proud to call home.

So come along with us as we take to the highways and back roads and see what our weird state has to offer!

— Troy Taylor

Local Legends and Lore

Spread out across the prairies of Illinois and lurking within the pages of the state's history are many mysterious places and strange tales that would have been forgotten long ago if they had not been told and retold over the years. Whether these stories are really true will probably never be known. But almost every legend, no matter how wild it may seem, has a kernel of truth at its core. And though the tale itself may have changed over time, this kernel remains.

Local legends like the ones that follow are different from the "urban legends" with which we are all familiar. Urban legends are merely myths and make-believe unwittingly deemed true by the people who pass them along. They vow that it really did happen—albeit to a friend of a friend—or claim that it comes from a real news source, never realizing that scores of similar stories are simultaneously being spread across the country. Unlike these urban myths, Illinois' local legends are connected directly to a particular location.

Almost everyone loves mysteries that take us beyond our mundane daily existence. When we come across an eerie, crumbling old house in a desolate area and strange things happen, it's not hard to believe that the place might be haunted. What better way to test your mettle than to journey to a place like this on a dark, fog-shrouded night?

And one stormy night, long ago, *Weird Illinois* did just that. We went with a group of friends to a derelict cemetery said to be so haunted that a true test of courage was just to walk across it and back again. This cemetery had more legends told about it than it had permanent occupants, and on that night, we had firsthand experience with one. As we stood there among the fallen tombstones and broken crypts, the headlights on the car we came in inexplicably went off! When we dared approach the car, we found that somehow, through locked doors, the headlights had been physically turned off. As you can imagine, we left the cemetery as fast as humanly possible.

Because of this strange occurrence—not to mention many others over the years—*Weird Illinois* respects the letters and e-mails we get about our state's spookiest spots. We may have little use for ordinary urban legends, but we always listen when a local legend comes our way. As long as people still wonder about the light that burns in the old abandoned house and quicken their step as they pass the moonlit graveyard, yesterday's legends, like yesterday's ghosts, will never truly die.

Devil Baby of Hull House

Hull House, located at 800 South Halsted Street on Chicago's Near West Side, was legendary in its heyday as the setting for the pioneering work of social reformer and activist Jane Addams. However, it is also legendary for something not quite so morally uplifting: the Devil Baby—said to have inspired the famous 1968 horror flick *Rosemary's Baby.*

Built in 1856 in what was then one of the most fashionable sections of the city, Hull House and the surrounding neighborhood were abandoned by their wealthy inhabitants after the Great Chicago

Fire of 1871. Soon the area began to attract a heavy flow of Italian, Greek, and Jewish immigrants. By the 1880s, factories and overcrowded tenements surrounded Hull House and the neighborhood had become a jungle of crime and vice. Referred to as the "darkest corner of Chicago," the Near West Side was awash in crooked cops and politicians, brothels, saloons, and dope peddlers. Exiled criminals from other parts of the city sought refuge here, attracting even more hoodlums. It was a depressing and dangerous place, and in the midst of it all, the immigrants struggled to carve out a living.

These were the people Jane Addams vowed to help, and Hull House was where she began her lifelong struggle for social equality. Addams, the privileged daughter of a wealthy merchant, graduated from the Rockford Female Seminary in the same year that her father suddenly died. Deeply depressed and unsure of what to do with her life, she was using her inheritance to travel through Europe with her college friend Ellen Gates Starr when she found her calling in the sordid slums of London's Whitechapel area.

It was here that Jane became intrigued by Toynbee Hall, a settlement house for the poor where affluent students lived and worked alongside the poor while pushing for social reform and better standards of living. After Jane returned to Chicago, she and Ellen began making plans for such a place in the city. In 1889, they acquired the run-down Halsted Street mansion and turned it into a settlement house to educate and improve the lot of immigrants. Hull House became a comfortable home and community center that offered food, shelter, education, and protection from the rough streets outside.

Yet despite their hard work, Hull House eventually became better known more for its ghostly inhabitants than its human ones. Long before Jane Addams took over Hull House, the wife of the builder, Charles Hull, had died of

natural causes in a second-floor bedroom of the mansion. Mere months later her ghost began haunting that room. Before Jane Addams moved in, earlier tenants, including the Little Sisters of the Poor and the proprietors of a secondhand-furniture shop, always kept a bucket of water on the stairs at night, believing that the ghost would be unable to pass over it.

After Jane Addams arrived, several years after Mrs. Hull's death, the ghost continued to make her presence known. Addams, who occupied Mrs. Hull's bedroom, was awakened one night by loud footsteps in the room. After a few nights of this, she confided her story to Ellen, who admitted she heard the same sounds from her room. Jane quickly moved to another room.

She was not alone in noticing the unusual occurrences. Other guests were disturbed in their sleep by footsteps and what they described as "strange and unearthly noises." Author Helen Campbell reported seeing a ghostly figure standing next to her bed when she spent a night in the "haunted room." When she lit the gas lamp, the apparition vanished. Louise Bowen, a lifelong friend of Jane's, and Canon Barnett of Toynbee Hall, who visited Hull House in 1893, heard peculiar sounds and saw mysterious figures. To everyone who saw her, however, the ghost of Mrs. Hull seemed a rather sad but harmless visitor, and residents and guests alike learned to live with her presence.

But a second supernatural visitor was not considered quite so innocuous, and Hull House earned its greatest notoriety after it was alleged to be the refuge of the Devil Baby. It was said that a devout Catholic woman gave birth to the Devil Baby after she attempted to display a picture of the Virgin Mary in their house and her atheist husband tore it down. He said that he would rather have the devil himself in the house than that picture. Apparently, he got his wish: His wife gave birth to a child with pointed ears, horns, scale-covered skin, cloven hoofs, and a tail.

Unwilling to raise the child themselves and hoping to spare the deformed creature a lifetime of torment and teasing, the parents begged Addams to take the child in, and she eventually agreed.

It was said that Addams and her staff took the baby to be baptized. During the ceremony, the baby escaped from the priest and began dancing and laughing. Not knowing what to do with the possessed child, Addams reportedly kept it confined to the attic. Rumors spread quickly throughout the Near West Side about this freak of nature, and within a few weeks, hundreds of people had passed by the house to try to catch a glimpse of the Devil Baby. Many came right to the door and demanded to see the child, while others quietly offered to pay admission.

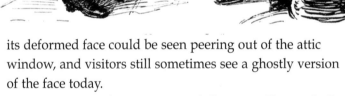

Each day Jane turned people away and tried to convince them that the story was fabricated. Later she even devoted forty pages of her autobiography to debunking the legend. Even though most of the poorly educated immigrant residents left the house still believing in the Devil Baby, the stream of visitors eventually dried up and the story became a curious side note in the history of Hull House.

Even today some people still maintain that the story of the Devil Baby is true—or that it contains at least some elements of truth. Some have speculated that perhaps the baby was actually a badly deformed infant brought to Hull House by a young immigrant woman who could not care for him.

Whatever the truth is, local legend still insists that at some point a disfigured child was hidden away on the upper floors of the house. Some say that on certain nights its deformed face could be seen peering out of the attic window, and visitors still sometimes see a ghostly version of the face today.

In the 1960s, the University of Illinois at Chicago built their campus around Hull House, turned the mansion into a historic site, and opened it to the public. It is still a popular attraction, not only to tourists and those with an interest in its history but also to those with an interest in the Devil Baby. Its force frequently triggers the motion sensors of the alarm system, but whenever campus police respond, they find the house empty, and there is never any sign of a break-in or disturbance. Who or what still lurks in Hull House? The ghosts of the many desperate people that Jane Addams tried so passionately to save in her day? The sad ghost of Mrs. Hull? Or is it the Devil Baby, that horned and scaly creature that some people believe has never really left the attic?

Grave of the Chesterville Witch

Chesterville is a small town that no longer appears on maps of the state. The tiny burg still exists, however, and is located just west of Arcola, in the heart of Illinois' Amish country. Most of its remaining residents belong to the Amish or Mennonite faiths, which shun the use of electricity and modern conveniences.

Just outside the village and across an ancient one-lane bridge is the small, secluded Chesterville Cemetery, where the curious will find the Witch's Grave. It reportedly belongs to a young Chesterville woman, whose name no one recalls, who was regarded as a witch in the community and whose ghost is rumored to appear near the grave.

Apparently, she was very liberal minded and liked to challenge the Amish faith, speaking out against the treatment of women in the area; as a result, she was branded a witch. She continued to disobey the elders of the church, and eventually they banished her. As few ever questioned decisions made by church elders, rumors quickly spread through the community that she had indeed practiced witchcraft and was a servant of the devil.

She disappeared soon afterward, and a short time later her body was discovered in a farmer's field. Regardless of what may have happened, the authorities ruled that her death was from natural causes. Her remains were taken to the local funeral home, and people from all over the countryside came to view the "witch's" body.

Eventually she was buried in the Chesterville Cemetery and a tree was planted on her grave to trap her spirit there. That tree still stands, and many believe that if it ever dies or is cut down, the witch's spirit will escape and take her revenge on the town. A fence was later placed around the gravesite to keep people away.

The witch has allegedly appeared to passersby and visitors to the cemetery, although because of the tree she is confined to the area around her grave. As the sightings increase, some people are beginning to believe that the story of the Chesterville Witch may not be just a folktale after all.

Run-in with the Chesterville Witch

When I was growing up in Chesterville, I used to run on the school track team. One day when I was out for a run, I went past the cemetery as I usually did and went on down the road. On the trip back, something different happened: The weather seemed to turn cold, and this occurred about the same time that I saw someone looking at me from inside the cemetery. They were standing next to the grave of the witch. I really thought it was just someone playing around in there, and I yelled that the cemetery was closed. The lady I saw standing in the cemetery laughed and then disappeared! Boy, I almost wet my pants. She looked so real. I ran the quickest hundred-yard dash that I ever ran back to the house! I never ran that course again. –*Ed H.*

Seven Gates to Hell

Located along the lonely back roads east of Collinsville are a series of daunting bridges and tunnels that for many years have been called the Seven Gates to Hell. There doesn't seem to be any agreement as to how these passageways received their ominous name, but legends abound. According to one source, the bridges, many of which are actually railroad trestles that provide passage beneath them for automobiles, were once commonly used by local Ku Klux Klan members as spots for lynching African Americans. Needless to say, no records of such events exist, but this is one of the reasons the bridges and trestles are said to have acquired their evil reputation over the years.

The most popular legend is that if you drive through all the gates, you will suddenly find yourself swept into the depths of hell. Variations on this theme state that you have to drive through the last gate at the exact stroke of midnight to make it to hell or that if you park your car under the seventh gate and turn out your lights, the spirits will send the "hounds of hell" to carry away your soul.

One of the bridges, dubbed Acid Bridge in recent times, has acquired a distinct reputation of its own. It is said that in the 1980s, some local students were out drinking and driving around on the back roads one night, and they apparently dropped some LSD, or acid. They went to look for the Seven Gates to Hell and managed to track down six of them, but could not find the last. They continued to drive around until they came upon what they thought was the final one. They were driving very fast when they missed the entrance and crashed into the concrete support walls. The automobile was burned up, and all of the occupants were killed. The accident was not discovered for several hours, when passersby noticed the flames. Today some claim to see a ghostly reenactment of the accident on the road near the bridge.

When this legend first came to the attention of *Weird Illinois,* we became curious about it, although we have to confess that we were mostly curious about why anyone would want to find the gateway to hell. Nevertheless, we began trying to track down the location of the seven bridges and railroad trestles. According to everyone we talked to, the gates were located in the countryside between Collinsville and O'Fallon, and most were scattered across the hills and ravines of Lebanon Road. Driving east from downtown Collinsville, we turned onto Lebanon Road and went in search of hell. But the big question in the car that night was, What do we do if we find all seven gates?

As you can surmise by the fact that this book has been written, we did not get sucked into the pit of hell from the back roads of Illinois that night. In fact, we have not yet been able to find all the bridges in question. As we drove along, we found five of the seven, which means that at least two are still out there waiting for us to discover them. The question now is, Do we dare look?

Ghost Riders at the Acid Bridge Gate to Hell

There is one bridge that always terrified me more than any other. It is called Acid Bridge. These kids were supposed to have been high on acid one night and crashed their car into the bridge. I drove out there once with two friends. We pulled up to the bridge and stopped before we got there. We were looking at all of the stuff painted there and saw lights coming toward us in the distance. So we pulled over until they passed us from the other direction. We turned around and were about thirty feet behind them. We saw them slow down when they made it to the bridge, and then they just disappeared. We were so freaked out that we just kept going. We figured it was those kids reliving the night they died over and over again.

—Dennis S.

The Albino Railroad Tracks

Some of the most popular legends that *Weird Illinois* has run across in our years of searching for ghosts, hauntings, and strange happenings involve bridges and railroad tracks where phantoms are said to assist the cars that cross over them. Several years ago we investigated such a place near Monmouth with a group of students from Knox College in Galesburg. They had heard about a bridge where a group of teenagers had been killed in an accident many years ago and had also heard, from those who had experienced it, that if you parked your car on the bridge and placed it in neutral, the ghosts of the teenagers would push you across.

Excited at the prospect, the students took us out to the bridge on a snowy winter night. We traveled downhill on a long, curving road to reach the beginning of the bridge, parked the car, put it into neutral, and waited for the spirits to do their work.

A few moments later the car suddenly began to move!

We steered the car as it crossed the bridge and then went down a short slope to the roadway again. We were excited about what had happened, and we ran back to take another look at the bridge. It certainly appeared to be level, and we couldn't see any reason why the car would have rolled on its own from a complete stop. We got out a carpenter's level to check whether it was angled at all. We soon learned that it was and that the angle would certainly account for the movement of the car. What seemed like a great story had now been debunked.

Ever since then we have been on the lookout for other bridges and railroad tracks that seem to defy gravity. One by one, we have learned that stories that seemed too good to be true . . . were. But then we learned about the Albino Railroad Tracks.

As with all of the bridges and tracks we had investigated, the story behind these tracks involved horrific deaths and gentle spirits helping passing motorists make it to the other side. But the tale of the Albino Railroad Tracks was a little bit more original than most of the others.

According to the legend, the tracks were the scene of a terrible accident in the late 1800s. There are several variations on what actually occurred. In one story, several children from a nearby farm decided to take the family's horse and wagon out for a drive without their parents' permission. They were crossing the railroad tracks when the wagon got stuck on the rails. A train was approaching, and the children, who ranged from five to thirteen years old, were unable to escape in time and were all killed. There is a cemetery a few miles down the road, near the family's former farm, which contains only the graves of the children who died in the accident.

Another version of the story explains how the railroad crossing came to be dubbed the Albino Tracks. In this legend, also set in the late 1800s, albino twins were born to a local farm family near a little railroad-crossing town called Rentchler Station. The birth sparked a lot of gossip in the area. When the twins were a few years old, an epidemic broke out in the community and a number of people died. Some of the more superstitious residents came to believe that the albinos were to blame for the sickness. The children were kidnapped and tied to the railroad tracks so that a train could run them over and free the community from its afflictions. The albinos were killed, and ever since then, they have haunted the railroad crossing.

It has never been clear whether they are trying to help or hinder the cars that cross the tracks. Some believe they are assisting people so that they won't get hit by a train, but others insist that they are looking for revenge—hoping to push cars into the path of an oncoming locomotive.

No matter what the intention, the common thread in all versions of the story is that spirits lurk around the tracks, pushing cars from one side to the other. Some witnesses have claimed to hear the sound of gravel crunching under invisible feet and to see small handprints appear in the dust on the back of the car. It's said that the children make these marks as they push the cars over the tracks. And there is no downhill slope here as there is near Monmouth. Cars here are inexplicably pushed uphill to get to the other side of the crossing! *Weird Illinois* was determined to check out this phenomenon.

The Albino Tracks are located off Rentchler Road between Belleville and Mascoutah. This rural area of farm roads, fields, and woods appears fairly isolated to the casual visitor. We spent quite a bit of time getting directions to the site, but we finally got them from the locals. We were told that the railroad tracks that once crossed the roadway are now gone. They had belonged to the Louisville & Southern Railroad, but were taken out years ago. We were assured that this does not stop the mysterious occurrence from taking place.

We drove through the countryside until we reached Rentchler Road, then turned past a house on the site of the tiny town's former hotel. We traveled west for a short distance, past an abandoned tavern, and then, on the far side of the hill that once held the railroad tracks, we spotted the weather-beaten DEAD END sign we were told to look for. This was where the albinos were said to push cars along the roadway. Following the directions we were given, we drove over the hill where the tracks used to be, turned our truck around, and faced back toward the tracks. We pushed the gearshift into neutral and waited for the mysterious to occur. The truck paused for a few moments, and then . . .

We'll leave what happened next for you to discover on your own. We have come to discover that the "truth" in tales like this can sometimes be as elusive as the mystery spots themselves. If we write about what did or

didn't happen during our visit to the Albino Tracks, this might dissuade readers from discovering this unusual spot on their own. Ghostly hands and spectral albinos or not, the old tracks are a part of the deep-seated weirdness in Illinois that we would hate for anyone to miss.

Didn't Believe It Until He Saw It for Himself

I myself did not believe in the haunted railroad tracks until I saw it with my own eyes. You drive out there at night and pull to the side of the road a few feet from where the tracks were, put your car in neutral, then turn it off and take the key out of the ignition. Your car then gets pushed backward, and you hear people talking and walking on the gravel. If you put baby powder on your car, you'll see small handprints on it when it gets pushed away.–*Terry D.*

The Sounds of Children's Laughter

I went to high school in Mascoutah, and my friends and I went to check out the tracks one night for ourselves. We drove out there and did exactly what we had been told. And it did happen! The car was in neutral, but it rolled over the tracks. We freaked out! I put the car into drive and took off! I drove farther down the road and came across what looked like an old schoolhouse. There was a story about this school that all of the kids here were killed in an accident. I don't know if it was true. I just figured that it was a tall tale to keep kids from wandering there, because it's heavily wooded, no houses really, just old narrow roads and cornfields. We turned back because we didn't want to get lost and stopped again at the schoolhouse. Just for laughs, I turned the car off, and we sat there in the dark for a little while. All of a sudden we heard laughing, like from a lot of kids, and something banging on the car like it was being hit with fists. Of course, we panicked, and I couldn't get the car started right away. Finally I did, and we took off! I was seventeen and haven't been back there since. We didn't find any handprints on the car, but we couldn't deny the sounds we heard that night when we went out to the old railroad tracks. We just weren't prepared for what else we would find.–*Jesse T.*

Axeman's Bridge

Just off Old Post Road in the south Chicago suburb of Crete you'll find the remains of an old rusted steel bridge that spans a trickle of river below. According to legend, a family lived in a house near the old bridge back in the late 1960s. The owner lived there with his wife, mother-in-law, and his children—a son and a daughter. This was not a peaceful home, and the police were often called to break up fights. One night the anger and violence reached a boiling point.

The story goes that the man took his mother-in-law and daughter to the old steel bridge and slaughtered them with an axe. Later that night he killed the rest of his family and left their bloody corpses scattered about on the lawn. He then set their house on fire, and the police surmised that he perished in the flames—although his body was never found.

From that night on, strange things began to occur near the bridge. Some have reported that at certain times the sounds of a man and a woman arguing can be heard in the darkness, followed by a woman's agonizing screams. At the site of the house, where only the blackened stone foundation remains, many have heard weeping and moaning. Others have reported seeing people running through the woods and hearing the clang of the killer's axe on the metal railings of the bridge. On some occasions, passersby have claimed to see lights of a house glowing through the woods, only to discover later that there is no house there.

These days the bridge has fallen into terrible disrepair and is no longer safe to cross. This doesn't seem to keep visitors away, though, and many still go in search of the murderous Axeman, whose ghost is said to lurk eternally near the structure.

Axeman Possessed Our Car!

If you park your car on the bridge, the car will usually stall or have some sort of weird problems. A friend and I were out there last year, and we parked off to the side of the bridge. The whole way home the doors kept locking and unlocking and the windows kept going up and down by themselves.

—*Jennifer W.*

The Demon Butcher of Palos Park

In Palos Park, across Southwest Highway from the Children's Farm, a small cemetery is nestled alongside the railroad tracks. One stone here, engraved with the name Butcher, has an eerie story of greed, murder, and cannibalism connected to it.

In the 1890s, a prosperous butcher owned a shop in Palos Park. His name was Butcher, as his family had been in the meat business since the time when people took their last names from their professions. A major depression struck America, and livestock was in short supply in the region, which put many other butchers and stockyards out of business. But thanks to good connections, this butcher was able to retain most of his customers, even though he was often forced to raise his prices as the meat supply became more and more scarce.

One day a large shipment of beef arrived, and Butcher and his apprentice began unloading the wagon. Because the butcher was getting older and had a bad back, the young man who worked for him usually carried the meat down to the basement meat locker. On this day, the apprentice tried to take a load that was too heavy, and he stumbled on the stairs and fell. He broke his neck on the bottom step and died instantly.

Butcher panicked. He knew that he should call the authorities but was worried that the scene looked suspicious, as though the boy had been pushed. Rather than tell anyone, he pulled the young man's body into the freezer with the butchered meat and hid it behind several packages and crates.

Days passed before anyone came looking for the young man. Butcher told the apprentice's family that he had no idea what had become of him. The last time he had seen the boy, the butcher said, was several days earlier, when he left work for the day. But the boy's father remained suspicious and went to the police. Two

detectives came by to question the butcher, and although they went away, the butcher grew even more nervous. Finally, as livestock became even scarcer, Butcher came up with his clever, albeit gruesome, idea.

Late one night he returned to his shop, and by the light of a covered lantern, he butchered part of the boy's body and packaged it up to sell as beef. Customers snapped up the packets the next day, and Butcher waited restlessly to see if anyone would complain. To his surprise, the customers loved the meat. They demanded more of it, so the butcher cut up the rest of the body and packaged it too. The body was soon gone, and he needed more. He feared that if he couldn't produce it, the people would ask what kind of meat it was and where they could get it themselves.

Here the legend takes an even more horrific turn. As the story goes, Butcher began prowling the streets at night, vanishing into his shop with hoboes from the railroad and bums that he was sure would not be missed. He lured them in with offers of free food, and then he slaughtered them and sold their flesh as beef. His customers were thrilled by the arrival of more of the delicious fare, but soon the hoboes were gone and Butcher again faced the dilemma of what to do for stock. At this point, he allowed his greed to get the better of him and he made his fatal mistake.

When the first of the local children vanished, townspeople were worried but never suspected that a killer was in their midst. After a few more disappeared, however, they began to wonder about what had really become of the butcher's young apprentice, who had also vanished without explanation. A mob of the local men, with weapons in hand, marched down the street to Butcher's shop. They broke the door open and began searching the place, ending up at the basement meat locker. They were stunned to find packaged body parts strewn about and the remains of a child hanging from a hook on the ceiling.

Outraged, the mob charged up the street to Butcher's house and pulled him out into the yard. The crowd screamed for justice and revenge. Their axes, hammers, and knives rose and fell, spraying

blood across the front of the house. The killer's head was severed from his body and was eventually buried under the fire pit on Indian Hill, on the present-day property of Children's Farm. His body was buried in the cemetery across the street, and his gravestone was marked with his last name, Butcher. This stone, which had no other inscription and offered no details, served as the only reminder of the grisly events that had taken place.

To this day, Butcher reportedly does not rest in peace. For years after his murder, local residents claimed to hear the sound of his meat cleaver cracking against his gravestone in the darkness. Is this really the ghostly sound of the butcher claiming his victims, or is this just the manifestation of the guilt of the community for taking the law into their own hands?

Butcher's Body Is Trying to Get a Head

The story is that the people who killed him cut off the butcher's head and buried him in two places because they were afraid that he would come back if they didn't. The problem is that the butcher's body keeps getting closer to his head. The grave has been moved from the far side of the cemetery, next to a pond, to just next to the street. My parents told me that the body has been moved four times because the coffin will not stay underground. It's supposedly because of underground water from the pond, but who knows?—*Ashley M.*

The Gate

If you are in the mood for a harrowing
experience some summer evening, take a trip out to
the Gate, a massive stone structure that is one of the most
bone-chilling locations on the north side of Chicago. Located near
Libertyville, the Gate can be found off the desolate and secluded River
Road, which borders the Independence Grove Forest Preserve.

Even the trip to the Gate can be unnerving. Those seeking the spot must travel
about two miles down River Road, with the dense trees of the forest preserve pressing
close on either side. There are no streetlights here, so only your headlights illuminate the path

ahead. On humid summer nights, fog rolls in from nearby ponds and obscures the lowest sections of the long and narrow River Road. Suddenly the road makes an abrupt turn, wends further into the darkness, and then offers up a menacing view of what locals refer to as simply the Gate.

According to legend, the Gate marked the entrance to a girl's finishing school back in the early 1950s. It was a peaceful and refined place where young women from wealthy Chicago families went to receive a proper education. The stillness of the school was shattered one night when the principal suffered a nervous breakdown and killed four of his young students, placing their heads on the metal posts of the Gate after he severed them from their bodies.

But this is just one version of the legend. In other versions, the Gate did not mark the entrance to a school, but to a summer camp or an asylum, and the killer is not always the person who was in charge. In some variations, he was a camp counselor or a madman who escaped from an asylum, found the summer camp, and slaughtered four children while they slept in their beds. Many who think that an asylum once stood here believe that the killer was a ward attendant who went insane and murdered four of his charges. All versions of this horrific tale of violence, bloodshed, and murder end with local residents and officials razing the school, camp, or asylum and trying to obliterate the remnants of the buildings.

To this day, it is said that the Gate is haunted by the souls of those who perished there. But few agree on exactly what kinds of ghostly happenings take place at the decaying structure. There are those who claim to have visited the Gate during the early hours of the morning and found blood dripping from the iron supports. Others say that at the stroke of midnight on the anniversary of the murders, phantom heads of the murdered girls appear on the fence posts, their mouths gaping in silent screams. There are also countless tales of apparitions, eerie screams, and mysterious sounds that cannot be explained.

If any murders took place here, they have been erased from public record, and when officials are asked about it today, they deny that anything ever occurred.

Many who believe that nothing actually happened at the Gate argue that if any brutal murders took place there, it would have been impossible to cover them up or forget about them. However, the saga of three chilling murders

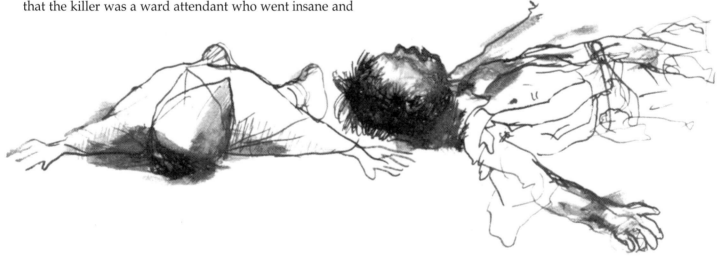

in more recent Libertyville history, all of which have already been glossed over and nearly forgotten, takes the wind out of this argument.

All three murders happened at the Rouse mansion, nicknamed Murder Mansion until it was demolished in 2003. In 1980, wealthy businessman Bruce Rouse and his wife, Darlene, were brutally murdered in their beds—shot at close range in the face, bludgeoned in the head, and then repeatedly stabbed in the chest. The grisly case went unsolved until 1996, when their son, Billy, a teenager at the time of the murders, finally confessed to killing them for their insurance.

A third murder took place at the Rouse mansion in 1982. This violent killing shed light on the history of organized crime in the Libertyville area, which since the 1920s had been a magnet for Chicago gangsters. At the time of the murder, prostitution and illegal gambling—abetted by the corrupt sheriff's department—were still rampant. The Rouse mansion had become the location of much of the vice, with the police camped out there ostensibly to keep watch over it during the murder investigation. Instead, they had turned Murder Mansion into a den of vice. The malfeasance came to an end only with the murder of Bobby Plumber, a bookmaker turned revenue collector for the mob. Mobsters beat Plumber to death in the house, and his body later turned up in the trunk of his car, parked at a nearby Holiday Inn. After his murder was solved, locals ousted the corrupt officials and the violence abated.

In spite of this murderous history, Libertyville has shown remarkable resilience and has gracefully weathered the killings. In fact, these days it is nearly impossible to find any information about the three murders or the corrupt law-enforcement officials. This begs the question: If Libertyville has successfully blocked the public from information about these more recent murders, could it also

be covering up the truth about vicious murders that occurred at the Gate more than a half century ago?

Weird Illinois did manage to turn up a little sketchy information that verifies some elements of the legend. The Gate was once a part of an orphanage, the Katherine Dodridge Kreigh Budd Memorial Home for Children, which opened in 1925. It was shut down for unspecified reasons in the late 1950s and became St. Francis Boys' Camp. The camp ceased operation without explanation and faded into oblivion some time ago.

Some surmise that whatever caused the orphanage to shut down may have been what spawned the blood-soaked legends of the Gate. Perhaps. What we do know, however, is that the Gate will continue to entice nighttime thrill-seekers for many years to come.

Tempting Fate at the Gate

The Gate up in the Gurnee area is one of the spookiest places that I have ever been to. A friend of mine was taking me around to places that were haunted, and we drove out there one night. It's in the middle of nowhere, out in the woods. They say that it used to belong to a school and one of the teachers went crazy and cut off some of the students' heads and stuck them on the Gate. I don't know if this is true, but I was so scared that I made my friend leave as soon as we got there.–*Jamie C.*

Escaped Inmate Haunts the Gate

Up in Lake County is this place called the Gate, and it used to be at the driveway back to this mental hospital. One of the inmates went crazy and killed some of the guards and then escaped. Well, he cut off their heads and hung them on the Gate for the cops to see when they got there. They were so scared that they never even chased the guy. Anyway, me and some buddies went out there one night, and just as we drove up, I swear that we saw somebody looking out from behind the Gate at us. When we stopped and put the headlights on him, there was nobody there. Man, we left fast!–*Todd R.*

Supposedly on certain nights of the year, a chair would rise from the ground in a graveyard. Anyone who sat down in it could make a pact with the devil and receive his or her heart's desire for the next seven years.

Sit a Spell in the Devil's Chairs

As I was growing up in Illinois, I was fascinated by the strange tales of the Devil's Chairs—stone seats found in graveyards across the state.

The story of the Devil's Chairs began in the Appalachian Mountains in the mid-1800s. Supposedly, on certain nights of the year, a chair would rise from the ground in a graveyard. Anyone who sat down in it could make a pact with the devil and receive his or her heart's desire for the next seven years. At the end of that time, the devil would return and take the hapless victim's soul.

The legend has been modified over the years, taking on a simpler yet dire mythology. The stories now state that if you sit down in one of these chairs, you are sure to die within the next year.

What are these eerie graveyard chairs? Most of them are simply what were called "mourning chairs" during the Victorian era. They were usually placed in cemeteries next to the grave of the recently deceased by a relative, creating a more comfortable place to sit when visiting the grave site.

The chairs are usually of plain design, but a few were elaborate—almost thronelike in appearance—and may have been what inspired the legend of the Devil's Chairs. Many of the throne-type chairs have been destroyed in recent years, supposedly by the grieving parents or friends of a luckless teenager who sat in a chair and then was killed a short time later, usually in an auto accident.

In one Illinois cemetery, a Devil's Chair stirred up such a fuss with local teenagers that they made nightly treks to the graveyard to get a look at it. A story made the rounds that a teen had sat in the chair one Halloween night and not long thereafter he died in a car accident. After that, more and more teenagers began sneaking into the cemetery at night to see the chair in question. Finally, with the family's permission, the superintendent of the cemetery removed the chair from the grounds and placed it in storage. It now sits in a dusty warehouse somewhere, its legend fading with time.

While most stories about Devil's Chairs are unsubstantiated, I do have a friend with real, and tragic, experience with one. The chair in question is in Peck Cemetery, a remote graveyard in a secluded section of central Illinois. My friend was present when his cousin sat down in the chair, laughing that nothing was going to happen to him. Less than a year later, my friend was in a car with his cousin when the car crashed. His cousin, who was not wearing a seat belt, was thrown through the windshield and killed.

Was this merely a coincidence that had nothing to do with the Devil's Chair? Perhaps, but his family did not believe so. Soon after the funeral, his father drove out to the cemetery and smashed the chair with a sledgehammer. That much of the story I know to be true, since I still have a piece of that chair to prove it.

As for the legend of the Devil's Chair in general, I'll let you decide the veracity of that for yourself. Just remember, though, the story had to get started for some reason; so if you run across an old stone chair in an Illinois cemetery some day, you may want to think twice before taking a load off your feet.

Ancient Mysteries

Who would have tied the history of Illinois to the French? Well, tie we must, because the first recorded history of the state began in 1673 with the arrival of French explorers. Those overseas visitors soon discovered strange mounds, altars, burial sites, and the ruins of many towns and villages, all attesting to the fact that an advanced ancient civilization once existed here. The dwellers have since been dubbed the Mound Builders, thanks to the monuments they left behind.

A few centuries after the French discovery, road builders found twenty-seven skeletons of the primitive people who once roamed the land in search of food and shelter. The bones are over eleven thousand years old and were found near Modoc, in Randolph County. Beneath an overhanging cliff here, early man found refuge from the elements and left behind remnants of their lives in the form of tools, weapons, and utensils. The site was later inhabited by tribes of Native Americans.

As time passed, more and more wanderers came to the region. Hunters, gatherers, and fishermen found Illinois to be a hospitable place. They traveled to distant places to trade for weapons, tools, and decorations; flint from Kentucky, Tennessee, and Indiana was used to make arrowheads and knives, and slate from Lake Huron was used to make ornaments.

Eventually, a rather advanced civilization, called the Hopewell culture, evolved; it received its name from a site discovered on the farm of Captain M. C. Hopewell in Ohio, where archaeologists unearthed objects such as mica, copper, axes, and volcanic glass. The first evidence that this culture existed in Illinois was found in Fulton County in 1926. On a local farm, a log tomb was discovered that contained a skeleton and a number of Hopewell-era artifacts, offering a picture of people who traded up and down the river, farming and producing works of art around the time of the fall of the Roman Empire.

The Hopewell culture buried their nobles and ruling class in elaborate tombs with adornments and possessions. The artifacts found include sharks' teeth and shells from the Gulf of Mexico, mica used for mirrors from Georgia and the Carolinas, copper from northern Michigan, and volcanic glass from Wyoming.

The Hopewell culture faded after a few centuries, most likely swallowed up by a newer and highly mysterious civilization—the Mound Builders. Forming a community perhaps as large as 100,000 inhabitants, the Mound Builders lived along the Mississippi River at a site that has been named Cahokia, after a tribe of Illiniwek Indians, who lived in the area when the French arrived. This society vanished at the end of the Middle Ages—where they went and why they left remain among the great mysteries of Illinois. And, not surprisingly, it's not the only one.

Illinois boasts a number of mystery sites for which no explanation exists. For instance, who built the mysterious stone forts in southern Illinois, and what were they used for? Some think their design was influenced by visitors who came from as far away as Egypt. Ridiculous, right? Maybe not. Consider the fact that in 1891, a Morrisonville woman was digging in her garden and, sixteen inches below the surface, unearthed an ancient Roman coin. Where did it come from? How did it get there? There's no logical explanation. It's just one of Illinois' many ancient mysteries.

Cryptic Cahokia Mounds

At Cahokia, near present-day Collinsville, are the remains of Illinois' most ancient city. The site boasts a number of mounds but one main centerpiece. It is sometimes called Monk's Mound, after Trappist monks who farmed the terraces of the structure in the early 1800s. It is a stepped pyramid that covers about sixteen acres. At the summit of the mound are the buried remains of some sort of temple, further adding to the mystery of the site. Pottery, carved pipes, stone trinkets, effigies of birds and serpents made from copper and mica, and vast numbers of human bones have been unearthed from the mounds.

Centuries ago there were more than 120 mounds at the Cahokia site, though the locations of only 106 have been recorded. Many of them have been destroyed or altered because of modern farming and construction, but 68 have been preserved inside state historic area boundaries.

It is generally believed that as many as 100,000 people may have once occupied Cahokia. They were a farming culture that lived close to the land. Their city consisted of well-made houses, with dirt floors and walls and roofs that were plastered with a mixture of dry grass and clay. They were sun and fire worshippers, and the advanced state of their civilization was evidenced in the early 1960s when Dr. Warren Wittry revealed numerous large oval-shaped pits, which seemed to be arranged in arcs of circles. Wittry believed the complex arrangement served as a calendar, which he dubbed Woodhenge. Solstices and equinoxes could have been predicted using Woodhenge, and there are indications that eclipses could have been predicted as well. Some of the alignments also suggest that the moon and certain stars were of significance to the culture.

So who built the mounds? It's easy to agree with Thomas Jefferson, who conducted one of the first systematic excavations at the site. He wrote in 1785 that he believed they were mass graves constructed by American Indians.

Other colonists maintained that the mounds were built by either European visitors or by some mystical cataclysmic civilization (like Atlantis) that left the mounds in its wake. Benjamin Franklin thought Hernando de Soto and his men might have built them during their wanderings in North America in the 1500s. A persistent belief in the nineteenth century was that the Mound Builders had been members of the lost tribes of Israel.

The desire for the Mound Builders to have been part of some exotic group came about for a couple of different reasons. One was that evidence of an ancient lost civilization in the Midwest would show that the United States had a deep and honorable heritage and that it was not just some upstart band of revolutionaries.

The other reason was a darker one, born of greed and racism. It was based on a lust for land and a hatred for the Native Americans who occupied it. If people were led to believe that the Mound Builders were part of an ancient civilization, founded by whites and then brought down by the "red savages," then the Indians would have no legal right to the land, and they could be run off it.

This myth was debunked in 1894 by Cyrus Thomas and William H. Holmes, who completed an exhaustive study for the Bureau of American Ethnology. They found that several tribes in the southeast, such as the Creek Indians, still built mounds. They also found that de Soto's explorations noted the discovery of mounds, as did many French explorers in the early 1700s. They compared artifacts from the mounds with objects made by Native Americans of the time and found them quite similar.

What happened to the Mound Builders of Cahokia? Perhaps they abandoned the area because of over-crowding or contamination of the local water supply, or there may have been a breakdown of the civilization itself. Around 1500, the Mississippi Valley was seized by a religious movement called the Death Cult, and a new type of grotesque artwork became prevalent, portraying winged beasts, skulls, and weird faces. The rituals practiced during this period of decline are unknown, but scholars have hinted at human sacrifice and cannibalism. Whatever was going on, believers in this theory say it was the death knell for the Mound Builders' society.

Even with this dark history, many people consider the Cahokia site a sacred place. In August 1987, the Monk's Mound was the meeting place of more than a thousand people who took part in a worldwide "harmonic convergence" that was designed to bring peace to the planet. Now there's something to converge for!

The Case of the Mysterious Stone Forts

Scattered throughout the southern states, in remote corners of Georgia and Tennessee, are collections of stone forts and barricades that were erected long before Columbus ever set foot on this continent. Some believe the forts were built by ancient visitors to these shores—Irishmen, Vikings, or people from other Old World cultures—while others contend that Native Americans built them.

Many such mysterious forts are located in southern Illinois. They have been studied numerous times over the years—although the first full-fledged excavations were carried out just a few years ago—however, so far no one has been able to determine their purpose.

As far as we know, there are at least ten forts in southern Illinois, but others may exist in the remote areas of the Shawnee Forest, a vast and mysterious wilderness that engulfs a large portion of the state. These walled structures form a rough alignment between the Ohio and Mississippi rivers. They are built in an almost straight line, cutting off the tip of the state. The forts that remain suggest that there may have once been a nearly solid line of structures spanning one side of the state to the other, sectioning off the tip of land that is surrounded by the Mississippi and Ohio rivers. The forts are all located on high bluffs, facing outward. While only one of them, near Stonefort in Saline County, has a water source inside it, all have stone-lined pits where water could be stored.

The most famous of the stone forts was located near Carbondale, in what is now Giant City State Park. The wall here was once six feet high and six feet wide, made of stones that were laid without mortar. There was a gateway that opened in one wall of the fort and may have been a bison pen, where the animals could be kept before they were driven off the cliff and then butchered for food.

There have been suggestions that the forts may have been used for defense against attackers. Although no sign of warfare has been unearthed at the sites, they would have made good defensive positions against attack. The puzzle of the stone forts may never be solved, but one has to wonder, What enemy were the builders trying to keep out of this region? Or were they trying to keep something or someone else from getting out?

Perplexing Petroglyphs in Fountain Bluff

Fountain Bluff, in southern Illinois' Jackson County, has a collection of authentic petroglyphs that were created by some of the earliest inhabitants of the state. It may also house an ancient American solar observatory.

Fountain Bluff has some of the oldest and best preserved sets of such carvings in the country. This four-mile-long rise of Pennsylvania sandstone looms more than four hundred feet above the small town of Gorham, which is nestled between the bluff and the Mississippi River.

The petroglyphs at Fountain Bluff, while not easily accessible, have unfortunately not escaped the hand of vandals, who have scrawled their initials on the rocks. Luckily the ancient images themselves have not been destroyed. Researchers who have studied the images believe that Fountain Bluff was once a place of initiation into the spiritual existence of a mysterious cult. The carvings were probably symbols of a shaman's religious experience.

The most commonly visited carvings are the petroglyphs at Painted Rock. The figures include handprints, animals, and even an encircled cross near a crescent moon and a bright star. Many think these designs signify ceremonial activities that are scheduled to occur at the rocks around the time of the vernal equinox. The circled cross is said to represent the shamanic activity, followed by the waning of the moon and the bright evening star.

Human figures carved into the walls walk toward the main body of images. Birds in flight that merge with hand-prints seem to imply the human striving after the divine. In front of these carvings is a large boulder decorated with an encircled cross emblem and a figure that is half man and half bird. The boulder has been dubbed the Rock of the Shaman. This particular site likely served a number of purposes, from the initiation of new shamans into the bird-man mystery cult to healing events.

Researchers who have studied the images believe that Fountain Bluff was once a place of initiation into the spiritual existence of a mysterious cult. The carvings were probably symbols of a shaman's religious experience.

The symbols seemed to have been placed here for instructional purposes, and some Native American legends may shed light on their meaning. In those legends, a shaman who was unable to cure his patient would go to a bluff near a river and fall asleep at its base after asking the resident spirits for assistance. When he awoke, he would recall his dream, in which the supernatural beings would tell him everything he needed to know to cure the sickness. He would go back to his village, exact the cure, and later return to the rock to depict his dream in symbolic figures that would help cure similar ailments in the future. Could the carvings at Fountain Bluff be part of the same type of instructional ritual?

Another mysterious site on the bluff is the Whetstone Shelter. This little-known place can be found only after a long and arduous hike up the bluff. The centerpiece of the Whetstone Shelter is a hemispherical depression. This depression, or chair, as some of the locals call it, is surrounded on all sides by petroglyphs. The carvings include encircled crosses, hands, weeping eyes, and numerous grooves in the sandstone that resemble those left in a whetstone. The chair faces northeast. About eight feet to the right is a seven-foot-high cleft in the wall that extends back about twelve feet into the bluff. It is a foot wide at the entrance and narrows to a mere six inches at the back. It is in this area, around the chair and the opening in the rock, that most of the carvings are concentrated.

The site's inaccessibility makes one wonder why the inhabitants would have chosen it. One theory is that the location was selected for its excellent acoustics. Words spoken in a normal tone of voice by someone across the river and nearly a mile away are distinct and easily heard by anyone sitting in the chair. You can hear water lapping on the far shore of the river, birds singing in the trees, fish splashing in the water, and even the distant rustling of leaves. Some researchers believe the ancient inhabitants may have been awed by this phenomenon and believed that the voice of the Great Spirit could be heard at this spot, and so they carved the symbols here to commemorate it. Yet there are many other shelters on the bluff that have identical acoustical properties but have no petroglyphs.

Another theory is that the shelter served as an observatory. The ancient inhabitants may have discovered a natural feature in the bluff that was fully illuminated near sunset only at the time of the winter solstice, an astronomically determined date. To commemorate this finding, they may have carved symbols into the rock around the stone chair, the best place to view the sun's arrival. Surely, this made it seem to be an awesome and magical place.

If this is true, it may call into question some of the theories about other sites on Fountain Bluff. Do the encircled crosses at the Painted Rock really symbolize healing or religious ceremonies, or are they a road marker to the observatory on the bluff high above? No one can say for sure, but these questions add to the mystery of the site.

Those who seek out the petroglyphs should do so with care. Traveling to this place in the summer can be hazardous, thanks to thick undergrowth and numerous snakes, but it is a somewhat easier journey during other seasons. See if you don't agree that Fountain Bluff has an atmosphere of the unexplained that even modern man, with all of his doubt and skepticism, cannot help but feel.

The Not Politically Correct Dickson Mounds

One of Illinois' most fascinating ancient sites is known as Dickson Mounds. It is located in rural Fulton County, not far from Lewistown.

Hundreds of years ago inhabitants buried their dead here in large mounds. As luck (at least for future archaeologists) would have it, the soil was ideal for preservation of skeletal remains. The soil, called loess, is rich in calcium oxide, and its content has almost none of the acids that break down the general structure of bone. In addition, loess soil is soft and very stable, which meant that the skeletal remains left behind at the burial grounds were in a nearly perfect state when discovered.

In the mid-1800s, William Dickson came to Illinois from Kentucky and settled the land where many of the mounds were located. He cleared the area of brush and trees with plans of turning it into an orchard. As he dug holes to set out the trees, he began uncovering human bones. Respectfully he removed all of the bones and buried them elsewhere. He also found a number of artifacts among the bones, but unfortunately, he discarded most of those. Word soon spread about what Dickson was

finding, and the mounds became a popular site for collectors—and for uncontrolled digging. The vast array of new holes, along with soil erosion, altered the shape of the burial mounds, and an unknown number of skeletons and artifacts were plundered.

In 1927, Don Dickson, one of William Dickson's sons, decided to excavate the remains of the burial ground. A chiropractor, Don Dickson was fascinated by pathology and hoped to find some connection between mass graves and the condition of bones. He left all the skeletons and the artifacts found with them exactly as he discovered them, knowing that the public would be interested in viewing what he found. The site soon became very popular for visitors. Much of Dickson's workday began to consist of explaining his work to the ever-growing crowd of tourists. Before long, he protected his excavation with a tent and began charging a small fee to cover the cost of building a museum. During the first year, the mounds attracted forty thousand visitors. During the years of the Great Depression

legislation that restricted or prohibited the excavation of Indian mounds. Most museums began to remove Indian remains from display, and many organizations and institutions adopted policies that prohibited the display of the human skeletons.

In 1989, Dickson Mounds was criticized for its open display of ancient remains. Anthropologists for the Illinois State Museum recommended to then governor Jim Thompson that the burial exhibit be closed. Governor Thompson agreed, but when his decision reached the newspapers, a huge cry of protest came from local residents who felt the exhibit was an important part of their history and should not be closed. A compromise was finally reached, allowing scientists time for a final study of the remains. Then the burials were all entombed under a concrete slab. The exhibit was closed for good in 1992. At that point, the museum was given funds to develop new exhibits, which were unveiled to the public in 1994.

Today some believe the closure of the mounds was nothing more than an abuse of political correctness, while others maintain that it was the right thing to do. But if these skeletal remains have been so carefully protected, what about the other ancient Illinois sites that have been so carelessly destroyed over the years? Don't the petroglyphs, village sites, and assorted carvings deserve to be protected from relic hunters and vandals?

There are nearly as many questions that remain about the future of the burial mounds as there are tales that such places still have to tell us.

and World War II, attendance dropped off, and in 1945, Dickson sold the land to the state of Illinois, which operates the museum today.

While Dickson Mounds remains fascinating, the allure of years past was not so much the history of the site but the eerie displays of skeletal remains. I can remember coming to Dickson Mounds as a child in the middle 1970s and being allowed to enter a dimly lit room with small spotlights shining directly on the skulls and bones of the mound's occupants. It's not hard to imagine that many children on school field trips went away from Dickson Mounds with nightmares! Regardless, the macabre scene was extremely popular, and it was one of the most often visited prehistoric sites in Illinois. But all of that was to change. . . .

In the 1960s, Native Americans began to gain a political voice, and they decried, among other things, the way their ancient burial sites were being treated throughout the country. Before long, many states passed

Burrows Cave: Hieroglyphics or Hoax?

In 1982, a spelunker named Russell Burrows from Olney discovered a deeply mysterious cave along a branch of the Little Wabash River. The startling contents of the cave would set American archaeology on its ear and would seem to provide evidence that visitors from the Old World may have reached the center of the North American continent long before the generally accepted date.

That was the claim, but were the contents of the cave real or an elaborate hoax? Did the weird figures and strange carvings challenge the state's history or just prove that trickery was alive and well in southern Illinois?

The Burrows Cave discoveries don't mark the first time that unexplainable mysteries have been found in our vast country, of course. For many years, scientists and ordinary people have happened upon everything from the skeletal remains of visitors that should not exist to ancient coins that logically cannot have ended up where they were found. Bizarre writings and carvings, stones written in mysterious ancient languages, and lots of other inexplicable artifacts have been talked about and written about for a long time.

So what makes Burrows Cave so different? Perhaps it is the sheer number of oddities. Burrows claims to have discovered ancient corpses, relics, strange inscriptions, and thousands of black stones carved with symbols and languages never seen before. Needless to say, mainstream scientists immediately dismissed the discovery as a hoax. Other researchers were not so quick to discredit the site and continue to study the artifacts today. They believe that the stones could be real and that ancient travelers journeyed up the Mississippi and ended up in southern Illinois. When members of the party died, the survivors created the hidden tomb and filled it with the stones, which were carved as the travelers passed the time in this harsh and uncivilized land. Is this possible?

One thing is sure, whether authentic or not, the cave was certainly well hidden. Russell Burrows was walking along a wooden path and literally stumbled onto the opening. As he fell, he dislodged a massive stone that, if it had not jammed, would have flipped over and deposited him into a stone chamber twelve feet deep. The stone had been designed to turn over and seal the intruder into the chamber—permanently. Happily for Burrows, this didn't happen. He noticed the strange carvings and writings on the bottom

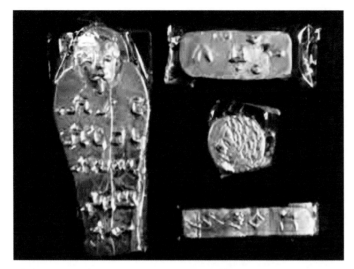

of the stone and peered deeper into the cavern. On one wall was a huge face that had its eyes fixed on the deadly trapdoor. Burrows's nearly fatal discovery began a mystery that remains unsolved today.

Those who have seen the carvings and artifacts from the cave confess to being either mystified or skeptical. The stones have an amateurish look to them that does not conform to the types of ancient drawings we are accustomed to seeing. Some would say that this is because of the conditions under which the ancient travelers were forced to work, while others would say this provides proof of the hoax.

What is always pointed out is that the writings on the stones (in tongues like Egyptian, Punic, Libyan, and Arabic) make no sense in the languages of their scripts. Skeptics point to this and say that the writings were obviously done by someone who simply gathered words from somewhere else and strung them together. But those who continue to study the stones offer alternate explanations. They point to the fact that the writings show a curious consistency and may actually be made up of an older language, one that provided a basis for the others. It's also possible that the language is merely similar to the others but is unique in its own right. Early American settlers noted that the Algonquin language of the

American Indians sounded like Hebrew. This is often pointed out by groups (like the Mormons) who believe the Native Americans were actually part of the lost tribes of Israel.

Another criticism is that the engravings are not at all typical of carvings found in ancient caves. They depict warrior profiles, animals, and ships of many periods and traditions. Yet why couldn't they simply represent something previously unknown to archaeologists? The cave is also a mausoleum containing skeletons and burial artifacts, as well as weapons and urns. Whether or not the bones have been studied closely is unknown.

At the time of this writing, the cave has received very little attention from archaeologists. No digs have been conducted, and supporters of the cave's authenticity have complained that the lack of attention is a conspiracy to suppress evidence that doesn't fit easily into scientific theories. However, these complaints don't really seem to be valid in light of the fact that Burrows and his associates have not discussed the exact location of the cave for over two decades. Burrows states that this is because he fears that it will be looted and destroyed by relic hunters. However, there are claims that Burrows and others have already removed "thousands" of artifacts from the cave and have sold them to private dealers. One man said that he purchased hundreds of pieces from Burrows, only to find that they were worthless fakes. Because of accounts like this, few scholars support the authenticity of the cave.

So, is the cave real or a hoax?

No one really knows for sure. To this date, Burrows and possibly some of his close associates are apparently the only ones who have been inside the cave. No one else has even been given its location, and the owner of the land where it rests remains anonymous. But who knows? At this point, Burrows Cave is as much a mystery as it was in 1982. Speculation, debate, and conjecture continue and are unlikely to stop anytime soon.

Fabled People and Places

The state of Illinois is filled with legendary places. There are unusual spots here that many of us have heard about and have never been able to find or simply did not really believe existed at all. They are often strange places where tragic and calamitous events have occurred—events that have attained a mythical quality for most of us. They are sites of mystery, death, destruction, and perhaps even of imagination, attached to characters that are sometimes bigger than life and more mysterious than we might have expected.

Keep that in mind when you go to seek out these locations. The highways and byways of Illinois can be both fascinating and spooky stretches of road. The people and places in this chapter show that there is a lot more to Illinois than Abraham Lincoln and cornfields. We may be proud of both those things, but we are also proud of the weird side of the state.

Outlaws of Cave-in-Rock

The rivers of southern Illinois provide a lot for our state. Things like shipping ports, riverfront hotels, flour and lumber mills, and all those good things. But even better are the mysterious shipwrecks, tales of lawlessness and pirates, and even ghosts. Now those are things you can write a book about.

One of the state's great watery locations was an outlaw hideout called Cave-in-Rock, which is located along the Ohio River at the southeastern edge of Illinois. The cave became the stronghold of pirates who plundered flatboats on the river and who murdered and robbed travelers. It was also here, around 1800, that thieves began operating a tavern and gambling parlor, right in the cave. Using whiskey, cards, and prostitutes to lure travelers in off the river, the outlaws beat, robbed, and sometimes murdered all those unsuspecting customers who thought they were tying up at the crude wharf for a good old time.

Cave-in-Rock, located close to a town of the same

name, was a perfect place for criminal enterprises. It boasted a partially concealed entrance and a wide view up and down the river. The cave is about one hundred feet deep, with a level floor and a vertical chimney that ascends to the bluff above.

The cave once provided shelter for Native Americans; later, in 1800, a man named Wilson brought his family to live there. He turned part of the cave into a tavern and erected a sign that said WILSON'S LIQUOR VAULT & HOUSE OF ENTERTAINMENT along the water's edge. Naturally, a sign like that would attract both river travelers and those who journeyed by land. Before long, it became a rough spot, famed for its hard cider, strong whiskey, and women of ill repute.

A band of robbers formed by Wilson became the first pirates to operate on this stretch of the river. Whole crews of boats on their way to New Orleans were killed when they docked at the cave, and their cargo was stolen and sold. After many months of robberies, word of criminal activities at the tavern was heard from Pittsburgh to New Orleans, and public indignation forced local authorities to act. Many of the pirates were arrested, but others were killed or fled the region. Wilson himself was murdered at the hands of his own men when they learned of the huge reward that had been placed on his head. There is, as they say, no honor among thieves. After Wilson's death, more than sixty bodies of luckless travelers were discovered hidden away in an upper room of the cave.

Samuel Mason was the next outlaw connected with Cave-in-Rock. Mason was a man of gigantic size and minuscule conscience. He killed for both pleasure and profit, but he had not always been a lawless man. Mason had been an officer in the army during the Revolutionary War and had served with distinction. He was promoted to captain and was cited twice for bravery.

Mason took over Wilson's tavern and renamed it the

Rock Cave Inn. He didn't make too many changes—women and whiskey were still the drawing cards to lure travelers. And he took up Wilson's methods of piracy as well. The prostitutes who worked for him would stand on the shore and pretend to be stranded. When a boat came by to help, the pirates would race from the cave and swarm over the craft, seizing the cargo and murdering the crew. Mason's pirates would also pose as river pilots who could be hired to steer vessels along a dangerous channel that ran nearby. The pirates would then purposely strand the boats, and their confederates would race up the river to raid the vessels.

River craft were looted in other ways as well. On rainy nights, welcoming lanterns were placed along the riverbanks to lure storm-tossed boats ashore. Just before the boat would reach the bank, it would plow into a sandbar or a line of rocks. The stranded vessel would then be overrun by Mason's cutthroats.

Still another approach was one that was frequently used by Mason's most brutal partners, Micajar and Wiley Harpe. The Harpe brothers were known as Big Harpe and Little Harpe and were remorseless butchers whose victims included innocent women and children. Big Harpe once admitted to smashing a newborn baby against a tree because its crying annoyed him.

The Harpes did not wait until nightfall or a storm to do their dirty work. They operated boldly in broad daylight. Their most effective method was to appear on the riverbank and flag down passing boats, saying that they had been attacked by Indians, or robbed, and needed help. When the sympathetic travelers came ashore, the Harpes would slaughter them on the spot and raid the boat. The trademark, so to speak, of the Harpes was to disembowel their victims, load their stomachs with stones, and then sink the bodies in the river.

Samuel Mason and his henchmen were eventually driven out of the Cave-in-Rock area, and he took up operations along the Mississippi and the Natchez Trace, a series of trails in the South that became known as a haven for thieves and pirates. He amassed a fortune during the five or so years that his criminal enterprise flourished in the region, but he did not survive to spend it. After the United States purchased the Louisiana Territory from France, a concerted effort was made to drive out the outlaw element that had existed along the river for years. Authorities offered a $10,000 reward for Mason's capture, dead or alive.

That was a grand sum in those days, but the man who finally ended Mason's life did not do it for the money. He did it so that he could take over Mason's criminal enterprise. That man was Wiley, Little Harpe. He contrived to get Mason alone, then buried his tomahawk into his friend's back. He then hacked off Mason's head, carried the grisly object off, and placed it on the desk of the judge in charge of dispensing the reward. Just as the judge was counting out the gold coins in payment, someone standing nearby recognized Little Harpe as an outlaw himself. Harpe made an effort to escape, but he was quickly captured and hanged soon after. The deaths of Mason and Harpe brought about the end of the gang, and Mason's men scattered to the winds.

By the late 1830s most of the outlaws, pirates, and counterfeiters had been driven away from Cave-in-Rock, and the bloody past of the place began to fade with time. As years went by, the cave became a recreation area, and it remains a natural attraction in southern Illinois today. However, the legends have never died completely, and many still remember the area's blood-soaked past. It's no surprise that travelers on the river often claim to hear the keening moans of ghosts echoing from the mouth of the cave, no doubt the hapless victims enticed ashore by the promise of rollicking good times.

The Hell of Hell Hollow

Legend holds that Native Americans believed the land where the city of Decatur is today was closely connected to the next world. Rather than live there, they considered it to be the perfect place to bury their dead, who would have a safe and easy passage to the world beyond. Decatur has been a weird place ever since.

The first home built by a settler near Decatur was a log cabin erected in 1820 by William Downing, a fur trapper and honey gatherer. More frontiersmen began to arrive from the east, and by 1829, the village of Decatur was platted. It was named after the naval hero Stephen Decatur, who had been noted for his spectacular feats of bravery during the wars with the Barbary pirates in the early 1800s.

The hardships and trials of early life in Decatur were much like those in other frontier settlements. Most of the settlers lived outside the village in log cabins in the forest and along the river. Many died from the bitter cold and fierce storms of the winter of 1830–31, but that winter also gave birth to one of the greatest legends of the Decatur area, a legend of death, depravity, and cannibalism in a place known today as Hell Hollow.

According to the legend, the wooded site that would someday be Hell Hollow was once the location of a small settlement. It was the most secluded of the outposts surrounding the village of Decatur and was in an area that was mostly avoided by the local settlers. They came here only to bury the dead. The hills above this narrow valley were part of an Indian burial ground that was soon taken over by the settlers. In later years, it would become Greenwood Cemetery.

During that bitter winter, snow seemed to fall constantly, alternating with sleet and ice, and it reached heights of three and four feet. The tiny collection of cabins was cut off from the rest of the settlers in the area. Food became scarce, and as the cold months wore on, the deer, turkey, squirrels, and prairie chickens all but disappeared as the settlers hunted all the game they could find. Soon stores of flour and dried meat were depleted. The outlook was grim, and there was a good chance that the settlers would starve to death long before spring arrived.

They made do with what they had, boiling tree bark into a bitter soup, even eating shoe leather and rawhide to stay alive. Finally, they had no option but to turn to the only food supply that was still available—each other.

In the early months of the winter, one of the older members of the community had passed away, and the body had been stored in an outbuilding—awaiting burial when the ground thawed. This was the first of two corpses that the settlers were forced to eat that winter.

When the weather finally broke, the remains of the devoured bodies were secretly buried on the hill, and the cannibals were sworn to secrecy. After a few months, someone discovered the horrible secret. The settlers vanished from the area and were never heard from again. While this may have been the first bizarre event to take place in Hell Hollow, it was most definitely not the last.

At some point in the late 1800s, the hollow became the territory of a gang called, for some unknown reason, the Biscuit-Necks by the local populace. They specialized in extortion and robbery and used the woods south of the cemetery as their base of operations. Then they committed a particularly vicious crime—thought today to be the robbery of a store, during which the owner was killed. When local authorities failed to find them, a vigilante group took up the chase and soon discovered their base. They captured the men and hanged them on the spot. As a message to other criminals operating in the area, the vigilantes left the bodies of the Biscuit-Necks hanging there in Hell Hollow, swaying in the wind, until the

elements and vultures finished off the corpses.

The years passed, and the edge of the hollow became known as a hobo jungle, where transients and small-time criminals lived. The railroad tracks passed close to this area, so it was convenient for the hoboes to hop off freight trains and camp here. In the spring of 1930, a caretaker from Greenwood Cemetery named Mel Savage was murdered in the hobo jungle. His murder was never solved.

In 1936, a series of Chicago newspaper articles pinpointed Hell Hollow as the hideout for a gang of grave robbers and killers. The gang, dubbed the Hounds of Hell Hollow, supposedly ruled the south end of the city. They often met in Greenwood Cemetery, robbed graves, and sold bootleg liquor. Even though Decatur officials hotly denied the stories, needless to say the articles did little to enhance the reputation of Hell Hollow.

The hollow grew smaller over the years as acres of woods and brush were cleared away. Finally only a small valley remained, just west of Greenwood Cemetery; it is the center for the strange activity that has continued to radiate outward from the region.

Eerie stories are still told: some about crazed killers with hooks for hands and horrifying murders that usually involved teenagers in parked cars. Not all the stories could be passed off as modern folk legends and campfire tales. Every once in a while someone encountered something truly inexplicable in Hell Hollow.

One story involved a couple that had gone down to the hollow for a romantic interlude and were surprised to hear what seemed to be open hands slamming down on the trunk of their car. The young man jumped out of the car and looked around, but no one was there. He heard a movement over to his left and turned to see the tall grass alongside the road being pushed aside, as if some invisible presence were passing through it. He quickly returned to the car, and there, on the dusty trunk, were the clear impressions of handprints.

A few years ago the road that ended in Hell Hollow was closed off and city crews cleared away the thick growth of trees that once filled the valley. Another roadway that passed through the area, running from South Main Street along the Sangamon River, was open until recently. It offered the only remaining access to the hollow, and thanks to this, it was also plagued with dark incidents and unexplained happenings. In the middle 1990s, two young men were executed here by drug dealers, and since that time, their phantom cries have been reported on occasion.

Strange things continue to happen in Hell Hollow today, as if some sort of weird and frightening energy still lingers there. The valley is no longer accessible by road, but a walking trail was cut through the forest a few years ago. Those curious about the macabre can still walk the same ground that both killers and victims walked in years gone by.

The Hell Hollow Suicide

When I was a teenager, I used to go down to Hell Hollow with my boyfriends. The road used to be open in those days, and I remember how dark and spooky it was. One story that I heard was that someone committed suicide there one time. I was down there one night, and my boyfriend and I saw a rope and a noose hanging from a tree. I found out later that this was where he was supposed to have killed himself.–*Janice D.*

Not Going Back to Hell Hollow Woods

Me and some friends went down to Hell Hollow one night because we were going to climb over the fence into the cemetery. We walked down the old road, and all of a sudden we heard this scream that came from the woods. I have no idea what it was, but it didn't sound human. We took off running, and I have never gone back down there.–*Jerry C.*

Dad's Full of It, but Hell Hollow IS a Spooky Place

I heard that the ghosts of Hell Hollow are the people who lived down there back in the 1800s. I guess they got snowed in and ate each other or something. Anyway, the place has been haunted ever since. My parents used to go parking down there when they were in high school, and my Dad said that he saw a ghost one time. I think he's full of it, but it's a pretty spooky place.–*Cindy E.*

The Legend of the Devil's Bake Oven

The small town of Grand Tower slumbers peacefully along the muddy banks of the Mississippi River. It's been a landmark for years, thanks to the vast array of tales that have been told about the area. One of the most haunting is the legend of the Devil's Bake Oven.

Not far from the town is a collection of menacing outcroppings that tower over the river. For centuries, Native Americans were convinced that evil spirits lurked here, waiting to claim the lives of unwitting victims. The white men who settled the area would later acknowledge these beliefs by giving the towering rocks suitable names. One, called the Devil's Backbone, is a rocky ridge about a half-mile long. At the north edge of the ridge is a steep gap and then the Devil's Bake Oven, a large hill that stands on the edge of the river and rises to almost one hundred feet.

The area has a strange past. Many years ago a band of immigrants were going up the Mississippi River, headed to Kaskaskia, when they were attacked and killed by Indians at the south edge of the Devil's Backbone. The only survivor was a boy named John Moredock, who somehow was able to hide among the rocks until the killers had departed. He buried his family and eventually was able to make his way to Kaskaskia. According to legend, he swore revenge on the Indians who had murdered his family, and one by one, he killed all the attackers.

Another legend still haunts the town of Grand Tower today, and the Devil's Bake Oven plays a major part in the story. When the first ironworks came to town, several attractive homes were built for the officials of the company, including a house for the superintendent. His home was constructed on top of the Devil's Bake Oven. The foundation of the old house can still be seen on the eastern side of the hill, and it is here that a lonely ghost is said to walk. People say that her voice is sometimes heard among the ruins of the old house, a once happy place that became one of tragedy and despair.

According to the story, the ghost is that of the superintendent's young daughter. The girl was said to be very beautiful but was also sheltered and naïve about life. Her doting father kept her away from the rough men of the foundry, and although she had a number of suitors seeking her hand in marriage, none were acceptable to her father. Finally the girl fell in love with one of the young men who came to court her. He was a handsome, roguish, and irresponsible fellow, and her father forbade his daughter to continue seeing him. She bravely disobeyed, and after she was caught slipping away during the night to see her suitor, her father confined her to the house.

The young man soon grew tired of waiting and moved away from Grand Tower. After he left, the young girl wept for weeks. At last, either because of grief or because of an illness brought on by despair, the young woman died.

Unable to cope with what he had done to his daughter, the girl's guilt-ridden father committed suicide. When the foundry closed down soon after, his once fine home was razed and its timbers were used to build a railway station.

It is said that the spirit of the girl has never left the Devil's Bake Oven. For many years after her death, visitors to the area reported seeing a strange, mistlike shape, resembling the dead girl, walking along the pathway and vanishing among the rocks near the old house. Her disappearance was often followed by the sound of moans and wails. When thunderstorms swept across the region, those moans and wails would become blood-curdling screams.

The town of Grand Tower has faded into a scattering of houses, with little to remind us of the young girl who died there of a broken heart and whose spirit refuses to rest in peace.

The Curse of Kaskaskia

Many years ago Kaskaskia was part of the mainland of Illinois. Situated on a small peninsula that jutted out just north of the present-day location of Chester, Kaskaskia was a thriving commercial and cultural center. Today it is largely a ghost town, consisting of a few scattered homes and a handful of residents. The remains of the town, while still considered part of Illinois, can now be reached only by an ancient bridge that stretches from the island to Missouri and is the only physical link this desolate spot has to the mainland.

What happened to change the fate of this once marvelous city? Was it simply nature taking its course, or were more dire circumstances behind the demise of Kaskaskia?

According to legend, a terrible curse was placed on the town that predicted that the city and the land around it would be destroyed in a flood and that the dead would rise from the graveyard in eternal torment.

The legend of the curse dates back to 1735, when Kaskaskia was flourishing. One wealthy inhabitant was a fur trader, remembered today only by the name of Bernard. He lived in a luxurious home with his daughter, Maria, a beautiful young girl who was the pride of his life. Bernard owned a trading post on the edge of the city, and he frequently hired local men, both French and Indian, to work for him. Most of the Indians were hired to do the menial work, as Bernard cared little for them and considered them not much more than a necessary evil.

One of the young Indians in his employ had been educated by French missionaries. Bernard actually became fond of the young man, until to his dismay he realized that his daughter had also become fond of him. In fact, Maria and the Indian had fallen in love.

Bernard became enraged and immediately fired the man. He warned his friends and other merchants to stay away from the Indian, and they all refused to hire him. Eventually the young man was forced to leave town, but before he did, he promised Maria that he would return for her.

Needless to say, Maria was heartbroken, but she wouldn't give up hope that one day her lover would return. Several local men attempted to court her, but while she feigned interest in their attentions, she secretly pined away for the young Indian.

A year passed, and one day a group of Indians arrived in Kaskaskia from the west. Among them was Maria's lover. He was secretly able to get in touch with Maria, and the two of them quickly fled Kaskaskia.

When Bernard learned what had happened, he vowed to seek vengeance on the Indian. He gathered several of his trapper friends and began hunting his daughter and her lover. They finally captured them near Cahokia. Maria begged her father to understand and to let the two of them be together, but he ignored her wishes. Her lover, he said, was to be drowned for his deeds.

The Indian was silent as the trappers tied him to a log and prepared to set him adrift on the Mississippi. But just as they placed him in the water, he uttered a terrible curse. He swore that Bernard would be dead within the year, and that he and his beloved Maria would be reunited forever. Kaskaskia was damned and would be destroyed, along with all of the land around it. The altars of the churches would be ruined and the homes along with them. Even the dead of Kaskaskia would rise from their graves.

Then the river swallowed the Indian beneath the muddy water. He was silenced forever, but his curse eventually came to pass. Within the year, both Maria and her father were dead. Maria had been so distraught over her lover's fate that she had refused to eat and soon died, joining her lover on the other side. Bernard became involved in a bad business deal, challenged the man he believed had cheated him to a duel, and was shot dead.

And then the rest of the curse played out as the river began to seek the Indian's revenge on Kaskaskia. The river channels shifted and flooded the peninsula over and over again until, by 1881, Kaskaskia was completely cut off from the Illinois mainland. Homes and farms were abandoned, and residents began to leave the island. The last church left standing was moved several times, but that did no good. Its altar was eventually destroyed in the 1973 flood. By this time, Kaskaskia had become a desolate ghost town, but not before its cemetery was washed away; the bodies of those buried there rose to the surface and then vanished beneath the river. The dead of Kaskaskia, as the Indian had predicted, had indeed risen from their graves.

Lost Souls of Flight 191 Still Arriving and Departing from Crash Site

Before the horrific events of September 11, 2001, the worst airline-related disaster in American history occurred in Chicago in 1979 on Memorial Day weekend. On Friday, May 25, American Airlines flight 191 fell from the sky, killing all 271 passengers and crew on board. The flight was meant to be a nonstop journey from Chicago to Los Angeles—but as fate would have it, the plane would never leave the Windy City.

It was a beautiful holiday weekend in Chicago, and throngs of people filled busy O'Hare International Airport. The passengers of flight 191 included a number of Chicago literary figures who were bound for Los Angeles and the annual American Booksellers Association conference.

As passengers boarded the McDonnell-Douglas

DC-10 shortly before three in the afternoon, nothing seemed out of the ordinary. The plane had logged more than 20,000 trouble-free hours since it left the assembly line, and its experienced crew had almost 50,000 flight hours among them.

At 3:02 p.m., the plane started down the runway. All went smoothly until just prior to takeoff when an air traffic controller saw parts of the port engine pylon fall away from the aircraft and a white vapor came from the area. A moment later the aircraft lifted off. As it did, the entire engine and pylon tore loose from its mounting,

flipped up and over the wing, and crashed down onto the runway.

About ten seconds later the aircraft banked to the left—then fell to the earth.

A fireball erupted, and the aircraft slammed into an abandoned hangar on the site of the old Ravenswood Airport, just east of a mobile home park. Two people were killed on the ground, and all the crew and passengers were killed instantly.

The National Transportation Safety Board began a long and grueling investigation that eventually revealed a stress crack in a flange that held the engine pylon as well as flawed maintenance methods. These answers, logical as they were, did not solve the mysteries that were plaguing Chicagoans who lived in the vicinity of the crash.

Ghostly tales soon began to spring up near the site. According to police officers in Des Plaines, northwest of Chicago and near O'Hare, motorists began reporting odd sights within a few months of the crash. They called in about seeing strange bobbing white lights in the field where the aircraft had gone down. While officers thought the lights were simply from flashlights carried by ghoulish souvenir hunters, they always found the field silent and deserted when they arrived. No one was ever found, despite patrols arriving on the scene just moments after receiving a report.

More unnerving were the accounts that came from the residents of the mobile home park that was adjacent to the crash site. Many of these reports came within hours of the disaster, when residents claimed to hear knocking and rapping sounds at their doors and windows. The residents, who included a number of policemen and firefighters, opened their doors and found no one there. Dogs in the trailer park would bark endlessly at the empty field where the plane had gone down. Their masters could find no reason for their erratic behavior.

This continued for weeks and months and escalated to the point where people reported that doorknobs were being turned and rattled, footsteps were heard approaching the trailers, and on some occasions, actual figures were confronted. According to some reports, a few residents opened their doors to find a worried figure who stated that he "had to get his luggage" or "had to make a connection" standing on their porch. The figure then turned and vanished into the darkness.

The tragedy and the strange events that followed caused many people to move out of the park, but when new arrivals took their place, they too began to report weird happenings. A recent sighting was described by a man who was walking his dog one night near the area where flight 191 went down. He was approached by a young man who explained that he needed to make an emergency telephone call. The man looked at this person curiously, for he seemed to reek of gasoline and even appeared to be smoldering. At first, he just assumed the man had been running on this chilly night and steam was coming from his clothing, but when he turned away to point out a nearby phone and then turned back again, the man had vanished. The man with the dog had heard stories from other local residents about moans and weird cries emanating from the 1979 crash site, but he never believed them until this encounter. He was now convinced that he had met one of the restless passengers from flight 191.

And he's likely not the only one, for the stories of weird knockings, inexplicable sounds, and apparitions continue to this day. Even some of the people who had loved ones on the flight claim to have had supernatural visitations. What is it about the flight 191 disaster that seems to invite such high strangeness? No one knows, but its impact is still being felt today.

Flight 191 Tourists in the Trailer Park

Since I moved into the trailer park at 400 West Touhy Avenue two years ago, I thought perhaps you might be interested in my experience. It happened when I only lived here a month and a half. I was sitting outside in front of my home with my neighbor late one evening when we saw two women coming from the north. They were walking in the middle of the street, looking straight ahead. Most people turn to look when they pass by, or even say hello. These two didn't look or say anything. They weren't even talking with each other. My neighbor commented that she wondered who they were, because she had never seen them before. I quickly answered, "They look like tourists." Not really thinking about my answer at the time, I didn't know where it came from. But after a few minutes, I began to think about the crash, the site of which is at the end of my street to the north. They didn't walk back by the location again.–*Edie R.*

And the Clock Stopped, Never to Chime Again

My husband was aboard flight 191. It was the Memorial Day weekend, and he had a return trip ticket on a later plane. He finished his conference early and arrived at the airport early. He was a standby on 191 and was able to board it for an earlier flight to Los Angeles. I live in Orange County next to Los Angeles County. At the time of his death, we were selling our home and moving to another area in Orange County near the ocean. I remember receiving a call from my real estate agent, who was a very good friend, saying that another agent was bringing some people after one p.m. to look at our home. I was sitting on the couch, and I glanced at the antique wall clock my husband had purchased for me as a gift several years earlier. It chimed one p.m., and several minutes later I heard the doorbell ring. I started to get up to answer the door, when I started feeling like I was losing consciousness. I had extreme dizziness and actually felt like I was dying. I fell to my knees and leaned against the couch. I was aware the people were at the door, but I could not move to get up and answer it.

About five minutes went by, and the people left. The telephone rang, and it was my real estate agent. I told her I became very ill and could not answer the door. Luckily, the phone was on an end table near the couch. My real estate agent came right over. We were standing in the living room, and suddenly it seemed the room and furnishings became very bright, almost like Technicolor. She did not notice this, but I did, and it disappeared in seconds.

It was getting close to midnight when American Airlines called to tell me my husband had lost his life in the crash. I was stunned, for I had not had the TV on and knew nothing of the accident. American Airlines had him listed on two flights, the original flight on his round-trip ticket and the flight that crashed. Because of all the confusion, they wanted to wait and see if he was on the original flight, but learned he was not on board when it arrived late that night in Los Angeles. Later, I walked into the living room and noticed the clock had stopped at 1:03 p.m. I could never get it to run again. That was twenty-five years ago, but I still remember that strange sad day I experienced, not knowing what the future was going to bring. –*Rita S.*

Talk About a Weird TV Show!

In 1986, television reporter and talk show host Geraldo Rivera took a national television audience into what was then one of the last remaining landmarks of the Chicago crime era and the reign of Al Capone—the old Lexington Hotel at the corner of Michigan Avenue and Twenty-second Street. Rivera was in search of lost treasure, a fortune that Capone had allegedly left behind in secret vaults in the hotel.

Capone had moved his headquarters to a luxurious fifth-floor suite of rooms at the Lexington in July 1928. He registered under the innocuous name of George Phillips and ran his operations from his suite, while in the Lexington's lobby, an armed gunman kept a careful eye on the front doors. Additional guards with machine guns patrolled the upper floors. But by this time, Capone's days as a gangster were number. The government charged him with income tax evasion; he was arrested on October 6, 1931, and was convicted. The remnants of Capone's gang abandoned the Lexington in 1932, and after that, its ownership changed several times. The place steadily declined.

Then, in the early 1980s, a local women's construction company investigated the possibility of restoring the hotel. As workers searched the building, they discovered a shooting gallery that had been used by Capone's cronies for target practice and dozens of secret passages and stairways. The tunnels had been designed to provide elaborate escape routes from both rival gangs and police raids.

This led to more interest in the hotel, and soon a researcher named Harold Rubin came to the crumbling old building and began

to search the premises. In addition to recovering many priceless artifacts from the days of the hotel's glory, Rubin stumbled across Capone's secret vaults in the lower levels of the Lexington. Capone had reportedly hidden away some of his loot there, and the vaults were so well hidden that even his closest accomplices were not aware of them. Rubin's discoveries led to a newspaper article in the *Chicago Tribune*, but his excellent research would be overshadowed by Geraldo Rivera, who stated that if treasure could be found in a secret vault, he would discover it—and would do so on national television. But the Lexington still had one last act left in its old bones.

On that night in 1986, Rivera and his camera crew went out live to America from the deserted and empty hotel. The place had already been picked clean by vandals and souvenir hunters, but Rivera was sure that secrets from the past remained there. In a basement chamber, the crew blasted away a seven-thousand-pound concrete wall that was believed to be hiding a secret compartment that contained thousands, perhaps millions, of dollars. The Internal Revenue Service even had agents on hand to claim its share of the loot. When the smoke cleared, though, only a few empty bottles and an old sign were found. The fortune, if it had ever been there at all, had long since been spirited away.

The Lexington Hotel finally gave up the ghost in November 1995 when it was torn down. Another chapter in the history of Chicago crime had been closed for good.

Unexplained Phenomena

it is human nature to love being tantalized by something that cannot be explained. That's why unsolved murder mysteries, ghost stories, and books about the paranormal have been immensely popular for decades. We love to question, to wonder, and to be baffled by those things that we believe to be unexplained.

Here at *Weird Illinois*, our interest in the unexplained came about at an early age. We were fascinated with anything that touched on the unknown and the unsolved. By the time we were in junior high, we had exhausted our local libraries, bookstores, and mail-order catalogues for any books that we could find on the subject.

And then we discovered a man named Charles Fort (1874–1932), the ultimate collector of the weird. Charles Hoy Fort was born in Albany, New York. He stood nearly six feet tall, was slightly heavy and fair in complexion. He sported a bristling brown mustache and wore thick wire-rimmed eyeglasses.

Fort had no real friends, and the only person he seemed to like well enough to be around—aside from his wife, Anna—was author Theodore Dreiser. He had no telephone, so all communication was through letter or telegram. His apartment was filled with books and papers; on the walls were framed specimens of giant spiders, butterflies, and assorted weird creatures. He had a photograph of a large hailstone and, under a glass, a specimen of strange shredded matter that was said to have fallen from the sky in such quantities that it covered several acres.

Fort was especially interested in oddities of nature and strange sightings that seemed to suggest something of an other- worldly nature.

Fort supported himself and Anna through his writing—a novel that received little notice—and through occasional odd jobs. When he wasn't working, he spent hours in libraries, reading and taking notes. He was especially interested in oddities of nature and strange sightings that seemed to suggest something of an otherworldly nature. Over time, he accumulated something like forty thousand notes. Not knowing what to do with them, he threw them all out and started over again. Most of his notes merely identified a subject and then gave a date and a location for the phenomenon, along with indicating the source of the information. Many of his later notes, scribbled on small rectangles of paper, were preserved for posterity, but his original collections were lost.

Fort traveled to London for materials not available in America, and from his accumulated research, he wrote the *Book of the Damned* in 1919. The book electrified readers. It opened with these words: "A procession of the damned. By the damned, I mean the excluded. We shall have a procession of data that Science has excluded." The book included such far-reaching subjects as strange things that fell from the sky, like blood, rocks, fish, and what would be called, several decades later, unidentified flying objects. The book received enthusiastic reviews, and Chicago newspaperman Ben Hecht hailed Fort's "onslaught upon the accumulated lunacy of fifty centuries." Hecht coined the word Fortean, not knowing that it would remain in use for years to come. Fort published *New Lands* in 1923, another compelling look at strange encounters with objects from the sky. *Lo!*, published in 1931, focused strongly on UFOs and unknown animals. His interest in the latter subject foreshadowed the future study of cryptozoology. His final book, *Wild Talents*, was published in 1932 and dealt with bizarre phenomena associated with humans.

By the late 1920s, Fort's health had begun to fail, yet he was healthy enough to be amused when writer Tiffany Thayer organized the Fortean Society in 1931. The society, which was designed to continue the research begun by Fort, included such luminaries as Ben Hecht, Booth Tarkington, Theodore Dreiser, Alexander Woollcott, Buckminster Fuller, Oliver Wendell Holmes, and Clarence Darrow. Fort, being skeptical of his own authority as much as anyone else's, refused to join.

Inspired by Charles Fort, we here at *Weird Illinois* have collected instances of strange stuff and unexplained phenomena in our state. We have managed to track down reports of mysterious spook lights, a girl who could set fires with her mind, religious apparitions, accounts of strange doorways between dimensions, flying saucers, and more. We think Fort would have approved of our efforts.

Ghost Lights

Old Union Cemetery  is located on the grounds of Union Christian Church, in a remote section of central Illinois, in De Witt County, near Clinton. The graveyard saw its first burials in 1831, and it closed down one hundred years later in 1931 after a fire destroyed the church. As time passed, the road past the cemetery, which had once been a busy stage line between Bloomington and Springfield, was abandoned, and the graveyard was largely forgotten. Although it is well kept by the local township, the cemetery is no longer visible from the road because of a thick forest that now surrounds it. Historical records say that over five hundred people are buried in the grounds, but fewer than one hundred grave markers remain.

Old Union Cemetery first came to our attention thanks to reports from a sheriff's deputy and two independent witnesses—caretakers who had worked for the local township—all of whom told stories of glowing balls of light that were often seen among the tombstones. In addition, the caretakers mentioned one part of the cemetery they avoided working in if possible. Both men reported, independent of the other, that the section made them feel strange and uncomfortable. They had no explanation as to why it made their flesh crawl.

The eerie area was located in the far corner of the grounds, almost touching the woods, and was apparently some sort of private plot that contained a now unreadable tombstone. It was surrounded by an iron fence decorated with the images of willow trees. Each corner of the plot had a metal post to which the sides of the fence connected. The design of the posts was rather intricate as well.

We began to hear other slightly creepy stories. It was not that the graveyard was haunted, at least in the usual sense, but visitors who managed to find the fenced-off place told of feeling strange sensations there. They said that the hair on their arms stood on end and that the temperature was sharply lower than it was in the rest of the graveyard. One visitor told us that it was almost like someone opened the door of a giant icebox and let the cold air out. Moments later the cold air would be gone.

We decided to check out the place ourselves. The first day we went, we didn't see any of the mysterious lights, though we did find that the air was much colder inside the fenced area than anywhere else. But we came back at night and, like others who had visited here, found that small, glowing balls of light appeared. They even turned up in

photographs we took that night, and in almost every case, we determined that they seemed to be coming from that strange area near the woods.

One afternoon while we were there with some friends, we saw a yellowish colored light streak past us and vanish in the area of the woods. This single light was followed by others. We watched in amazement as the cemetery's spook lights put on a midafternoon show for us.

Why did all of the weird happenings seem to be connected to this part of the cemetery? It has been suggested that perhaps Old Union Cemetery is marked by what some call a portal, or doorway, between dimensions. Such portals are said to exist all over the world, providing access for entities to come into our realm. The entities may be the spirits of people who have lived before, or they may be something else altogether. Some researchers believe that they could be otherworldly beings from a dimension we cannot even comprehend.

We know this all sounds far-fetched, but it may not be as strange as it seems. If locations like this do exist and they are some sort of doorway, it's possible that these spots may have been labeled haunted over the years by people who saw something near them that they couldn't explain, isn't it? It's possible that some reports of ghosts, spook lights, and perhaps even ancient stories of fairies and little people came from areas where portals were located.

If you are looking for weird stuff that defies logic, you'll find Old Union Cemetery just the spot. It's worth searching for, and when you get there, hike back and look for the old metal fence where the weathered tombstones have all but fallen down. Just be sure to keep your head down—you never know what may be flying by.

Groundskeeper Hated Mowing That Plot

I used to cut the grass at Old Union Cemetery in De Witt County, and there is a part of the cemetery that I hated to work in. In the back, near the woods, is this old fence and tombstone. I hate that place. It always seems cold there, and every time that I cut grass I felt like someone was watching me. The place must be haunted.—*Gary H.*

Old Union Cemetery Is Worth Checking Out

There is a place that you should check out called Old Union Cemetery. It's not haunted like you might think, but I have been out there with friends and have seen these weird lights in the trees. They're like yellow and glow a little bit. I have no idea what they are.—*Becky S.*

Cop Is Witness to Lights

I have been on the sheriff's department for about six years now, and I used to patrol out east of Clinton. I used to get reports from people who lived out that way who said that they saw lights in Old Union Cemetery at night. Some of the lights were so bright, they said, that they thought vandals were in the graveyard. I never found any vandals or anyone else out there, but I did see these lights in the back. They flew around all over the place. The place gave me the creeps.—*Joan C.*

Watseka Wonder: The Possession of Lurancy Vennum

The small town of Watseka, Illinois, is located about seventy-five miles south of Chicago, just a few miles from the Indiana border. The sensation that would come to be known as the Watseka Wonder would first make its appearance here in July 1877.

It was at this time that a thirteen-year-old girl named Lurancy Vennum first fell into a strange catatonic sleep during which she claimed to speak with spirits. The attacks occurred many times each day and sometimes lasted as long as eight hours. During her trance, Lurancy would speak in different voices, and when she awoke, she would remember nothing. News of the strange girl, whom doctors diagnosed as mentally ill, traveled about the state, and during this time of popularity for the spiritualist movement, many visitors came to see her.

In January 1878, a man named Asa Roff, also from Watseka, came to visit the Vennum family. He claimed that his own late daughter, Mary, had been afflicted with the same condition as Lurancy. He was convinced that his daughter had actually spoken to spirits and that his daughter's spirit still existed—inside the body of Lurancy Vennum.

To understand the strange and fantastic events that took place in Watseka, we must first start at the beginning of the tale and try to piece together a puzzle that has disturbed historians for years.

Mary Roff was born in Indiana in October 1846. At the age of six months, she began suffering from strange fits, which gradually increased in violence. Mary's life ended on the afternoon of July 5, 1865, while hospitalized at the State Mental Asylum in Peoria. She had been committed there when she began slashing her arms with a straight razor. It was the final tragedy in Mary's descent into madness.

When she was a young child, Mary had complained of hearing mysterious voices. She also experienced long periods in a trancelike state. Then, when she awoke, she spoke in other voices and seemed to be possessed by the spirits of other people. Finally Mary developed an obsession with blood. She became convinced that she needed to remove the blood from her body, using pins, leeches, and at last, a sharpened razor.

In the asylum, Mary endured more tragedy, as the "cures" for insanity in those days were cruel. A favored treatment was the water cure, in which a patient would be immersed naked in a tub of icy water and then taken to a tub of scalding water. And there was more horror. Female patients, like Mary, received a cold water douche, and then wet sheets were wrapped tightly around them to squeeze the blood vessels shut. This was followed by vigorous rubbing to restore circulation. These treatments were administered several times each week. Not surprisingly, such techniques brought little success, and most patients never improved. Mary died not long after arriving at the hospital.

Lurancy Vennum had been born on April 16, 1864, and she and her family had moved to Watseka when she was seven years old. Since they arrived after Mary Roff's death, the Vennum family knew nothing of Mary's strange illness, nor did they have more than a nodding acquaintance with the Roff family.

On the morning of July 11, 1877, Lurancy felt sick and then collapsed onto the floor. She stayed in a deep catatonic sleep for five hours, but when she awoke she seemed fine. However, this was only the beginning. The next day Lurancy once again slipped off into the trancelike sleep, but this time she began speaking aloud of visions and spirits. In her trance, she told her family that she was in heaven and that she could see and hear spirits, including the spirit of her brother, who had died in 1874.

From that day on, the trances began to occur more and more frequently and would sometimes last for up to eight hours. While she was asleep, Lurancy continued to speak about her visions, which were sometimes terrifying. She claimed that spirits were chasing her through the house and shouting her name. The attacks occurred up to a dozen times each day, and as they continued, Lurancy began to speak in other languages, or at least in nonsense words that no one could understand. When she awoke, she would remember nothing of her trance or of her strange ramblings.

Rumors about Lurancy and her visions began to circulate in Watseka. The local newspaper even printed stories about her. No one followed the case more closely than Asa Roff. In the early stages of his own daughter's illness, she too had claimed to communicate with spirits and would fall into long trances without warning. He was sure that Lurancy Vennum was suffering from the same illness as his poor daughter. But Roff said nothing until the Vennum family exhausted every known cure for Lurancy. It was not until the local doctor and a minister suggested that the girl be sent to the State Mental Hospital that Roff got involved. He refused to see another young woman end up in the hands of the doctors who had so tortured his Mary.

On January 31, 1878, he contacted the Vennum family. They were naturally skeptical of his story, but he did persuade them to let him bring a Dr. E. Winchester Stevens to the house. Stevens, like Asa Roff, was a dedicated spiritualist, and the two men had become convinced that Lurancy was not insane. They believed that she was actually a vessel through which the dead were communicating.

The Vennums allowed Dr. Stevens to "mesmerize" the girl and try to contact the spirits through her. Within moments, Lurancy was speaking in another voice, which allegedly came from a spirit named Katrina Hogan. Then the spirit changed and claimed to be that of Willie Canning, a young man who had committed suicide. She spoke as Willie for over an hour; then she suddenly threw her arms into the air and fell over backward. Dr. Stevens took her hands until she regained control of her body. She was now in heaven and would allow a gentler spirit to control her.

She said the spirit's name was Mary Roff.

The trance continued into the next day, and by this time, Lurancy apparently was Mary Roff. She said that she wanted to leave the Vennum house and go home to the Roff house. When Mrs. Roff heard the news, she hurried to the Vennum house in the company of her married daughter, Minerva Alter. Lurancy watched the two women walk up the sidewalk and reportedly said, "Here comes Ma and Nervie," and ran up to hug the two surprised women. No one had called Minerva by the name Nervie since Mary's death in 1865.

It now seemed evident to everyone that Mary had taken control of Lurancy Vennum. She knew everything about the Roff family and treated them as her loved ones. The Vennums, on the other hand, although treated very courteously, were met with a distant politeness.

On February 11, Lurancy was allowed to go home with the Roffs. Mr. and Mrs. Vennum agreed that it would be for the best, although they desperately hoped that Lurancy would regain her true identity. The Roffs, however, saw this as a miracle, as though Mary had returned from the grave. Lurancy was taken across town, and as they traveled, they passed by the former Roff home, where they had been living when Mary died. She demanded to know why they were not returning there, and they had to explain that they had moved a few years earlier.

For the next several months, Lurancy lived as Mary and seemed to have completely forgotten her former life. As days passed, Lurancy continued to show that she knew more about the Roff family, their possessions, and habits, than she could have possibly known if she had been faking the whole thing. Many of the incidents and remembrances that she referred to had taken place years before Lurancy had even been born.

She seemed happy living in the Roff home, and she recognized and called by name many of the friends and neighbors known to Mary in her lifetime. In contrast, she claimed to not recognize any of the Vennum family, their friends, or neighbors. In spite of this, Mr. and Mrs. Vennum and the family visited her often at the Roff home, and after frequent visits, she learned to love these "strangers."

During her stay with the Roffs, Lurancy's physical condition improved. She no longer suffered from fits, and yet she was unable to function as anyone other than Mary.

In early May, Lurancy told the Roff family that it was nearly time for her to leave. She became despondent and would spend the day going from one family member to the next, hugging them and touching them at every opportunity. She wept often at the thought of leaving her "real family." Over the next couple of weeks, a battle raged for control of Lurancy's physical body. At one moment, Lurancy would announce that she had to leave, and at the next moment, Mary would cling to her father and cry over the idea of parting with him. On May 19, in the presence of Henry Vennum, Lurancy's brother, Mary yielded control for a time and Lurancy seemed to take full possession of her own body. Two days later Mary was gone altogether.

On May 21, Lurancy returned home to the Vennums. She displayed none of the strange symptoms of her earlier illness, and her parents were convinced that somehow she had been cured, thanks to intervention by the spirit of Mary Roff. She soon became a happy and healthy young woman, suffering no ill effects from her experience.

She remained in touch with the Roff family for the rest of her life. Although she had no memories of her time as Mary, she still felt a curious closeness to the Roffs. During visits to their home, Lurancy would sometimes allow Mary to take control of her so that she could communicate with her family.

When Lurancy turned eighteen, she married a local farmer named George Binning, and two years later they moved to Rawlins County, Kansas. They bought a farm and had eleven children. Lurancy died in the late 1940s.

Asa Roff and his wife received hundreds of letters, from believers and skeptics alike, after the story of the possession was printed on the front page of the Watseka newspaper. After a year of constant hounding and scorn from neighbors, they left Watseka and moved to Kansas. Seven years later they returned to live with Minerva and her husband. They died of old age and are buried in Watseka.

Dr. Stevens lectured on the Watseka Wonder for eight years before dying in Chicago in 1886.

Mary Roff was never heard from again.

The Macomb Fire Starter

The word poltergeist *is German for "noisy ghost."* Activities connected with poltergeist cases include knocking and pounding sounds, disturbance of stationary objects, doors slamming shut, and violent physical actions sometimes involving heavy objects. Despite what some believe, many cases like this have nothing to do with ghosts.

The most widely accepted theory in many poltergeistlike cases is that the activity is not caused by a ghost, but by a person in the household. This person is usually an adolescent girl and normally one who is troubled emotionally. It is thought that she is unconsciously manipulating the items in the house by psychokinesis, the power to move things using energy generated in the mind. The living person, or agent, subconsciously vents her repressed anger or frustration in ways that science has yet to explain. Most of these disturbances are short-lived because the conditions that cause them to occur often pass quickly.

One of the most famous poltergeist cases in America took place in Macomb in 1948 and appeared in almost every newspaper in the nation, often on the front page. That year, a disturbed thirteen-year-old named Wanet McNeill was forced to live with her father, Arthur, after her parents' bitter divorce. The girl, her younger brother, Arthur Jr., and her father moved to the farm of Charles Willey, Arthur's brother-in-law. Wanet's mother was living in Bloomington, and that's where Wanet very much wanted to be.

Mysterious fires began on August 7, when small brown spots appeared on the wallpaper of the Willey house. Seconds after they appeared, they would burst into flames. This happened day after day, and neighbors came to help keep watch and to dowse the small fires with water. Pans and buckets were placed all over the

house. Still, the fires materialized in front of the startled witnesses. The fire chief from Macomb, Fred Wilson, was called in to investigate, and he had the family strip the wallpaper from every wall in the house. Dozens of witnesses watched as brown spots appeared on the bare plaster and then burst into flames. More small blazes even spread to the ceiling.

"The whole thing is so screwy and fantastic that I'm ashamed to talk about it," Wilson said. "Yet we have at least a dozen reputable witnesses that say they saw brown spots smolder suddenly on the walls and ceilings of the home and then burst into flames."

During the week of August 9, fires appeared on the front porch, ignited the curtains in every room, and even engulfed an entire bed. Fire investigators, insurance investigators, as well as the Illinois State fire marshal, John Burgard, all visited the farm. "Nobody has ever seen anything like this," Burgard announced to the press, "but I saw it with my own eyes." No one could give an explanation for the fires.

That week, over two hundred fires broke out, and on August 14, fire finally consumed the entire house. Willey drove posts into the ground and made a shelter for his wife while McNeill moved his children into the garage. The next day the barn went up in flames, followed by the milk house, which was being used as a dining room. On Thursday, two fires were discovered in the chicken house, and that same afternoon the farm's second barn burned down in less than an hour. A company that sold fire extinguishers was on hand with equipment, but it did little

radio waves, underground gas pockets, flying saucers, and more. The authorities had a more down-to-earth explanation in mind. They suspected arson.

On August 30, the mystery was announced solved. The arsonist, according to officials, was Wanet. They claimed that she was starting the fires with kitchen matches when no one was looking. The officials ignored reports from witnesses that fires sprang up from nowhere, even on the ceiling, and often when Wanet was not in the room. Apparently, this slight thirteen-year-old girl possessed some pretty amazing skills, along with a seemingly endless supply of matches.

Fire marshal Burgard and a state's attorney named Keith Scott took Wanet aside for questioning, during which time she allegedly confessed. She stated that she was unhappy, didn't like the farm, and wanted to see her mother, and, most telling, complained that she didn't have pretty clothes. As far as the officials were concerned, the mystery was solved!

This explanation pleased the authorities, but not all the reporters who were present seemed convinced. The hundreds of paranormal investigators who have examined the case over the years have not been reassured either. One columnist from a Peoria newspaper, who had covered the case from the beginning, stated quite frankly that he did not believe the so-called confession. Neither did noted researcher of the unexplained Vincent Gaddis, who wrote about the case. He was convinced it was a perfect example of poltergeist phenomena.

What really happened on the Willey farm? We will probably never know. Wanet went to live with her grandmother. The insurance company paid Willey for the damage done to his home and farm, the reporters all had closure for the stories, and the general public was given a solution that could not have possibly been the truth.

But that's often the case, isn't it?

good. An employee of the company stated that "it was the most intense heat that I've ever felt."

The family escaped to a nearby vacant house, but the fires continued. The United States Air Force even got involved in the mystery. They suggested that the fires could be caused by some sort of directed radiation, presumably from the Russians, but could offer no further assistance. By this time, the farm was swarming with spectators, investigators, and reporters. Over one thousand people came on August 22 alone. Theorists posed their own explanations. They ran the gamut from fly spray to

The Virgin Mary Visits Illinois

Visitations from angels and the Virgin Mary are nothing new, although most believe that such miracles ended long ago. This may not be the case, however, especially in Illinois, where the Virgin Mary makes regular appearances, and where shrines, paintings, and relics bleed, ooze, and mystify the faithful.

One spot that Mary regularly visits is the Lady of the Snows Shrine in Belleville. She was first encountered there by Ray Doiron in 1993 and appeared for a number of years afterward. Before being visited by Mary, Doiron had been through three near-death experiences and was deaf in his right ear. He had been sleeping one afternoon when he heard a soft voice that instructed him to go to the nearby Lady of the Snows Shrine. He was told to first go on February 11 and then on the thirteenth of each successive month.

At first, the visitations were kept secret, but they were always the same. There would be a strong wind that would suddenly stop, and then a statue at the shrine would turn blue just before a bright light would appear. From the light would appear the form of Mary. She would speak and impart lessons, which Doiron would write down. Later he was allowed to bring a small number of friends to the shrine, and finally he was told to make the visitations public. Since then, hundreds have visited the site, and it's a popular attraction to this day.

In recent times, Mary has also reportedly appeared to six young people in war-torn Bosnia, an event that has attracted more than eleven million people from around the globe. One such man was Joseph Reinholtz, a retired railroad worker from Hillside, Illinois. He had been suffering from blurred vision and periods of blindness and journeyed to Bosnia to pray and meet with one of the young people who had reported seeing Mary. She prayed over Reinholtz in 1987, and after he returned to Illinois, his sight slowly returned.

Reinholtz went back to Bosnia in 1989. This time the young woman instructed him to return home and look for a large crucifix next to a three-branched tree. He was to pray there, she told him. He later discovered this location at Queen of Heaven Cemetery in Hillside and began to make frequent trips to the spot to pray. On August 15, 1990, Reinholtz had his first visitation from Mary, and it was repeated on November 1, when she returned, he claimed, with Saint Michael and three other angels. Soon word of the visitations leaked out, and thousands of people began flocking to the cross. It wasn't long before complaints about the number of spectators caused the cemetery officials to move the cross to another location. It is very accessible now and even has a paved parking lot next to it.

The visitations reportedly occur every day but Tuesday, which is coincidentally the day that the archdiocese of Chicago placed a "restriction of obedience" on Reinholtz and asked that he not visit the cemetery. But the Hillside man is not the only person to report miracles at the site of the cross. There have been dozens of photographs taken here that purport to show angels and various types of light phenomena. Others claim to have seen blood coming from the cross and have reported the scent of roses in the air.

Weird Illinois visited the site a couple of years ago and found it surrounded by the faithful, praying and passing out religious literature. We have been shown a number of the "miraculous" photos taken there and confess that it looked like bad photography and a lot of sun glare to us—but we cannot argue the importance of the photos in the lives of the believers.

Sadly, Joseph Reinholtz suffered a stroke in February 1995 and was hospitalized, where Mary continued to visit him. He passed away in December 1996, but his legacy remains in Queen of Heaven Cemetery, where a crucifix stands and where true believers still experience miraculous visitations.

Tears from Heaven

In addition to being the location of sightings of the Virgin Mary, Chicago has also played host to religious apparitions, weeping statues, and relics. Over the past three decades, there have been more than a dozen reported religious apparitions and unexplained happenings in the area, each of them drawing dozens, sometimes hundreds, of believers. The sites include statues, paintings, and icons that appear to weep and shapes and shadows that appear on windows, walls, and even tree trunks.

One strange event took place at St. Adrian's Church on Chicago's south side in May 1970. According to witnesses, the seventeen-hundred-year-old remains of Saint Maximina, a first-class relic, began oozing watery blood.

Another miraculous incident happened in December 1986, when a painting of the Virgin Mary that hung in St. Nicholas Albanian Orthodox Church began to weep. The phenomenon continued for the next seven months, during which time water also dripped from her fingers. Hundreds of people witnessed the event, but the icon abruptly ceased crying in July 1987. A year later the weeping started up again, but didn't last long. At that time, the tears that she produced were used to anoint nineteen icons in Pennsylvania, and they all began weeping too.

An icon panel of the Virgin Mary in St. George's Antiochian Orthodox Church in Cicero began weeping oil during April 1994 at the beginning of Holy Week. Eight orthodox bishops examined the tears and declared them to be genuine. Mary has continued to cry, and the relic has since been renamed Our Lady of Cicero.

The Virgin of Guadalupe was said to have visited Hanover Park in July 1997, appearing on the wall of an apartment complex located at 2420 Glendale Terrace. The image appeared from shadows created by a security light that was angled at the building. When the light was turned off, the image vanished, but the faithful remained, convinced that a holy miracle had taken place. Today, at the southwest end of the parking area, a tent stands next to the building where it happened. Inside are hundreds of votive candles and a statue of the Virgin Mary.

Mystery Airships over Illinois

People have been seeing strange things in the skies since the beginning of time, but during the late 1800s and early days of the 1900s, reports of mysterious flying aircraft drifted in from around the country. What were these strange craft? Who had built them, and perhaps most importantly, who was flying them?

The sightings of the airships, with their vast metal wingspans and arrays of bright lights, first began in California in 1896. Hundreds of people saw them as they began to make what seemed to be a leisurely tour eastward across the country. People also reported encounters with the passengers of the ships. Most of them were said to carry strange messages to the witnesses on the ground, while others seemed to have superior intelligence, odd complexions, and weird speech patterns.

One of the first airship sightings took place in Sacramento, California, on November 22, 1896. A deputy sheriff named Walter Mallory spotted a bright white light with a dark body behind it. The next day it was seen in Tacoma, Washington, and in San Jose, California. On February 2, 1897, a giant airship was spotted in Hastings, Nebraska, and then on March 27, in Topeka, Kansas.

The airship arrived in Illinois on April 3, when it flew over Evanston and several other communities near Chicago. The local newspapers promoted fears that the airship was filled with "English spies." Over five hundred people witnessed the craft over Evanston, and it was in full view for over forty-five minutes. One description noted that the airship was "composed of two cigar-shaped bodies attached by girders," and others claimed that it had wings and sails.

The airship reportedly stayed in the Chicago area for three days and was there long enough to be photographed by a newsdealer named Walter McCann. After the plates were developed, McCann gave copies of the photos to all

> The airship arrived in Illinois on April 3, 1897, when it flew over Evanston and several other communities near Chicago. The local newspapers promoted fears that the airship was filled with "English spies."

the newspapers that requested them, but he refused to sell the negatives. Staff artists for the *Chicago Times-Herald* subjected the photos to acid tests and proclaimed them authentic. Sadly though, they have since been lost.

After the airship left Chicago, it began a tour across the state and was spotted in dozens of cities. There seemed to be no rhyme or reason to its route; it appeared in both northern and southern Illinois within a day or so of its appearance elsewhere. Even if we discount many of the reports as jokes generated by newspaper stories, there are still scores of credible accounts.

Several of the Illinois sightings from April 1897 stand out as particularly strange. One of the encounters took place about two miles outside Springfield, when two farmhands reported that the airship landed in a field where they were working. The occupants of the ship, two men and a woman, came out and told the field workers that they would make a report to the government about their journey "when Cuba is declared free." Modern readers who are confused about this should note that this period of history was marked by the Spanish-American War over the issue of Cuban independence. After this bizarre announcement, the occupants of the airship waved and climbed back into the craft. It lifted off again into the skies.

The airship was seen again near Mount Vernon a few days later. The city's mayor was looking at the sky with his telescope when the ship came into range. In addition to the airship, he also claimed to see one of the occupants of the craft hovering in the sky around it. He said that the man had some sort of device strapped to his back.

The airship landed several more times over the next few days—in Nilwood, Downs Township, and Green Ridge—but the occupants always left when they were approached by witnesses. In two of the cases, the passengers were seen checking over some of the machinery on the airship before they took off.

The last airship sighting in the state took place in Rossville on April 25. Then the ship moved on to Indiana before vanishing for good.

How can we explain the mysterious airship that visited Illinois in April 1897? Was it a hoax, or a case of mass hysteria? Perhaps, but this seems unlikely based on the completely unconnected witnesses who reported it.

If the ship was real, then who were its passengers? They had strange messages to pass along and seemed to be almost constantly at work on their vessel. During one earlier encounter that took place in Texas, an airship passenger actually asked for help in repairing his craft. He handed the witness American money and asked him to get supplies from the local hardware store.

The mystery remains unsolved. The airship could not have been built by any mechanical means of the time period, and yet it apparently existed. The passengers on the ship appeared to be normal humans, taking what seemed to them to be a normal trip, aboard a machine that could not exist—and yet did.

Illinois Versus the Flying Saucers

Illinois has hundreds of sightings of UFOs in its history. Aside from the weird airship sightings of 1897, most of the reports began at the dawn of the modern UFO age, in 1947, when, two years after the end of World War II, the public embraced the idea of watching the skies for mysterious visitors.

One of the most thrilling UFO flaps to occur in Illinois history took place on the night of July 4, 1997. For three hours, hundreds, if not thousands, of Illinois residents saw a blue-green UFO, or several UFOs, along with the holiday fireworks in the sky.

The excitement began with a sighting in Lenzburg around eight thirty p.m. A local man was outside with his wife, daughter, and the daughter's boyfriend, shooting off some fireworks, when they saw a bluish white light in the sky. It was so bright that they ducked for cover. Then, as they looked up, they saw a bright blue, ball-shaped object moving from east to west at great speed. There was no sound—the light simply passed over and disappeared.

At nine fifteen, in Elmwood, another witness was watching a local fireworks show and saw an unusual object come down from the clouds. It first appeared as a bright flash and then seemed to be a solid object with a bluish glow to it. It descended straight downward, with no sound, and vanished below the edge of the horizon.

A few minutes later a group of people in Granite City saw the same object. They also described it as being bluish green, and it traveled from east to west. It was gone within a moment or two.

At nine thirty-five, a group of relatives who were driving through Fairview Heights on their way to St. Louis spotted a blue UFO with a wispy blue trail. At the same time, it was seen over Millstadt, where one of the witnesses claimed that it vanished in a red flash.

Meanwhile, a similar object was seen over

Southwestern Illinois College in Belleville during a fireworks display. Hundreds, perhaps thousands, of people saw it. Most of them assumed that it was a firework that did not explode. Then they realized that it was much too large—and much too weird. It was royal blue in color, most agreed, and left a white, sparkling tail behind it. As the light was appearing over the campus, it was also being seen by several hundred people at the Skyview Drive-in Theater in Belleville.

Five minutes later, at nine forty p.m., spectators at the fireworks presentation in Collinsville saw the blue light. At nine forty-five, it was flying over East Alton. A family there saw a bright blue-and-green object traveling from east to west. Moments later it was seen again in Millstadt, and then at nine fifty-three, it flashed over Dupo. Witnesses here added that it had red lights along the edges. The blue light in this report was said to be a flashing beam that moved back and forth over the ground. The UFO moved over a house, and then just as it started to pass over some woods, the light turned off.

At ten p.m., the blue object was reported over Granite City and also over Alton. At the same time, it appeared above Valmeyer, traveling about two hundred to four hundred feet above the ground. Witnesses watched as it appeared over the bluffs on the Illinois side of the Mississippi River and sped off toward Missouri.

If it was the same craft, then it changed directions to appear over the eastern Illinois town of Olney at ten twenty-five p.m. Strangely, it was seen again over Freeport, on the opposite side of the state. Witnesses here also described a bright blue object, this time shaped like a diamond. It moved from east to west and then vanished.

At ten forty-five p.m., the object was spotted over a field in Brighton, again moving from east to west, and was seen again in Columbia and then, on July 5, in

One of the most thrilling UFO flaps to occur in Illinois history took place on the night of July 4, 1997. For three hours, hundreds, if not thousands, of Illinois residents saw a blue-green UFO, or several UFOs, along with the holiday fireworks in the sky.

Caseyville. And with that, the flap came to an end.

April 1998 brought major UFO sightings in northern Illinois. They began on April 4 in Bedford Park when a man leaving work saw a green sphere streaking through the sky. The sphere left a white trail behind it. It traveled for some distance and then vanished. Later on the next night, at around nine thirty-five, the man saw the same object heading west before it disappeared again.

Two hours later, in Channahon, a young student saw a much different object. He was driving home from a friend's house when he noticed three lights in the sky. They seemed to be hovering over a field, and as he rounded a curve to the right, he lost sight of them behind some trees. As he came around the stand of woods, he saw that the lights formed a perfect triangle and that the craft they were connected to was hovering over a quarry. The lights rotated clockwise; then the ship banked and turned, moving in the direction of the student's car. As it came closer, he sped off down the winding road, only looking back to see that the object was keeping pace with him. The road curved, and he lost the lights in the trees again, but a few moments later, as he stopped to turn left onto U.S. Route 6, he saw that they were still there. In fact, the craft had banked, so that the bottom of the object was turned in the direction of the car. The student raced away, and when he finally dared a look into the rearview mirror, the object was gone.

On April 14, in Texico, an encounter took place at nine thirty p.m. A woman and her two children were in their car driving home and noticed a bright light in the sky. It seemed to follow their automobile and kept growing brighter. As they pulled into their driveway, the object passed slowly over them, then traveled southward and west before disappearing.

On March 11, 1999, the crew of an airliner coming into Chicago was allegedly burned by a UFO. Around nine that night, the pilot and copilot were watching a display of what they thought were the northern lights. They were coming in for a landing and were amazed to see the lights start to "stretch above and over the aircraft." There was a short pulse of green light, and then the light turned into a bright ball, which quickly approached the plane from the north. According to reports, the members of the cockpit crew experienced a sensation on their faces as if they had been sunburned. As soon as the green light vanished, the burning sensation went with it. The next morning, however, one crew member noticed that his skin was red and sore.

A young man and his girlfriend were on their way home from a movie on February 23, 2002, when they saw a cylinder-shaped object giving off a blue light in the sky over Belleville at around eleven p.m. As they approached a stoplight, they saw that passengers in a nearby car were also looking at the object. A few moments later the blue light faded out. It was dark for several seconds, and then the object let out a white light and shot across the sky. Within a minute, two military jets (presumably from nearby Scott Air Force Base) streaked past, following in the wake of the mysterious object.

On October 15, 2002, a motorist was driving on Missouri Avenue in East St. Louis and stopped at a railroad crossing. As he was waiting for the train to pass, he noticed what he first thought was a large object in the sky moving up and down and in a spiral motion. It soon became apparent that he was not watching one object, but many, possibly as many as one hundred to two hundred lights that were all moving in sequence. The lights were part of round metallic objects that glinted as they reflected the light from the afternoon sun.

Once the train had passed, he followed the lights out on Highway 15, and he kept them in sight for nearly ten minutes. Suddenly they split up, and a large group of them headed southeast in a V formation. Another small group headed off to the west. About thirty seconds later two military fighter jets appeared out of the north, flying toward the objects. At that very moment, the two groups of UFOs just disappeared.

These reports are merely a sampling of the strange events that have occurred in Illinois over the years. There are hundreds of others.

The Alien in the Attic

I was the Illinois State Director for an organization called MUFON (Mutual UFO Network) in the 1970s and 1980s. I was always interested in stories that people had to tell about strange things they had seen in the skies or even on the ground, like typical UFOs. One of the strangest reports that I investigated alleged that a UFO had crashed on a farm in central Illinois and that the farmer had pulled a dead alien from the craft and put it into a box. The box was then placed in his attic and hidden there. A friend of mine and his wife actually saw the dried-up alien, but I could never get the farmer to talk to me, because he did not want any publicity. As far as I know, that alien is still in the farmer's attic to this day.—*Leonard S.*

Extra, Extra, Extraterrestrial!

My neighbors had a weird encounter with something back when I was a kid. My friend's little brother was out delivering newspapers one morning in early December and saw a small UFO fly overhead. It stopped right over his head, and he was so scared that he stopped his bike and sat down on the ground. He could never explain why. Anyway, his dog always came with him on the route; the dog ran home, and when he got there, everybody knew that something was wrong. His dad drove over and picked him up. The kid was so scared that his dad told the whole family to never mention the incident again. My friend told me later that one of his brothers did ask about the UFO one time at Christmas dinner, and the younger kid turned white and threw up! My friend always said that he never had a doubt that the boy had had a real close encounter.—*Donny W.*

Fighter Jets Track Bogey over Belleville

I was a teenager in 1979, and I was working on my parents' farm one day and saw a UFO. I was on the tractor near Belleville and had just turned around to start back down the rows when I saw something silver and shiny come streaking out of the sky from the south. It was moving really fast, and then all of the sudden it stopped and shot straight upward. It sort of banked and then swooped back down again. A moment or two later it took off again to the east. I couldn't really believe what I was seeing, and I must have been just sitting there when all of the sudden, two fighter jets came from the direction of Scott Air Force Base and chased after the UFO. They had obviously picked it up on radar or something and came to investigate it. I watched the newspapers for a few days after that, but I never saw any mention of something in the sky.—*Tom R.*

Keep Watching the Sky! The 2000 UFO over Illinois

Something very strange visited southwestern Illinois on January 5, 2000 — but what it was remains a mystery to this day.

The first person to notice anything weird was Melvern Noll, the owner of a miniature golf course in Highland. During the winter months, Noll worked as a truck driver. He was just returning from a delivery at around four a.m. and decided to make a quick stop at his golf course, just to make sure everything was in order during the off-season. As he climbed out of his truck, he noticed a bright star in the northeastern sky. He didn't give it much thought and went into the building.

After a few minutes, he returned to his truck and again noticed the bright light. This time he realized that the "star" was moving in his direction and now looked like part of a giant rectangle, roughly the size of a football field. It was very tall and had two floors with windows that emitted a very bright light. He also spotted a number of dim red lights on the bottom of the rectangle. The object was black or dark gray, and he described it as looking like a "two-story house" in the sky.

Noll watched as it moved silently across

the sky and then vanished. The entire sighting lasted almost five minutes.

Noll immediately drove to the Highland police station. He was sure that no one would believe him but hoped that whoever was on duty might be open-minded enough to at least contact a neighboring town's police department and see if the strange object in the sky could be verified. The dispatcher in Highland was skeptical of Noll's account, but he agreed to put a call into the police in Lebanon and ask them to be on the lookout for anything unusual.

Officer Ed Barton received the call at around four fifteen a.m. Not surprisingly, he asked the dispatcher if he was joking. When he was assured that it was a serious call, he drove to the north end of town, past Horner Park, and onto Widicus Road. He saw nothing out of the ordinary but followed the road as it turned to the north and the east toward Illinois 4. A short distance along this road, Officer Barton looked up and saw two large, brilliant white lights in the sky. Curious, he drove a little faster. When he arrived at Route 4, he turned south and headed back toward Lebanon, watching the lights from his driver's-side window as he drove. He noticed that the two lights seemed to merge into one, and he became convinced that they were from a low-flying aircraft that was experiencing mechanical problems.

The object seemed to stop and then to move again. Barton turned off his lights and his car radio in order to hear any sound the craft might be making. As far as he could tell, though, it was completely silent.

As the dark shape got closer to him, he could make

Police Report Sketch, *January 2000, Officer Martin; Shiloh, Illinois' Police Department*

out more details. It appeared to be a massive elongated narrow triangle, and at each corner was a bright white light. The lights appeared to be pointing straight down. They did not light up the ground, but they were still very bright. Amid them, he also saw a smaller red light that was flashing. The ship moved closer and blotted out the rest of the sky. Even at this close distance, which Barton guessed was no more than one thousand feet from the ground, the object made no noise. Then it turned in a southwesterly direction, never banking like a normal aircraft would, but rotating, always remaining completely level.

Barton now scrambled for his radio and called in to describe what he was seeing. In between transmissions, he saw the aircraft pick up speed and shoot away from him.

By the time he finished his call, he told the dispatcher that he estimated the object was now above the town of Shiloh, about eight miles to the southwest.

At this time, Officer David Martin of the Shiloh Police Department joined in on the sighting and radioed back that he could indeed see something in the sky. He had been driving along the southern end of town when he saw the mysterious object, which was moving to the west. Martin noticed the three brilliant white lights, as well as the flashing red one, before he saw the dark mass of the ship's body. He thought the object resembled a wide triangle or an arrowhead, and as he chased after it, he stuck his head out the window to see if he could hear any sounds coming from it. He too heard absolutely no sound. Finally the craft picked up speed and moved out of the area.

By this time, the weird radio transmissions were

attracting the attention of other officers on early-morning duty in surrounding small towns. One was Craig Stevens, a cop in nearby Millstadt. After hearing the other calls, he drove to the east end of town in an attempt to see this thing. When he got to Liederkranz Park, he looked out the windshield of his squad car and spotted a large triangular-shaped object in the sky. He described it as moving very slowly, and he said that it made no noise except for a "low-decibel buzzing sound" that he could barely hear. He watched it move to the north, and he saw the white lights and the single red light on the bottom. Stevens called his dispatcher, then grabbed his Polaroid camera and jumped out of the car. He aimed the camera at the object and took a photo. Unfortunately, the cold morning air and the dark of the early-morning hours produced only a murky and barely discernible image.

What was this bizarre ship? Was it really a UFO that would have passed over Illinois without incident if not for the watchful eyes of a miniature–golf course owner and a few small-town police officers? If it was, one has to wonder how it could have passed within one mile of Scott Air Force Base without causing grave concerns on the part of the military. The base would later state that they knew nothing of the large ship, leading many to believe that they were hiding the fact that this was some sort of test plane. But my brother was in the air force for many years and spent a few of them stationed at Scott. He told me flat out that there are no test planes at Scott.

UFO? Secret test plane? Or something else altogether? No one knows, but one thing is certain, those officers saw something that night. For now, though, what it may have been remains unexplained.

Bizarre Beasts

Legend has it that wild things lurk in the dark woods and remote regions of Illinois. They can be found on land, in the water, and even in the air. Sightings and stories abound, and yet no real proof has ever been found for some of the most legendary creatures in the state, including our own homegrown Bigfoot. Still, the lack of proof has not stopped many locals from believing that you shouldn't walk alone at night in rural areas if you don't want to encounter some nightmarish beast.

Ah yes, you may be thinking, those escaped house cats can be real terrors! But before you laugh off the state's many tales of terrifying beasts, consider this: Illinois is home to more Bigfoot sightings than any other state east of the Mississippi. And a wide variety of other strange critters abound here too. From kangaroos and monstrous, flesh-eating birds to albino squirrels, there's no denying that the state is home to some very weird creatures.

Even if you have never been afraid of solo strolls before, you will be by the time you finish this chapter! So take heed, and if you find yourself stranded in the woods or fields of Illinois with only the light of the moon to guide you, make sure you are ready to do battle with the eerie and sometimes vicious fauna of our strange state.

Bigfoot Makes His Home Here Too

Without a doubt, America's most famous Bigfoot sightings come from the Pacific Northwest, but such creatures do turn up in Illinois too. For more than a century, reports have filtered out of rural and southern Illinois of encounters with strange hairy beasts that resemble a cross between a man and an ape. Such stories have been passed along from generation to generation and have long been chronicled by both professional and amateur researchers, becoming deeply embedded in Illinois history and lending the region an air of mystery unrivaled by any other midwestern state.

According to many eyewitnesses, the creatures average around seven feet tall and give off a horrible odor. Their limbs appear unusually powerful and are described as proportioned more like human limbs than those of an ape. However, their broad shoulders, short necks, flat faces and noses, sloped foreheads, ridged brows, and pointy heads make them appear apelike. The creatures are usually reported to be almost completely covered in dark auburn hair, although reports of brown, black, and even white and silver hair do occasionally pop up. They are said to eat both meat and plants, are largely nocturnal, are usually seen wandering alone, and are less active during cold weather. The footprints these monsters leave behind are about seven inches wide and average about eighteen inches in length—clearly much larger than a human foot.

The earliest sighting that *Weird Illinois* could find occurred in 1912 when a woman named Beaulah Schroat reported that she and her brothers often used to spot some kind of huge hairy creature near their home in Effingham. The next brief report asserts that a manlike beast covered in brown hair and with the face of an ape was spotted near Alton in 1925.

Then, in July 1929, a creature described as looking like a huge gorilla was seen in the woods near Elizabeth. In 1941, more than a decade later, the Reverend Lepton Harpole was hunting squirrels near Mount Vernon when he encountered a beast that "looked something like a baboon." He struck it with his rifle and fired a warning shot that sent it scurrying back into the underbrush. More sightings of a similar creature occurred the following year.

From the 1940s through the 1960s, huge prints were

often discovered along the marshy areas of Indian Creek in southwestern Illinois. The creature leaving the tracks was dubbed the Gooseville Bear, taking its name from an area of farmland and small businesses about three miles east of Bethalto. Some insisted that the tracks belonged to a bear, while others claimed they were more manlike. Whatever this beast was, no one actually saw it, and after leaving its mark on the area for almost two decades, the Gooseville Bear simply disappeared.

But a similar creature reared its furry head in the state in 1962. Steven Collins and Robert Earle were standing in a river east of Decatur, just off East Williams Street Road, when they spotted a large grayish creature. The monster was looming upright in the water and looking straight at them, but then it quickly vanished into the woods. They had thought it was a bear at first, but then they noticed its strangely humanlike features. The two men later told the local newspaper that it was "like no other animal we had ever seen before."

In May 1963, a similarly strange creature reared its ugly head in Centreville. It also was sighted just across the Mississippi in St. Louis, where several children spotted a "half man, half woman with a half bald head and a half head of hair." They said they had seen it lurking around the Ninth Street housing project and that it often disappeared into an old tunnel around Twelfth Street. Patrolman Bill Conreux of the St. Louis Police Department took the sightings seriously, insisting, "Those kids were sincere. They saw something." He added, "Supposedly it scuffled with a man near the Patrick Henry School."

The St. Louis sightings began on May 9, but by May 18 the beast had moved back to Centreville. When it appeared in front of the house of James McKinney, he quickly summoned the police, but they never managed to catch up with what he described as "half man and half horse." According to reports, authorities received over fifty calls in a single night about the creature, but the sightings eventually dropped off. By May 23, the monster was apparently gone. But was it gone for good? Some claim that the sightings continued around Centreville until the 1980s but were never publicized.

One of the most memorable appearances of Illinois' Bigfoot occurred in an undeveloped area outside Decatur called Montezuma Hills, in September 1965, when a massive black manlike shape approached a parked car in which two young couples were sitting. A night at a lovers' lane quickly turned to panic, and the terrified teenagers drove away in a hurry. But after dropping their dates off at home, the two young men returned to the area for another look. Once again the monster walked up to the car as if curious. The boys were too scared to get out, but even with the windows rolled up, they could smell the monster's terrible stench. They brought police to the site, and several officers helped them complete a thorough, but fruitless, search of the woods. The police officers on the scene said they had no idea what the young people had witnessed, but they were obviously badly frightened by it.

Another manlike monster was encountered near Chittyville on August 11, 1968. Two young people, Tim Bullock and Barbara Smith, were driving north of town when a ten-foot-tall creature covered in black hair began throwing dirt at their car. They drove off quickly to summon the police, and when they all returned they found a large depression in the grass that was apparently a nest, but there was nothing in it.

This is just a small sampling of the many Bigfoot sightings reported in Illinois over the years. In several instances, strings of sightings in certain areas became so infamous that the creatures earned nicknames, such as the Farmer City Monster. These reports stand out very vividly to this day and make us all wonder what's really lurking in the deep dark woods.

The Freaky Farmer City Monster

One of the most well-known beast sightings took place in July 1970 near Salt Creek, a ten-acre section of woods and fields outside Farmer City. One night three teenagers decided to camp out in the area. Late in the evening, they heard something approaching their campsite through the tall grass. They turned a flashlight in that direction and saw a huge black shape crouching nearby. It had gleaming yellow eyes, a detail repeated in every sighting that followed. The terrified screams of the teenagers apparently scared the creature, which ran off into the darkness.

Stories about the Farmer City Monster quickly spread, and over the next several days dozens of people reported seeing the creature in the wooded area outside town. Robert Hayslip, a Farmer City police officer who was charged with investigating the reports, had his own encounter in the early-morning hours of July 15 when he saw the broad back of the beast moving among the trees. Eventually the creature turned in his direction, and Hayslip noted its yellow eyes. Following this report, the police chief, who until that point had been skeptical about the sightings, decided to close off the area.

But apparently the creature had already moved on. A few days later a woman driving north of Bloomington caught the reflection of piercing yellow eyes with her car headlights. She thought it might be an injured dog, so she stopped and approached the ditch where she had seen the eyes. Suddenly a large creature jumped out and ran away on two legs. Later that same week another witness reported an identical beast near Heyworth.

Three young men claimed to have seen a large dark-haired creature near Waynesville on August 11, and then, on August 16, construction workers saw the creature near the same location, when it ran across the highway in front of their truck and disappeared into the forest. These were the last reported sightings of the so-called Farmer City Monster. We can't help but wonder if the beast continued its solitary journey across central Illinois. If it did, it was never reported again.

Dark Shadows Outside My Tent

When I was about twelve, my brother and I went camping at Carlyle Lake, which is near Vandalia. Back then, he liked to tease me and play a lot of pranks on me, so I didn't take him too seriously when he told me he had found these Bigfoot tracks out in the woods. He showed them to me, but I was sure that he made them himself and was just trying to scare me. That night, after we had gone to bed in the tent, we left a fire burning outside. It was kind of chilly that night, and the fire helped us stay warm. Some time after midnight my brother woke me up and told me that something was outside. I just laughed at him, right? I was sure that he was still trying to scare me. Then, all of a sudden, I saw this huge shadow between us and the fire! There was something out there, and it grabbed onto the guylines of the tent and started shaking it. My brother, who was always this tough guy, started to scream, and when he did, whatever was outside ran away. Neither one of us set foot outside that tent until morning. When we did, we found all of these huge footprints on the ground near the campfire. Guess what—they looked just like the footprints that my brother had shown me the day before!—*Rob S.*

A Creepy Thing Called Cohomo

Cohomo made his hairy debut in early May 1972 when news reports of a gigantic fur-covered beast starting flooding in from the Pekin and Peoria areas. It all started in late May when a young man named Randy Emmert and his friends spied the hulking hairy creature near Cole Hollow Road. Reports of sightings became so common that the beast quickly became known as Cohomo, short for the Cole Hollow Road Monster. This particular monster was eight to ten feet tall and covered in whitish hair, and made a loud screeching sound when encountered. Its very unusual tracks showed that it had only three large toes on each foot.

By May 25, local police departments had logged more than two hundred calls about Cohomo, and by July, there had been so many more sightings that the Tazewell County Sheriff's Department, though skeptical, organized one hundred volunteers to search for Cohomo. However, the department had to send them home empty-handed when Carl R. Harris, one of the volunteers, accidentally shot himself in the leg with a .22-caliber pistol.

Cohomo dropped out of sight for a while and was not seen again for over a year. On June 6, 1973, police in Edwardsville received three reports that a very large humanlike creature with a terrible odor was lurking in a wooded area near Mooney, Little Mooney, and Sugar creeks east of town. It was broad-shouldered but short and reportedly made no sound when it walked. The witnesses claimed that the creature chased them, and one man told police that it had clawed at him and ripped his shirt.

Since then, sightings of Cohomo and other Bigfoot-like creatures have been few and far between, but they do still occur, and *Weird Illinois* has talked to a number of people who have encountered these creatures in places like the American Bottoms region along the Mississippi River. The most recent sighting of Cohomo that we know of took place near Essex in July 2000. A man named Andrew Souligne was driving into a local cemetery one night when a bulky, furry shape walked in front of his car. The creature froze in the headlights and turned toward his vehicle, apparently stunned by the bright lights. Souligne and his passenger were pretty shocked themselves, and Souligne immediately backed his car away from the monster. Moments later the ape-man loped into the woods and vanished.

We're sure that many other recent encounters with Cohomo haven't been reported, for the simple reason that most people don't want others to think they're crazy! But crazy or not, most witnesses believe that Cohomo—and perhaps his brothers and sisters—is still out there, skulking through Illinois' deep dark woods. Who knows? Maybe you'll be the next one to see him.

The Murphysboro Mud Monster

The heavily wooded and sparsely populated reaches of southwestern Illinois, which include the sprawling Shawnee National Forest, seem to invite weirdness that might not occur in more crowded locales. This lonely wilderness area—sometimes referred to as the Devil's Kitchen because of its long history of eerie phenomena—seems almost untouched by humans, so it should come as no surprise that mysterious creatures apparently pass through here.

In the summer of 1973, the town of Murphysboro in this region became infamous for a series of hairy monster sightings. The enigmatic creature, dubbed the Murphysboro Mud Monster or the Big Muddy Monster, appeared without warning and disappeared just as suddenly two weeks later. In its wake, it left a number of confused and frightened witnesses, baffled law-enforcement officials, and, of course, an enduring legend.

A young couple, Randy Needham and Judy Johnson, first spotted the beast around midnight on June 25, 1973. On that humid and steamy evening, they were parked near a boat ramp on the Big Muddy River, enjoying the peaceful setting. Suddenly an eerie roar from the nearby woods shattered the silence. They looked up and froze when they saw a huge shape lumbering toward them out of the shadows. The beast walked on two legs and continued roaring as it lurched toward them. They later described the noise as "not human."

According to their account, the monster was about seven feet tall and covered with matted whitish hair streaked with mud from the river. As the creature loomed closer, its cry began to intensify, alarming them even more. When it was about twenty feet away, they were finally able to start their car and leave the scene, heading directly to the Murphysboro police station.

In 2003, the thirtieth anniversary of the sightings, former police chief Ron Manwaring agreed to be interviewed by *Weird Illinois* and related every detail he remembered about the case. "They were absolutely terrified," the retired officer recalled. "I'm convinced that they saw something that night. I can't tell you what it was that they saw, whether it was a bear or something else. But something was definitely there."

That night, shortly after the couple reported the sighting, officers Meryl Lindsay and Jimmie Nash had gone to the area to survey the scene. Although skeptical at first, they did in fact find a number of gigantic footprints in the mud. Their report states that the footprints were "approximately 10 to 12 inches long and approximately three inches wide." At two a.m., Nash, Lindsay, a Jackson County sheriff's deputy named Bob Scott, and Randy Needham returned to the scene. They discovered more tracks, and Lindsay left to get a camera while the others followed the footprints along the river.

Suddenly, from about one hundred yards away in the woods, came a terrifying, otherworldly scream. Instead of waiting to see if they could spot the monster, they beat a quick retreat to the patrol car. After a while, they got out again and spent the rest of the night trying to track down a splashing sound they could hear in the distance. They never did find the source of the sound, and the next night the creature was back in force.

This time the first person to spot the monster was a four-year-old boy named Christian Baril, who told his parents that he had just seen "a big white ghost" in the yard. They didn't believe him at first, but after learning that neighbors Randy Creath and Cheryl Ray had seen an identical monster in their yard just ten minutes later, Christian's parents reconsidered their son's comment.

At about ten thirty p.m., Randy and Cheryl were sitting on the back porch of their neighbors' house when they heard something moving in the woods near the river. They then spotted a muddy white-haired creature staring at them with glowing pink eyes. It stood about seven feet tall and had long, apelike arms, and they estimated that it weighed at least three hundred and fifty pounds. Cheryl turned on the porch light, and Randy went for a closer look. The creature seemed unconcerned and ambled off into the woods. Investigators later found a trail of broken tree branches and crushed undergrowth, along with a trail of huge footprints. The monster also left a strong foul odor in its wake, but that didn't last long.

The Murphysboro Mud Monster was glimpsed at least twice more that summer. In a July 4 sighting, traveling carnival workers found the creature checking out some Shetland ponies that were being used for the holiday celebration at Riverside Park. The carnival owner didn't report the encounter until July 7 because he was concerned it might scare away customers. He eventually told police that his workers had noticed the ponies straining to break loose from the trees where they had been tied up for the night. When they investigated, they came face-to-face with a monster seven to eight feet tall and covered in light brown hair. It stood erect and weighed at least three hundred pounds.

As the sightings continued, accounts were posted to the wire services and began turning up in newspapers, where they made big headlines. Even the *New York Times* sent a reporter to investigate. The story of the Big Muddy Monster was reported around the world, and soon letters came pouring into the Murphysboro Police Department from all over the country — and even from as far away as South Africa. Everyone, from curiosity-seekers to actual scientists, pleaded with the local authorities to release more information.

The police department also received many letters from hunters and trappers who offered to track down the monster and kill or capture it. Two men from Oregon proposed that they do the job, writing that they "would be willing to take on this adventure at only the cost of expenses and materials for doing so." Some wrote suggesting that the police try using bait to snare the creature. A Florida man asked, "Why don't you put bread and cheese and eggs out for your creature? You would have a splendid attraction if you could have it in a little hut to show people."

Despite all the media attention and scrutiny — or perhaps because of it — there was only one other sighting of the Murphysboro Mud Monster, and it occurred in the fall of 1973 several miles southwest of a town near the Mississippi River. A local truck driver told police that he had seen something that resembled the famous monster along the edge of the road, but it had vanished before he could get a good look at it. It did, however, leave some large prints behind in the mud. Researchers made casts of the prints but were unable to determine if they matched the previous footprints or were the work of a prankster. After that one last gasp, the Big Muddy Monster simply disappeared.

So what was the Murphysboro Mud Monster? In thirty years, no one has ever come forward with a logical explanation. One of the officers involved in the case said, "A lot of things in life are unexplained, and this is another one. We don't know what the creature is, but we do believe what these people saw was real." Randy Needham, one of the first to see the monster, recently said, "It would be kind of naïve for us to think that we know everything that's out there." He went on to admit that he never goes into the woods at night anymore.

The Enfield Horror

"It had three legs on it . . . a short body, two little short arms coming out of its breast area, and two pink eyes as big as flashlights."

While Illinois seems to have more than its fair share of Bigfoot sightings, it also seems to be home to even creepier creatures, like the Enfield Horror—a terrifying little beast seen in Enfield in April 1973. This tiny community in southeastern Illinois was the scene of some bizarre happenings during a brief period of time.

When local resident Henry McDaniel began telling folks about the weird events that took place at his home on April 25, 1973, the county sheriff threatened to lock him up. In spite of the threats, McDaniel stuck by his story, and his report brought about a living nightmare for the town.

According to McDaniel, he was at home that evening when something started beating on his door. When he opened it, he couldn't believe his eyes. "It had three legs on it," McDaniel stated, "a short body, two little short arms coming out of its breast area, and two pink eyes as big as flashlights. It stood four and a half to five feet tall and was grayish colored. It was trying to get into the house."

Needless to say, McDaniel did not want to let it in. He quickly retrieved a pistol, kicked open the door, and started firing. After the first shot, McDaniel knew that he had hit the creature. It "hissed like a wildcat" and scampered away, covering seventy-five feet in three jumps, then disappeared into the brush along the railroad tracks near McDaniel's house.

He called the police, and the state troopers who responded found tracks "like those of a dog, except they had six toe pads." Two of the footprints were four inches across, and the third was slightly smaller.

Investigators soon learned that a young boy, Greg Garrett, who lived just behind McDaniel, had been playing in his yard about a half hour before the ominous pounding on McDaniel's door. According to the boy's account, a deformed-looking creature had suddenly appeared and attacked him, stomping up and down on his feet with its sharp, misshapen claws and tearing the boy's tennis shoes to shreds. He managed to escape from the bizarre creature and ran into the house crying hysterically.

Less than two weeks later, on May 6, Henry McDaniel was

awakened in the middle of the night by howling neighborhood dogs. He looked out his front door and saw the monster again, standing out near the railroad tracks. "I didn't shoot at it or anything," McDaniel reported. "It started on down the railroad track. It wasn't in a hurry or anything."

McDaniel's incredible story soon brought a flood of publicity to Enfield and eventually prompted the threat of arrest from the county sheriff, but the damage had been done, and hordes of curiosity-seekers, reporters, and scientists descended on the town. Among the monster hunters were five young men who were arrested by Deputy Sheriff Jim Clark for being "threats to public safety" and for violating hunting regulations. This was after they had opened fire on a gray, hairy thing they had seen in some underbrush on May 8. Two of the men thought they had hit it, but it sped off.

One of the more credible reports of an encounter with the Enfield Horror came from Rick Rainbow, who was then the news director of radio station WWKI in Kokomo, Indiana. He and three other people spotted the monster near an abandoned house just a short distance from McDaniel's place. They didn't get a very good look at it as it ran away from them, but they later described it as about five feet tall, gray, and stooped over. Rainbow did manage to tape-record its strange hissing cry, which was also heard by others who tried to track down the creature. Over the next several days, the cries were heard frequently near the railroad tracks close to McDaniel's home.

A short time later the sightings ended as abruptly as they began. No reasonable explanation has ever been given for what this truly strange creature was, where it came from, or where it went. Some think it was connected to UFO activity reported in the general area at the time, but we will most likely never know for sure the true origin of the Enfield Horror.

The Man-Eating Piasa Bird

Visitors leaving the city of Alton north along the River Road are often surprised to pass a petroglyph, or ancient rock painting, on the side of a bluff that portrays a vicious-looking winged creature. The original rock painting actually once showed two such creatures, called the Piasa by the Illiniwek Indians, and was first described in the journals of Père Marquette in 1673 as he explored the Mississippi River:

> As we were descending the river we saw high rocks with hideous monsters painted on them and upon which the bravest Indian dare not look. They are as large as a calf, with head and horns like a goat, their eyes are red, beard like a tiger's and face like a man's. Their tails are so long that they pass over their bodies and between their legs, under their bodies, ending like a fish tail. They are painted red, green and black and so well drawn that I could not believe they were drawn by the Indians, for what purpose they were drawn seems to me a mystery.

Other early explorers also described paintings of the Piasa and recounted the bird's colorful history, which is one of the most enduring native legends of the region, beloved by children and adults alike. But this entertaining tale also has a gruesome, modern-day component that is not as well known.

According to the legend, which can be traced to the Illiniwek who lived along the Mississippi just north of present-day Alton, the original bird was so huge that it could carry away a full-grown deer in its talons. Yet once it obtained a taste for human flesh, it would eat nothing else. Every morning after it took its first human victim, the great bird appeared in the sky and carried away another member of the tribe, earning its name, Piasa, or "the bird that devours men."

Owatoga, the chief of the tribe, and six brave young men came up with a plan to slay the Piasa. The great bird was shot repeatedly with arrows and fell to its death over the edge of a tall bluff on the Mississippi River. To celebrate their victory, the Illiniwek painted a colorful tribute to the Piasa on the stone face of the bluff where they had battled it.

When white men settled this region, they heard the legend of the Piasa, but they found no evidence to suggest that the creature had really existed. That is, until July 1836, when Professor John Russell discovered something very unusual in the region of the Piasa bluff painting. Russell's fascination with the legend had led him to explore the nearby cliffs and caves, where he apparently made a gruesome discovery:

> After a long and perilous climb, we reached the cave. . . . The floor of the cavern throughout its whole extent was one mass of human bones. Skulls and other bones were mingled in the utmost confusion. To what depth they extended I was unable to decide; but we dug to a depth of three or four feet in every part of the cavern, and still we found only bones. The remains of thousands must have been deposited here.

To Russell, the existence of this cave and its grisly contents was proof of the Piasa's terrifying reign over the region's Native American inhabitants. The cave was nearly impossible for humans to reach, but a gigantic, man-eating bird could have easily accessed it, using it to feast on its human victims and scattering the bones of its meal afterward.

Throughout the remainder of the century, other

renowned explorers and academics supported Russell's account with first-person reports of the bone-filled cave. But was this cave really the lair of the Piasa Bird? Did this bird, always thought to be merely a mythological creature, actually exist? And did it really carry off and feast on the Native Americans who once lived in this region?

No one really knows for sure, and the mystery of the Piasa Bird remains unsolved today. While many have gone in search of this elusive cave in recent years, no one has ever been able to find it again. But this is not as strange as you might think. This remote area contains overgrown forests that may have concealed the bluff over time. Homes, buildings, churches, and cemeteries have all been reclaimed by nature in this way, so it's very possible that the same thing could happen with caves, hundreds of which are scattered along the river below the bluffs. *Weird Illinois* has spoken to people who have found caves with Indian drawings on the walls, and has met a man who recalls seeing an ancient depiction of the Piasa above the Illinois River past Grafton. This petroglyph, however, has proven to be as elusive as the bone cave of the Piasa. But, as with all great mysteries, the search will surely go on.

Terrifying Thunderbirds over Illinois

It's a chilling image: gigantic birds swooping across the sky, frightening the unsuspecting, and then vanishing back into the clouds. Illinois seems to have an inordinate number of such sightings—certainly enough to keep us watching the sky as we make our way through the woods and fields of the state.

American Indian lore is filled with legends of huge flying beasts like the Piasa that could carry away full-grown adults. These birds are often called thunderbirds because their flapping wings sound like rolling thunder. They've been described as having wingspans of twenty feet or more, hooked talons, and razor-sharp beaks that can rip their human prey to shreds in seconds.

Aside from Indian legends, however, there are also many modern accounts of thunderbirds attacking and carrying off people.

A rash of sightings began in Alton in 1948. On April 4, former army colonel Walter F. Siegmund reported that he had seen a gigantic bird in the sky above Alton. He had been talking with Colonel Ralph Jackson, head of the Western Military Academy, and a local farmer at the time. "I thought there was something wrong with my eyesight," Siegmund said, "but it was definitely a bird and not a glider or a jet plane. It appeared to be flying northeast. . . . From the movements of the object and its size, I figured it could only be a bird of tremendous size."

A few days later a farmer from Caledonia named Robert Price saw a similar bird. He called it a "monster bird . . . bigger than an airplane." On April 10, Mr. and Mrs. Clyde Smith and Les Bacon spotted a huge bird in Overland. They said they thought the creature was an airplane until it started to flap its wings furiously.

On April 24, E. M. Coleman and his son, James, sighted the bird back in Alton. "It was an enormous, incredible thing with a body that looked like a naval torpedo," Coleman later recalled. "It was flying at about five hundred feet and cast a shadow the same size as a Piper Cub."

On May 5, the bird was sighted for the last time that year in Alton by a man named Arthur Davidson, who called the police to report that it was flying above the city. Later that same night Mrs. William Stallings of St. Louis informed authorities that she had also seen it. "It was bright, about as big as a house," she said. A number of sightings then followed in the St. Louis area, but ironically, just when the public excitement over the bird reached its peak, the sightings came to an end.

Another rash of sightings took place in 1977, beginning with a frightening encounter, the famous Lawndale attack, which took place in this small town in Logan County. On the evening of July 25, several witnesses reported two giant birds circling and swooping in the sky. Finally they dived straight down and reportedly attacked three boys who were playing in the backyard of Ruth and Jake Lowe. One of the birds grasped the shirt of ten-year-old Marlon Lowe, snagging its talons in the cloth. The boy tried in vain to fight the bird off and cried loudly for help.

His cries brought Marlon's mother running outside, and she later reported that she had actually seen the bird lift the boy into the air and peck at him as it tried to carry him off. She screamed loudly, and the bird released the child after it had carried him about thirty-five feet at a height of about three feet. She was sure that if she had not come outside, the bird would have carried her son away.

Four other adults had appeared on the scene within seconds of the attack, and they described the birds as black with bands of white around their necks. They had long, curved beaks and a wingspan of at least ten feet. The two birds were last seen flying toward some trees near Kickapoo Creek.

Luckily, although he was scratched and badly frightened, Marlon was not seriously injured. However, he did have trouble coming to terms with the frightening encounter, and it took years for the shock of the incident to wear off. Ruth Lowe had vivid flashbacks of the event and spent years trying to identify the huge winged creatures that had almost taken her son. She spent long hours looking through books, determined to prove that the creatures had not been turkey vultures, as an area game warden tried to convince her. "I was standing at the door," she told investigators afterward, "and all I saw was Marlon's feet dangling in the air. There aren't any birds around here that could lift him up like that."

The Lawndale incident was not the last sighting in Illinois that year. Three days later a McLean County farmer named Stanley Thompson spotted a bird of the same size and description flying over his farm. He, his wife, and several friends were playing with radio-controlled airplanes when the bird flew close to the models. He too told McLean County Sheriff's Department sergeant Robert Boyd that the bird had a wingspan of at least ten feet and a six-foot-long body. Boyd commented that Thompson was a "credible witness" who had lived in the area for a long time and

had absolutely no reason to make up stories.

The next day James Majors, a mail truck driver, spotted the two birds above the highway as he was driving from Armington to Delevan. One of the birds dropped down into a field and snatched up a small animal. Not prone to believing fantastic tales, Majors reported that the two birds were probably condors—but with ten-foot wingspans! Condors or not, Majors quickly drove to the next town, jumped out of the truck, and smoked four cigarettes to regain his composure.

Reports of giant birds continued to come in from Bloomington and north-central Illinois, then from farther south, around Decatur, Macon, and Sullivan. On July 30, the same day the birds were reported near Bloomington, a writer and construction worker named Texas John Huffer spotted and filmed two large birds while he was fishing with his son at Lake Shelbyville. Huffer frightened the birds with his boat horn, and when they took flight, he managed to shoot over one hundred feet of film, part of which he sold to a television station in Champaign for a newscast. Huffer said that the largest bird had a wingspan of over twelve feet.

After the footage aired, experts were quick to dismiss Huffer's claims, along with the accounts of everyone else who had recently seen the birds. Officials from the department of conservation insisted the birds were merely turkey vultures and their size was nothing out of the ordinary. These claims were disputed by wildlife experts, however, who stated that turkey vultures could not reach the size reported by witnesses. The largest bird in North America is the California condor, which has a wingspan of up to nine feet, but the condor is on the endangered species list and is restricted to a few areas in California.

The following month eyewitness reports of the still unidentified bird came from numerous people farther south near the towns of Odin and Herrick. All were

amazed by the bird's incredible wingspan and insisted that they had simply never seen anything that large before. Paul Harrold told *Weird Illinois* that he saw a giant bird in the sky near the south-central town of Fairfield on August 20, 1977, and insisted that it was no vulture or buzzard.

Another sighting occurred near Alton in late 2003, along the Mississippi River. In this case, a hunter told *Weird Illinois* that he had seen a "big bird" that drifted overhead with "hardly any wing movement" and landed in some trees. He added that it was of huge size and that "I doubted my sanity when I saw it because it looked just like a prehistoric pterodactyl."

So, what are these creatures? Some will try to convince you that the giant birds that have been seen, and on rare occasions have carried away children, are nothing more than turkey vultures or condors. In many cases, though, the birds have been spotted by people who would have recognized these commonly known species, and even if they did not, only a small percentage of the reports could be so easily dismissed. Some cryptozoologists, who study extinct prehistoric species, believe that these thunderbirds may be teratorns, a supposedly extinct bird that once roamed the skies of North and South America. If these prehistoric monsters are still around today, that could certainly account for these reports of giant birds. But could some of these winged creatures be something else altogether?

One thing is for sure, the sightings still occur, and an occasional report still trickles in from Illinois. So keep that in mind the next time you are standing in an open field and a large dark shadow suddenly fills the sky overhead. Was that just a cloud passing in front of the sun—or a prehistoric monster ready to carry you away and eat you for lunch?

Creatures of the Watery Deep

A vast number of creepy creatures are said to lurk in the lakes and ponds of Illinois. One of the most famous was the gigantic serpentlike Lake Michigan Water Monster. Hundreds of people on shore and at sea, including fishermen and crewmen on tugboats, reported sightings of the beast throughout the 1800s, but by the early 1900s, it had sunk quietly back into the depths and has not been seen since.

In the summer of 1879, people also began to report another Illinois water monster, this time in Stump Pond on the Hayes Fair Acres Estate near Du Quoin. One evening a local named Paquette was fishing on the lake when something rushed through the water beneath him with enough force to rock his boat. The experience frightened him so much he vowed never to venture out onto the lake at night again.

The following summer two other local fishermen claimed that they saw a twelve-foot-long "serpent" in the water. The dark green body was as thick as a telephone pole. After this brief appearance, it vanished back into the depths. Meanwhile, the men decided they were no longer in the mood for fishing.

Reports continued to come from Stump Pond for many years. One night a retired miner named Allyn Dunmyer was fishing near shore when a large serpent-like creature suddenly passed directly underneath his boat. Whatever it was, it had apparently been hiding in the muddy shallows when it was startled by a noise and quickly headed for deeper water, bumping its head on the boat so hard that it nearly turned it over. This wasn't the first time Dunmyer had seen the monster. "I think there are more than one of the critters in the pond," he said afterward. "I've seen them so near the surface that their back fins were sticking out of the water."

Herb Heath, a Du Quoin businessman, was wading in the pond one night when he stumbled upon some kind of large creature sleeping under the moss covering the water. The beast quickly sped away. Heath stated that it looked like an overgrown alligator and claimed that the monster was "as big as I am, maybe bigger."

The stories of the Stump Pond Monster continued until 1968, when the water was partially drained from the pond and the fish cleared out of it with electric stunners. What locals found there in the muddy remains led some to believe the monster was nothing more than an overgrown catfish. A number of the fish they hauled in weighed more than thirty pounds, which is awfully big for a catfish. Even so, it's hard to imagine how one of them could have been mistaken for a creature so large that it was dubbed a monster.

Kangaroos on the Loose

More than ten thousand miles away from their native "land down under," kangaroos have apparently made themselves at home in northern Illinois. Reports of these jumpy critters, sometimes called hopping monkeys by locals, date back several decades, but it was not until the mid-1970s that kangaroo mania swept across the state. Are these creatures escapees from zoos, refugees from circus trains, or mystery beasts that come and go without explanation? No one seems to know.

The sighting that kicked off kangaroo mania occurred in the early-morning hours of October 18, 1974, when a resident on the northwest side of Chicago called police to report that a kangaroo was sitting on his front porch. The call got a good laugh out of the officers and radio dispatchers until two cops showed up to investigate and ended up cornering an ornery five-foot-tall animal in a dark alley. Patrolmen Leonard Ciagi and Michael Byrne approached the growling animal with caution and inexplicably decided to try to handcuff it. When Byrne gave this a try, the kangaroo suddenly started screeching and became vicious. It began punching the officers in the face and kicking them in the shins. Understandably, the officers backed away, and short of using their guns, they found they had no way to subdue or capture the animal. A minute or two later the kangaroo took off at high speed. It cleared a fence and vanished, leaving behind some puzzled officers with sore shins.

This incident opened a floodgate, and other reports from around the area began pouring in. That afternoon a kangaroo was seen hopping down the street in Oak Park. The next morning Kenneth Grieshamer was delivering papers when he heard car brakes screech behind him. He turned to see what the trouble was and saw a kangaroo hopping across the intersection of Sunnyside and Mulligan streets. "He looked at me, I looked at him, and away he hopped," Grieshamer recalled.

An hour later it was seen again near Austin and Eastwood roads, and later that evening it was spotted around Belmont and Mango avenues. The following morning police dispatchers fielded calls from residents who had seen the kangaroo rummaging through their garbage cans. Finally, on the night of November 1, John Orr, an off-duty Plano police officer, spotted the kangaroo on Riverview Road, just outside town. From the edge of a cornfield, the animal jumped about eight feet and landed in the road, directly in front of Orr's headlights, paused, then hopped away and disappeared. "I'm positive that I saw him," Orr insisted. "If I hadn't slowed down, I would have hit him. My cousin was in the car behind me, and when she saw him, she just plain ran off the road."

The next night Jerry Wagner, Steve Morton, and Shawnee Clark were driving along Shafer Road in Plano when their headlights illuminated something in the road. As they swerved to avoid it, they realized they were staring at a kangaroo. The animal hopped over a fence and took off. "I never believed the stories about people seeing a kangaroo around here," Wagner said the next morning, "but I do now."

Apparently, more than one kangaroo was hopping around Illinois in November 1974, because just as the three men were reporting it to the Kendall County Sheriff's Office, fifty miles away Cathy Battaglia and Len Zeglicz spotted another kangaroo hunched on the side of South New England Avenue in Chicago.

Since that last sighting, no one has reported seeing a kangaroo on the loose in Illinois. Most likely we will never know where they came from and what became of them, but if you are out driving around Plano some night, keep your eyes peeled for this big mean hopper.

Albino Squirrels of Olney

Although they are rarer than kangaroos, there is nothing truly mysterious about the albino squirrels of Olney. Unknowing visitors to this small town are often startled to encounter these bizarre-looking creatures in a local park, but their reports to police officers are always met with knowing smiles and the explanation that these squirrels are supposed to be here and are a local phenomenon. In fact, the people of Olney are so protective of their albino squirrels that state law prohibits them from being taken outside the city limits, and the squirrels always have the right of way when crossing the street.

Olney is not the only town that claims to be the home of these strange white squirrels—towns in Tennessee, Missouri, North Carolina, and Connecticut also have some—but the residents of Olney scoff at their claims. Most of their squirrels have dark eyes, they insist, not the pink eyes of true albinos. The people of Olney are so proud of their special critters that they have an annual squirrel count and hold a festival in honor of them. The patches of the local police officers even have the outline of a white, bushy-tailed albino on them! Perhaps not the most threatening mascot to have, but certainly a unique one.

No one knows for sure when white squirrels ended up in Olney, but one legend traces their arrival to a day in 1902, when William Yates Stroup was hunting for squirrels in the woods near his home. He saw a gray squirrel run into a nest and fired a shot at it, killing the mother and knocking two baby squirrels, which happened to be pure white, out of the nest. He took the little critters home and let his two sons, George and Era, raise them by hand. Later that fall Stroup sold the squirrels to Jasper C. Banks

for $5 each, and Banks displayed them in the front window of his saloon. They became quite a draw for the tavern and remained on display until the Illinois legislature passed a law prohibiting the confinement of wildlife, including squirrels. The albino creatures were then released in Tippit's Woods. Just as the male albino climbed out of the box, however, a large fox squirrel darted out and ripped it to shreds, but the female managed to escape and built a nest in the trees. She later bore an all-white litter, establishing the Olney albino colony.

The population of white squirrels increased as the years passed, and by 1925, Olney had established various city ordinances to protect them. Dogs and cats are not allowed to run loose within city limits, because the albino squirrels are unable to see very well, making them easy targets for predators.

In the 1940s, the albino population reached one thousand, but today it holds steady at around two hundred. These famous little critters have been featured in magazines, newspapers, and even national television programs, but if you come to Olney to look for them, be prepared to wait—they can be elusive! The best time to see them is in the early morning at Olney City Park on Route 130. If you stand around quietly for a little while, they will likely come scampering across the grass to you and will even eat out of your hand. You'll definitely look twice when you first see them, but you're not imagining things—they really are true albinos and just one more addition to Illinois' weird animal menagerie.

Local Heroes and Villains

Illinois is a place of unusual people and strange characters. Even revered Illinois icons like Abraham Lincoln had their weird sides, as you'll soon see.

And speaking of Lincoln—when I was growing up in the Decatur area, there was a man named Don Turney who lived in town and used to dress up like old Abe. He would wander around town and show up at local football games and shopping malls in full Lincoln attire. Whatever the weather, he always wore a long black overcoat, a black bowtie, and a black stovepipe hat, and he had the Lincoln beard without the mustache. He walked in an almost regal manner, and when some kid would call out, "Hey, Abe!" he would proudly turn and wave. Mr. Turney continued to wander around as Mr. Lincoln until his death several years ago. Many people considered him a true eccentric, but I always thought of him as just another red-blooded resident of Illinois.

So, enjoy this look at some of Illinois' true eccentrics. I think you'll find that we grow them pretty weird here in the Prairie State.

Many people who knew Lincoln during his Illinois years described him as seeming to be in a world by himself, ignoring his surroundings and, at times, even visitors to his law office.

The Dark Prophecies of Abraham

No book about the unusual characters and eccentric figures of Illinois would be complete without mention of Abraham Lincoln. The death of his mother when he was still a child, hard labor to make an existence for himself in the wilderness, and his struggle for an education all combined to make him a serious man. While he always stated that he longed for a life of peace and contentment, he seemed to know that he would never live to find it. It's not surprising that legend has it that Lincoln's ghost is one of the most restless in American history.

Many people who knew Lincoln during his Illinois years described him as seeming to be in a world by himself, ignoring his surroundings and, at times, even visitors to his law office. He would sit for several minutes in complete silence, staring straight ahead. A few friends described him as rejoining the visitors "like one awakened from sleep" when such an interval ended. Years later, in Washington, a number of distinguished foreign visitors noted this strange habit. One French nobleman counted "twenty such alterations" in a single evening.

One of his closest friends and longtime law partner, William H. Herndon, stated that Lincoln was "a peculiar, mysterious man with a double consciousness, a double life. The two states, never in a normal man, coexist in equal and vigorous activities though they succeed each other quickly."

Lincoln was elected to the presidency in 1860, and while he may have won the day, he fared poorly in the popular vote. He had soundly defeated Stephen Douglas in the electoral college but had won just forty percent of the vote among the people. When Lincoln returned home in the early-morning hours after the votes had been counted and he knew he had won, he went into his bedroom for some much needed rest and collapsed onto a settee. Near the couch was a large bureau with a mirror on it, and Lincoln stared for a moment at his reflection in the glass. He then experienced what many would term a vision, one that he would later believe had prophetic meaning.

In the mirror, he saw that his face appeared to have two separate, yet distinct, images. The tip of one nose was about three inches away from the other one. The vision vanished but appeared again a few moments later. Lincoln realized that one of the faces was actually much paler than the other, almost with the coloring of death. The vision disappeared again, and Lincoln dismissed the whole thing to the excitement of the hour and his lack of sleep. But he talked of the strange experience for many years to come.

Mary Todd Lincoln

As the Civil War raged, its bitter turmoil and the great loss of life took their toll on Lincoln. He became bitter and dark, his times of prayer and contemplation grew much longer, and he seemed to turn inward. He spoke often of the "hand of God" in certain battles, and it was almost as if an uncanny perception somehow strengthened as the war raged on. Documents of the Union War Department refer to one occasion when Lincoln burst into the telegraph office of the department late one night. He ordered the operator to get a line through to the Union

commanders. He was convinced that Confederate soldiers were just about to cut through the Union lines.

The telegraph operator asked where he had obtained such information, and Lincoln reportedly answered, "My God, man! I saw it."

While the war affected President Lincoln deeply, there is no doubt that the most crippling blow he suffered in the White House was the death of his son Willie, in 1862. Lincoln and his wife, Mary, grieved deeply over the twelve-year-old boy's death. It was probably the most intense personal crisis in Lincoln's life.

After his son died, Lincoln tried to work, but his spirit had been crushed. One week after the funeral, he closed himself up in his office and wept all day. Some said he was on the verge of suicide, and he withdrew even further into himself. He also began to look more closely at spiritual matters.

While Lincoln never publicly discussed having interest in spiritualists, Mary embraced them openly and invited a number of them to the White House. Each claimed to be able to allow Mary to communicate with Willie. Mary's closest spiritualist companion was Nettie Colburn Maynard. Many are familiar with a tale told about a séance held by Maynard in 1863 where a grand piano levitated. The medium was playing the instrument when it began to rise off the floor. Lincoln and Colonel Simon Kase were both present, and it is said that both men climbed onto the piano, only to have it jump and shake so hard that they climbed down. It is recorded that Lincoln would later refer to the levitation as proof of an "invisible power."

Perhaps the most famous weird incident connected to Lincoln would be his prophetic dream of his assassination.

One of Lincoln's old friends from Illinois was a lawyer named Ward Hill Lamon, whom Lincoln appointed to a security position in the White House. Lamon would never forgive himself for Lincoln's assassination—especially since he believed that he had had a forewarning of the event from the President himself. For just shortly before Lincoln was killed, he had recounted to Lamon and Mary an eerie dream of death.

About ten days ago, I retired late. I soon began to dream. There seemed to be a death-like stillness about me. Then I heard subdued sobs, as if a number of people were weeping. I thought I left my bed and wandered downstairs. There the silence was broken by the same pitiful sobbing, but the mourners were invisible. I went from room to room; no living person was in sight, but the same mournful sounds of distress met me as I passed along.

It was light in all the rooms; every object was familiar to me, but where were all the people who were grieving as if their hearts would break? I was puzzled and alarmed. What could be the meaning of all this? Determined to find the cause of a state of things so mysterious and so shocking, I kept on until I arrived at the East Room, which I entered. Before me was a catafalque, on which rested a corpse wrapped in funeral vestments. Around it were stationed soldiers who were acting as guards; and there was a throng of people, some gazing mournfully upon the corpse, whose face was covered, others weeping pitifully.

'Who is dead in the White House?' I demanded of one of the soldiers.

'The President,' was his answer, 'He was killed by an assassin.'

Then came a loud burst of grief from the crowd, which awoke me from my dream. I slept no more that night; and although it was only a dream, I have been strangely annoyed by it ever since.

Lincoln spoke of death and prophecies to other members of his staff also, like Colonel W. H. Crook, one of his bodyguards. On the afternoon of April 14, Lincoln told him about the strange dreams that he had been having. Crook pleaded with the President not to go to the theater that night, but Lincoln dismissed his concerns, explaining that he had promised Mary they would go. Lincoln had a habit of bidding Crook a good-night each evening as he left the office. On that fateful day, according to Crook, Lincoln paused as he left for the theater and turned to the bodyguard. "Good-bye, Crook," he said significantly.

"It was the first time that he neglected to say good night to me," Crook would later recall. "And it was the only time that he ever said good-bye. I thought of it at that moment, and a few hours later, when the news flashed over Washington that he had been shot, his last words were so burned into my being that they can never be forgotten."

The Gentle Giant

Robert Pershing Wadlow was born in Alton, Illinois, on February 22, 1918, and during his all-too-brief life, he gained lasting fame as the tallest man in history. Robert died at the age of only twenty-two, but during his life, he remained vigilant about not being cast in the role of a "freak." He simply wanted a normal life, but even when he was very young, his family realized that this would be impossible.

When Robert was born, he weighed in at just over eight pounds, an average weight for a baby boy, but his height and weight would not stay average for long. By the time he was five years old, Robert weighed 105 pounds and was five feet four inches tall, and by age eight, he was over six feet tall and weighed 195 pounds. His parents, brothers, and sisters were all of normal size.

Robert became a regular visitor at the Barnes Hospital in St. Louis. After diagnosing that his rapid growth was caused by pituitary gigantism, doctors explained to his parents about a dangerous operation that could be attempted on his pituitary gland. The decision was made not to try the procedure.

Robert attempted to live a normal life, joining the Boy Scouts, running a soft drink stand in front of his home, and doing other things that average boys did. He attended public schools, and throughout his life, he was known for his very quiet, sedate manner. He was called the Gentle Giant.

Robert was a good student and a likable and remarkably well-adjusted young man, but he had many problems with even the simplest things in life. When he entered college, those problems began to cause great complications. At eight feet three and a half inches tall, Robert found it hard to do something as simple as take notes, as even the biggest fountain pen was dwarfed by his massive hand. He also ran into trouble in the biology lab, where the delicate instruments were impossible for him to handle. A chair, an automobile, and just about every object around him was an obstacle. Even the weather was a problem. When the ground was covered with ice, he had to gingerly work his way along, flanked by his friends, holding on to their shoulders as he walked. His weight was enormous and his bones fragile. If he fell, it could mean a long stay in the hospital, or worse.

Realizing that earning a living in a normal career was impossible, he turned to the only avenue that was offered, promotion and entertainment. For years, Robert's shoes had been specially made for him by the

International Shoe Company, which agreed to not only supply Robert with shoes, which cost more than $150 per pair to make, but also to pay him to make appearances. He soon began traveling for International Shoe and appeared in their advertising as well. Obviously, Robert's height was being exploited to draw large crowds, but he refused to think of it that way. He preferred to think of the exhibitions as advertising work.

By age nineteen, Robert had grown another two inches, and he found himself making quite a bit of money from his shoe promotion work. The idea struck him that he would open a shoe store of his own, or even a whole chain of them. To do this, however, he would need more money.

In 1937, Robert was offered a job with the Ringling Bros. and Barnum & Bailey Circus. Their salary offer was enticing, and Robert decided to accept. One of his conditions was that the Ringling organization would provide a hotel suite for him and his father and would take care of all of their expenses. Robert also said that he would not appear in the sideshow, but in the center ring of the circus, three times each day.

Robert made other appearances as well, always accompanied by his father. He operated concessions at fairs, where great crowds of people turned out to see him.

As time went on, Robert found himself pursued by showmen and promoters as well as by doctors. His father once stated that Robert was more concerned with how physicians would present him than how circus showmen would. All that came to a head in June 1936, when Dr. Charles D. Humberd made an unannounced visit to the Wadlow home. Robert, disheveled by a rainstorm, was surprised to find Humberd sitting in his living room when he got home. The doctor asked Robert to agree to a physical examination, and when he was quickly rebuffed, he became disgruntled and stormed out of the house.

The following February an article by Dr. Humberd appeared in the *Journal of the American Medical Association* that greatly upset the Wadlows. Entitled *Giantism: Report of a Case,* the article did not mention Robert by name but did state that the subject was from Alton, Illinois, and his initials were "R.W." He was referred to as a specimen of "preacromegalic giant." The doctor wrote that "his expression is surly and indifferent and he is definitely inattentive, apathetic and disinterested, unfriendly and antagonistic . . . his defective attention and slow responses hold for all sensory stimuli, both familiar and unexpected but he does manifest a rapid interest in seeing any memoranda made by the questioner. All functions that we attribute to the highest centers in the frontal lobes are languid and blurred."

The family filed suit against Humberd and the American Medical Association but lost when the judge ruled that the doctor's observations might have been accurate on the day the young man was examined. Unfortunately, even though he had never appeared in a freak show, Robert felt that his worst fear had been realized—he had been exhibited like a sideshow attraction.

Robert and his father continued to make personal appearances and to work with the Ringling Brothers circus. They traveled extensively, visiting forty-one states and the District of Columbia. Door frames, elevators, awnings, and hanging lights bedeviled the young man, and to ride in an automobile, he almost had to fold himself in two. Three beds, turned crossways, provided him the only sleeping arrangement suitable in a hotel room.

In 1940, Robert reached eight feet eleven and a half inches. His weight was a massive 490 pounds, and he was forced to walk with a cane. He was traveling and making personal appearances throughout the year and on July 4 was in Manistee, Michigan, at a lumbermen's festival. At lunch, Mr. Wadlow noticed that Robert was not eating, but they were scheduled to ride in a parade. Later Robert complained that he didn't feel well; however, since their car was trapped in the parade route, it would be several hours before they could get to a doctor.

As soon as the parade was over, Robert's father rushed him to the hospital. When they arrived, the doctors found that Robert was running a very high fever. He was wearing a new brace on his ankle, and it had scraped through the flesh, which became infected. Robert never noticed, because one of the consequences of his enormous size was that sensation in his legs was diminished. Finally, after ten fever-racked days, doctors performed surgery on his foot, but it was too late. His temperature continued to rise, hovering near 106 degrees. In the early morning hours of July 15, 1940, Robert passed away in his sleep.

His remains were returned to Alton, and huge crowds came to the Streeper Funeral Home. A special casket, measuring ten feet long and thirty-two inches wide, was constructed for his body. Since the casket was too big to fit through the doors of the church, the services were held at the funeral home. Twelve pallbearers and an additional eight men were required to manage his casket.

At Robert's request, special measures had been taken to protect the coffin. He had once read the story of Charles Byrne, the Irish Giant, and John Hunter, the anatomist who coveted his bones and had stolen his body to get them. Robert was not taking any chances with his own remains, so a thick shell of reinforced concrete was used to encase the coffin for eternity. Robert's wish not to be exploited in either life or death was fulfilled.

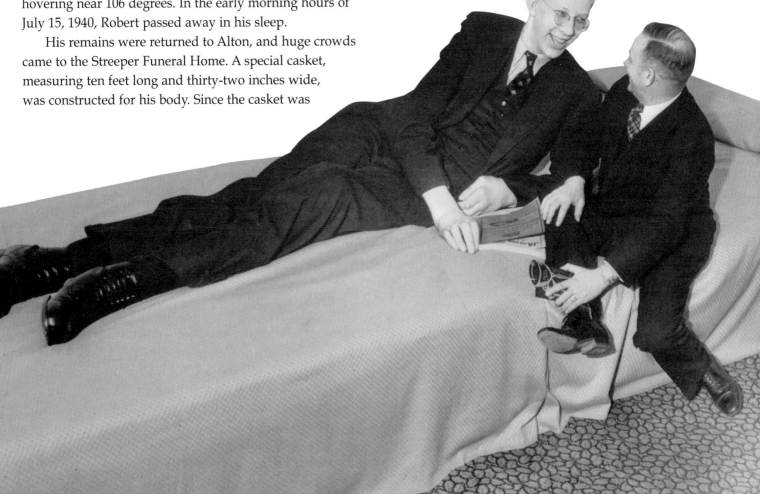

The Mummy of "Deaf Bill" Lee

One of the greatest odd characters in the history of Alton was a figure known as "Deaf Bill" Lee, a man who spent more than eight decades as a mummy in a local funeral home.

Bill Lee—or Deaf Bill as he was nicknamed, since he was hard of hearing—was born in 1863 and made his living fishing the Mississippi River. He was a legendary drinker and brawler and, when roaring drunk, would loudly deliver convoluted religious sermons along the riverbanks, on street corners, and even in church on Sunday mornings.

Bill got to know a man named Bill Bauer, owner of the Bauer Funeral Home. When Deaf Bill started to get along in years, Bauer kindly signed him into the Madison County poor farm so that he would have someone to care for him. Bill died on the farm in November 1915.

There were rumors that Bill might have relatives somewhere, possibly in West Alton, Missouri, and Bauer wanted to see if he could track them down to arrange for burial. He decided to hold on to Bill's body until he could find them.

While Bauer truly was searching for Deaf Bill's relatives, he was also experimenting with an embalming procedure that he had devised to see how long a person's body would remain preserved. Deaf Bill was embalmed with the new fluid, but the plan was to keep him only as long as it took for his family to come forward. Unfortunately, no one ever came.

As the years passed, Bill remained unclaimed, and new owners took over the funeral home. Although a traveling showman offered to pay the morticians $2,500 for Bill, the owners refused to sell. But they realized they could get all kinds of free publicity by exhibiting him in the funeral home, so they put him on display. The mustachioed mummy was around five feet three inches tall and weighed about sixty pounds. His legs were crossed, and his arms were folded across his waist. Thanks to the embalming fluid, the skin had turned dark and leathery and felt like wood to the touch. He was clad only in a loincloth the entire time he was left on display. Eventually the body was removed to a closet, where Bill spent the next several decades.

When Tom and Dallas Burke purchased the funeral home in 1948, the mummy was part of the package. They weren't sure what to do with him, but as time passed, the novelty of having a dead man in the downstairs closet started to wear off. At one point, they offered the mummy to the Alton History Museum, but the museum declined the offer.

Finally in 1996, Dallas Burke and Brian Fine, now co-owners of the Burke-Fine Funeral Home, decided that it was time to put Bill to rest. Deaf Bill was taken out of the closet, and some makeup was applied to his face to make him appear a bit more lifelike. And he was given some clothes: For his final viewing, Bill wore a turn of the century tuxedo coat, trousers, and a shirt with a black string tie. His dark hair and thick mustache were nicely trimmed, and his hands were crossed over a spread of red and white carnations. Hundreds came to see Deaf Bill one last time, and members of the Knights of Columbus served as his pallbearers.

The Reverend Michael Sandweg learned that several Lees were buried in the Immaculate Conception Cemetery in West Alton. While there was no proof that Bill was related to them, a plot was obtained, and Bill was buried next to an Edward Lee, on June 25, 1996.

Deaf Bill Lee could finally rest in peace—more than eighty years after he died.

H. H. Holmes: The Diabolical Druggist and His Murder Castle

In 1893, Chicago was host to a spectacular World's Fair, the Columbian Exposition, which celebrated the anniversary of Columbus's discovery of America. But everything was not as shiny and beautiful as the advertising for the exposition's "White City" would have people believe. "A devil" that would become known as America's first serial killer was alive and well on the city's south side, and visitors were vanishing without a trace—never to be seen again.

In the late 1800s, Englewood was a quiet community on the southern outskirts of the Windy City. Among the decent folk who lived there was a Mrs. Dr. Holden, as the newspapers mysteriously referred to her, who ran a drugstore at Sixty-third and Wallace. An increase in business led her to hire an assistant, the handsome and capable Dr. Henry H. Holmes.

It was not long before Holmes seemed to be more the manager of the store and less the prescription clerk. He spent more and more time on the ledgers and chatting pleasantly with the ladies who came into the place, some of whom took a very long time to make a small purchase. Trade at the drugstore continued to improve, making Mrs. Dr. Holden exceedingly happy. But Holmes was not satisfied with his lot, and he had many plans and visions that drove him onward. Strangely, in 1887, Mrs. Dr. Holden vanished. A short time later Holmes announced that he had purchased the store from the widow, just prior to her "moving out west." The lady had left no forwarding address.

Henry H. Holmes, whose real name was Herman W. Mudgett, was born in 1860 in Gilmanton, New Hampshire, where his father was a respected citizen. Early in life, Mudgett dropped his given name and became known as H. H. Holmes. He was constantly in trouble as a boy and young man and in later years was remembered for his cruelty to animals and children. His only redeeming trait was that he was an excellent student. In 1878, Holmes married Clara Lovering, the daughter of a prosperous farmer in Loudon, New Hampshire, and soon began studying medicine at a small college in Burlington, Vermont. He paid his tuition with a legacy that had been inherited by his wife.

In 1879, Holmes transferred to the medical school at the University of Michigan in Ann Arbor, and while there, he devised a method of stealing cadavers from the laboratory. He would then disfigure the corpses and plant them in places where it would look as though they had been killed in accidents. Conveniently, Holmes had already taken out insurance policies on these "family members," and he would collect on them after the bodies were discovered.

After a particularly daring swindle, he left Ann Arbor and abandoned his wife and

He was constantly in trouble as a boy and young man and in later years was remembered for his cruelty to animals and children.

infant son. Clara returned to New Hampshire and never saw her husband again. Holmes dropped out of sight for six years and then turned up in Englewood in 1885, where he soon took over the drugstore. A new era in his criminal life had begun.

Two years after arriving in Illinois, Holmes bought property across the street from the drugstore and began erecting a huge edifice on it. With three stories and a basement, false battlements, and wooden bay windows that were covered with sheet iron, the castle had over sixty rooms and fifty-one doors that were cut oddly into various walls. Holmes acted as his own architect for the place, and he personally supervised the numerous construction crews, all of whom were quickly hired and fired with great fury. He refused to pay the workers' wages, and as far as the police were later able to learn, he never paid a cent for any of the materials that went into the building. In addition to the eccentric general design, the castle was fitted with trapdoors, hidden staircases, secret passages, rooms without windows, chutes that led into the basement, and a staircase that opened out over a steep drop to the alley behind the structure.

The first floor of the building contained shops, while the upper floors could be used for spacious living quarters. Holmes had an office on the second floor, but most of the rooms were to be used for guests—guests who would check into the hotel and never be seen again. Evidence would later show that Holmes used some of the rooms as "asphyxiation chambers," where his victims were suffocated with gas. Other rooms were lined with iron plates and had blowtorchlike devices fitted into the walls. In the basement, Holmes installed a dissecting table and a crematory. There was also an acid vat and pits filled with quicklime, where bodies could be conveniently disposed of. All of his "prison rooms" were fitted with alarms that buzzed in Holmes's quarters if a victim attempted to escape. How many visitors actually fell prey to Holmes's evil ways is a mystery, but no fewer than fifty people who were reported to the police as missing were traced to what became known as the Murder Castle.

An advertisement for lodging during the fair was not

In 1893, Chicago was host to a spectacular World's Fair, the Columbian Exposition.

the only method that Holmes used for procuring victims. A large number of his female victims came through ads that he placed in small-town newspapers, offering jobs to young ladies. When a woman was accepted for a job, she would be instructed to pack her things and withdraw all of her money from the bank because she would need funds to get started in a new city. The applicants were also instructed to keep the location and name of his company a secret. He told them that he had devious competitors who would use any information to steal his clients. When the applicant arrived, she would become his prisoner.

Holmes placed newspaper ads for marriage as well, describing himself as a wealthy businessman who was searching for a suitable wife. Those who answered this ad would remain his prisoners until he disposed of them.

In 1893, Holmes met a young woman named Minnie Williams, heir to a Texas real estate fortune. She was in Chicago, working as an instructor at a private school. It wasn't long before she and Holmes were engaged. Minnie lived at the castle for more than a year, and police would later state there was no way that she could not have known about many of the murders.

One of those she would surely have known about was Emmeline Cigrand, a beautiful young woman who came to the castle—and never left it. Holmes later confessed that he locked the girl in one of his soundproof rooms and raped her before killing her.

A visit to Chicago by Minnie's sister, Nannie, provides evidence of Minnie's murderous ways and her willingness to go along with Holmes. In June 1893, Holmes seduced Nannie while she was staying at the castle and had no trouble persuading her to sign over her share of some property in Fort Worth. She disappeared a month later, with Holmes explaining that she had gone back to Texas. Holmes later claimed it had been Minnie who killed her. When Minnie found out that Nannie had been consorting with Holmes, the two of them got into a heated argument. Minnie hit her sister over the head with a chair, killing her; then Minnie and Holmes dropped the body into Lake Michigan.

A short time later Holmes and Minnie traveled to Denver in the company of another young woman, Georgianna Yoke, who had come to Chicago from Indiana and had applied for a job at the castle. Holmes told her that his name was Henry Howard and that Minnie was his cousin. On January 17, 1894, Holmes and Georgianna were married at the Vendome Hotel in Denver with Minnie as their witness! After that, the three traveled to Texas, where they claimed Minnie's property and arranged a horse swindle. Holmes purchased several railroad cars of horses with counterfeit banknotes and signed the papers as O. C. Pratt. The horses were then shipped to St. Louis and sold. Holmes made off with a fortune, but it would be this swindle that would later come back and destroy him.

The threesome returned to Chicago, and their return marked the last time that Minnie was ever seen alive. Holmes explained to police that he believed Minnie had killed her sister in a fit of passion and then had fled to Europe. They believed him, as he was known for being an upstanding citizen, and it was not until much later that he confessed to killing Minnie too.

Holmes's next scheme took place at a seaside resort in Rhode Island. He took a cadaver to the resort, burned it, disfigured the head, and dumped it on the beach. He then shaved his beard, altered his appearance, and returned to the hotel, registering under another name and inquiring about his friend Holmes. When the body was discovered on the beach, he identified it as H. H. Holmes. He presented the insurance company with a policy for $20,000, but the company suspected fraud and refused to pay. Holmes returned to Chicago without pressing the claim.

In November 17, 1894, he turned up in Boston and was arrested for the horse swindle that he, Minnie, and Georgianna had pulled off in Texas. Meanwhile, the authorities had learned of Holmes's insurance scheme. He was given the choice of being returned to Texas to be hanged as a horse thief or of confessing to the insurance scheme. He chose insurance fraud and was sent to Philadelphia. On the way there, Holmes offered his guard $500 if the man would allow himself to be hypnotized. Wisely, the guard refused.

After Holmes's arrest, a Pinkerton man, Detective Frank Geyer, slowly started to uncover the man's dark secrets. He was beginning to sift through the many lies and identities of Henry Howard Holmes, hoping to find clues as to the fates of the missing people. At this point, he had no idea how many potential victims there might be. Meanwhile, in June 1895, Holmes entered a guilty plea for a single count of insurance fraud and Georgianna, finally realizing the evil of her husband's ways, began cooperating with the police.

Now the door was open for Geyer and Chicago detectives to search Holmes's residence. Geyer entered the place with several police officers—neither he nor the veteran investigators would ever forget what they found there.

On the second floor, with its hidden stairways, secret panels, and labyrinth of narrow, winding passages, was a clandestine vault only big enough for a person to stand in. The room was alleged to be a gas chamber, equipped with a chute that would carry a body directly into the basement. The investigators found a single scuffed footprint on the inside of the door. It was a small print that had been made by a woman who had attempted to escape the grim fate of the tiny room.

In addition to all of the bizarre additions to the floor, the second level also held thirty-five guest rooms. Several were without windows and could be made airtight by closing the doors. Others were lined with sheet iron and asbestos with scorch marks on the walls, fitted with trap doors that led to smaller rooms beneath, or equipped with lethal gas jets that could be used to suffocate or burn the occupants.

The chamber of horrors in the basement stunned the men even further. Here they found Holmes's blood-spattered dissecting table, his gleaming surgical instruments, his macabre laboratory of torture devices, jars of poison, and even a box that contained a number of female skeletons. Built into one of the walls was a crematorium that still contained ash and bone. A search of the ashes revealed a watch that had belonged to Minnie Williams, some buttons from a dress, and several charred tintype photographs.

Dozens of human bones and several pieces of jewelry were found, as well as scraps of cloth and a bloody dress. One set of bones was believed to be those of a small child between the ages of six and eight.

Following the excavation, the Murder Castle sat empty for months. The newspapers were not yet filled with stories about Holmes's crimes, but rumors quickly spread about what had been discovered there. The neighborhood people were stunned and sickened.

Then, on August 19, the castle burned to the ground. Three explosions thundered through the neighborhood just after midnight, and minutes later, a blaze erupted from the abandoned structure. In less than an hour, the roof had

Following the excavation, the Murder Castle sat empty for months. The newspapers were not yet filled with stories about Holmes's crimes, but rumors quickly spread about what had been discovered there.

caved in and the walls began to collapse. A gas can was discovered among the ruins. The mystery of who burned down the house—an accomplice of Holmes or an outraged neighbor—was never solved, but regardless, the Murder Castle was gone for good.

The trial of Herman Mudgett began in Philadelphia just before Halloween 1895. The jury deliberated for just two and half hours before returning a guilty verdict. Afterward they reported that they had agreed on the verdict in just one minute but had remained out longer "for the sake of appearances."

On November 30, the judge passed a sentence of death. Holmes was scheduled to die on May 7, 1896, just nine days before his thirty-sixth birthday. Through it all, he remained unrepentant. He was led to the gallows, and

a black hood was placed over his head. The trapdoor opened beneath him, and Holmes quickly dropped. Although the force of the fall had broken his neck, his heart continued to beat for nearly fifteen minutes.

There are a couple of macabre legends associated with Holmes's execution. The most enduring legend is that of the Holmes Curse. A short time after Holmes's body was buried, Dr. William K. Matten, a coroner's physician who had been a major witness in the trial, suddenly dropped dead from blood poisoning. More deaths followed in rapid order, including that of the head coroner, Dr. Ashbridge, and the trial judge who had sentenced Holmes to death. Both men were diagnosed with sudden deadly illnesses. Next the superintendent of the prison where Holmes had been incarcerated committed suicide. Then the father of one of Holmes's victims was horribly burned in a gas explosion.

Not long after, the office of the claims manager for the insurance company that Holmes had cheated caught fire and burned. Everything in the office was destroyed except for a framed copy of Holmes's arrest warrant and two portraits of the killer.

Several weeks after the hanging, a priest who had prayed with Holmes before his execution was found dead in the yard behind his church. The coroner ruled the death as uremic poisoning, but according to reports, the priest had been badly beaten and robbed. A few days later the jury foreman in Holmes's trial was electrocuted in a bizarre accident involving electrical wires above his house.

In the years that followed, others involved with Holmes also met violent deaths. Perhaps H. H. Holmes was simply a man so adept at murder that not even his own death could dissuade him from practicing this gruesome trade.

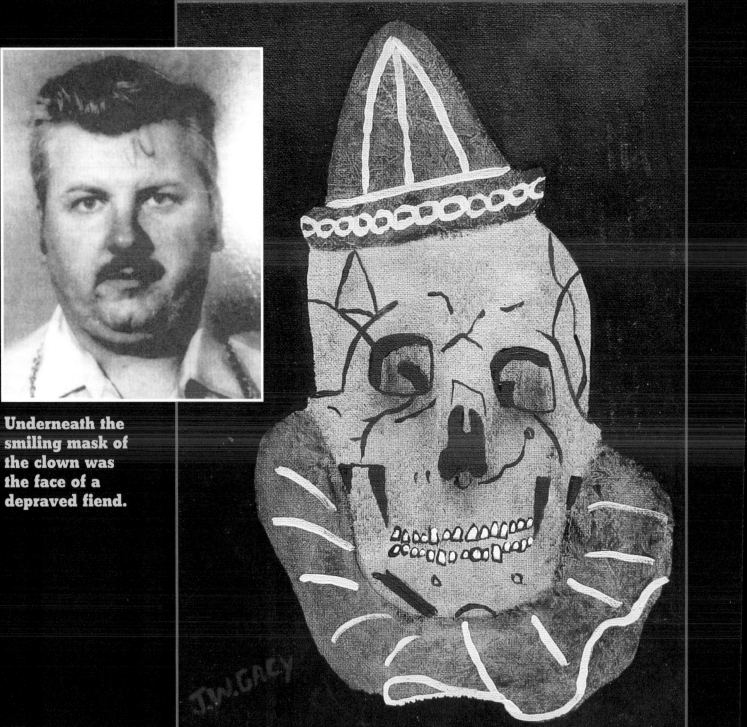

Underneath the smiling mask of the clown was the face of a depraved fiend.

J.W. GACY

John Wayne Gacy—The Killer Clown

To everyone who met him, John Wayne Gacy seemed a likable man. He was widely respected in the community and easy to get along with. He was a sharp businessman who, when not running his construction company, was active in the Jaycees. He also hosted elaborate street parties for his friends and neighbors, and entertained children at area hospitals dressed as Pogo the Clown. That was the side of John Wayne Gacy that he allowed people to see.

Underneath the smiling mask of the clown was the face of a depraved fiend.

Gacy was born in Chicago, and grew up in Illinois. In 1964, he married Marlynn Myers, whose parents owned a number of Kentucky Fried Chicken restaurants in Iowa. Gacy's father-in-law offered him a position with the company, and soon the newlyweds moved to Iowa.

Gacy worked hard and was active with the Waterloo, Iowa, Jaycees. He and Marlynn had a son and daughter, and they all seemed to have the picture-perfect life. It almost seemed too good to be true. And it was. . . .

Rumors were starting to grow around town about Gacy's sexual preferences. Stories spread that he had made passes at some of the young men who worked in the restaurants. Then, in May 1968, a grand jury in Black Hawk County indicted Gacy for committing an act of sodomy with a teenage boy named Mark Miller. The boy told the courts that Gacy had tricked him into being tied up while visiting Gacy's home and had raped him. Gacy denied the charges but did say that Miller willingly had sex with him in order to earn extra money.

Gacy entered a guilty plea to the charge of sodomy. He received ten years at the Iowa State Reformatory, the maximum time for the offense, and entered prison at the age of twenty-six. Shortly after, his wife divorced him.

Gacy was a model prisoner and was paroled after only eighteen months. On June 18, 1970, he made his way back to Chicago, where he moved in with his mother and obtained work as a chef in a restaurant. After four months, he decided to live on his own, and his mother helped him buy a house at 8213 West Summerdale Avenue in Norwood Park Township. He quickly made friends with his next-door neighbors, an older couple named Grexa, who had no idea of Gacy's criminal past.

In June 1972, Gacy married Carole Hoff, a newly divorced mother of two daughters. Carole knew about his time in prison but believed that he had changed his life. She and her daughters soon settled into Gacy's home and forged a close relationship with the Grexas. The older couple were often invited over to the Gacys' house for elaborate parties and cookouts. However, they were bothered by the horrible stench that frequently wafted throughout the house. Lillie Grexa was convinced that an animal had died beneath the floorboards of the place, and she urged Gacy to do something about it. He blamed the odor on moisture buildup in the crawl space under the house.

In 1974, Gacy started a contracting business called Painting, Decorating and Maintenance or PDM Contractors, Inc. He hired a number of teenage boys to work for him, explaining to friends that hiring young men would keep his payroll costs low. But Gacy could no longer deny what he was, and he confessed to his wife that he preferred young men to women. She filed for divorce.

Gacy's need for recognition and success continued. He volunteered himself and his employees to clean up and repair Democratic Party headquarters, and became secretary-treasurer of the organization. But his political career was short-lived—rumors were circulating about Gacy's interest in young boys.

His web of secrets began to unravel with the vanishing of Robert Piest. Robert, fifteen, disappeared mysteriously

just outside the doors of the pharmacy where he worked. He had just told his mother, who had come to pick him up after his shift, that he would be back in a minute because he needed to talk to a contractor who had offered him a job. He went back inside—and never returned. His mother began to worry and went in to search the pharmacy, but Robert was nowhere to be seen. Finally the Des Plaines police were notified. Lieutenant Joseph Kozenczak led the investigation.

The officer quickly obtained the name of the contractor who had offered Robert the job, and Kozenczak went straight to Gacy's home. Gacy refused to accompany him to the police station, explaining that there had been a recent death in his family and he had to make some telephone calls. He agreed to come down later. Several hours later Gacy arrived and gave a statement to the police. He said that he knew nothing about the disappearance, and he was allowed to leave.

Something about Gacy did not sit right with Kozenczak, and he decided to do a background check on him. He was stunned when he discovered that Gacy had earlier done time for sodomy with a teenage boy. He quickly obtained a search warrant, and on December 13, 1978, police officers entered Gacy's house. Gacy was not at home at the time.

Some of the items recovered included a box containing marijuana and pills, a stained section of a rug, a number of books with homosexual and child pornography themes, a pair of handcuffs, police badges, sexual devices, a hypodermic needle and small brown bottle, clothing that was too small for Gacy, nylon rope, and a box containing two driver's licenses and several rings, including one that was engraved with MAINE WEST HIGH SCHOOL CLASS OF 1975 and the initials J.A.S. The police then entered the crawl space under Gacy's home. They thought the rancid odor was sewage. The earth in the crawl space had been sprinkled with lime but appeared to be untouched. They left the narrow space and returned to police headquarters to run tests on the evidence they had obtained.

Gacy was again called to headquarters and was told about the evidence that had been removed from his house. Enraged, he immediately contacted his attorney, who told him not to sign anything. The police had nothing to charge Gacy with and eventually had to release him, but they placed him under twenty-four-hour surveillance. Soon they decided to book him on possession of marijuana.

While Gacy was being charged with possession, the police lab and investigators were coming up with critical evidence against him from the items taken from his home. One of the rings found in his house belonged to another teenager who had disappeared a year earlier—John Szyc. Furthermore, a receipt for a roll of film that was found in Gacy's home had belonged to a co-worker of Robert Piest's, who had given it to Robert on the day of the boy's disappearance. With this new information, the investigators began to realize the enormity of the case that was starting to unfold.

Detectives and crime lab technicians returned to Gacy's house. With

everything crumbling around him, Gacy finally confessed to the police that he had killed someone but that it had been in self-defense. He said that he was frightened and had buried the body under his garage. He told the police where they could find it. Before digging there, the investigators decided to search the crawl space—and minutes after starting to dig, they found the remains of the first corpse.

That evening Dr. Robert Stein, the Cook County medical examiner, was called in to help with the investigation. He organized the search by marking off areas of earth in sections, as would be done with an archaeological site. For the next several days, the digging progressed under the medical examiner's watchful eye.

On Friday, December 22, 1978, detectives confronted Gacy with the fact that digging was being done under his house. With this news, the monster finally broke down.

He admitted to the police that he had killed at least thirty people and that most of their remains were buried beneath the house. He explained that he lured his victims into being handcuffed, and then he would sexually assault them. To muffle their screams, Gacy stuffed a sock or their underwear into their mouths and would often kill them by placing a rope or board against their throats. He also admitted to sometimes keeping the corpses under his bed or in his attic for hours or days before burying them.

By December 28, the police had removed twenty-seven bodies from Gacy's house. Two more victims were eventually found in the Des Plaines River, another in the concrete of Gacy's patio, and another in the Illinois River. The last body found at the house was discovered beneath Gacy's recreation room. After that discovery, the house was destroyed.

The body of Robert Piest was found in the Illinois River in April 1979. The death toll was thirty-three.

Eventually all but nine of the young men were identified.

John Wayne Gacy's murder trial began on February 6, 1980, at the Cook County Criminal Courts Building in Chicago. It took jury members only two hours to convict Gacy of the deaths of the thirty-three young men. No one in American history has ever been convicted of more murders. Gacy was sent to the Menard Correctional Center to await execution. He spent much of his time on death row painting pictures, which he would sell to people on the outside. His favorite subject to paint was clowns, including his alter ego, Pogo, who was often pictured in full costume and makeup, smiling and passing out colorful balloons and flowers to children. After years of appeals, Gacy was put to death by lethal injection on May 9, 1994.

Finally Gacy's terrifying string of crimes could be relegated to memory—or could it?

After the remains of the house were cleared away, the muddy vacant lot was a constant reminder to the neighborhood of the monster who had once been in their midst. All vestiges of the house, even the driveway and barbecue pit, were hauled away, but curiosity-seekers still came to the site. Neighbors hoped the visits would stop when warmer weather came and the grass grew over the open scar where the house had once stood.

Unfortunately, though, the grass did not return. Even eighteen months after the house was destroyed, the land remained strangely barren. Some weeds had started to grow near the front sidewalk, but the back of the lot, where the house had stood and where the bodies had been buried, remained completely devoid of plant life, although there was no logical reason for the soil to be bare.

Those searching for an explanation suggested that perhaps the lime with which Gacy had dusted the bodies of his victims had contaminated the soil in some way, but police officers involved in the recovery of the bodies disputed this. They insisted that Gacy had never used enough lime to cause any damage to the ground. Besides, a backhoe had dug down eight to ten feet to be sure that nothing was missed. The small amount of lime that had been used would not have survived that.

It was as though the evil deeds that had occurred had left a mark on the site.

The mystery of the barren soil lasted a few more years, and then the lot was sold and a new house was built there. The new owners even changed the address of the location so that the stigma would be removed. Fortunately, their efforts worked. Once the construction was completed, the grass began to grow once again. The nightmare, it seemed, was finally over.

Mad Gasser of Mattoon

The Mad Gasser of Mattoon wreaked havoc in a small Illinois town in 1944. This creature turned out to be so elusive that law-enforcement officials eventually declared him nonexistent, despite dozens of eyewitness reports. Was it a mad scientist? A government agency? A visitor from another planet? No one will ever know for sure, but the annals of the unknown are plagued with cases of inexplicable attackers who vanish without explanation. Just remember, though, that if these attacks can happen in Mattoon, they can happen anywhere — even where you live!

Mattoon is located in the southeastern part of central Illinois, and it's a fairly typical rural midwestern town. The strange events that took place here in 1944, however, were anything but typical.

It all began in the early-morning hours of August 31. A Mattoon man was startled out of a deep sleep and complained to his wife that he felt sick. He asked her if the gas could be on in the kitchen, because his symptoms seemed similar to gas exposure. The woman tried to get out of bed and check the pilot light on the stove, but found that she could not move. Minutes later, according to published reports, a woman in a neighboring home also tried to get out of bed and discovered that she too was paralyzed.

The next evening a woman named Mrs. Bert Kearney was awakened by a peculiar smell in her bedroom. The odor was sweet and overpowering, and as it grew stronger, she felt paralysis creeping into her legs and lower body. The following day she complained of having burned lips and a parched mouth and throat. Police found nothing in her house or yard, but that would not be the last strange event to occur at this particular house.

Just after midnight Mr. Kearney spotted a man lurking near the house; he would later fit the descriptions of the Mad Gasser. According to Kearney, he was tall and dressed in dark clothing and a tight-fitting black cap, and was standing near a window when Kearney spotted him. He quickly ran away.

Panic soon gripped the town of Mattoon. The local newspaper reported the Kearney case and subsequent others in a wildly sensational manner. Skeptics later said that the town's frightened citizens had taken leave of their senses and had just imagined that a "mad gasser" was loose. Mass hysteria is a simple explanation, but it does not eliminate all the evidence that something bizarre had happened in Mattoon.

By the morning of September 5, the police department had received reports of four more "gas attacks." All of the victims complained of a sickeningly sweet odor that caused them to become ill and slightly paralyzed for up to thirty minutes at a time.

Late that night, when Carl and Beulah Cordes returned home, they found a white cloth lying on their porch. Mrs. Cordes picked it up and noticed a strange smell coming from it. She held it close to her nose and was overwhelmed with nausea. In minutes, she had a severe allergic reaction as her lips and face swelled and her mouth started to bleed. The symptoms would disappear in about two hours. The police took the cloth into evidence and began an investigation. They soon found a skeleton key and an empty tube of lipstick on the porch. They decided the prowler was probably trying to break into the house but had failed.

They also came to the conclusion that the cloth was connected to the other gas attacks. It should be noted, however, that the odor on the cloth caused different symptoms in Mrs. Cordes than in the other victims. She did feel sick to her stomach, but there were no sensations of paralysis. The case itself is also different because if this was the Gasser, it is the only time that he actually tried to gain access to the home of his victims. Could his intentions have been different this time?

The Gasser attacked again that same night, but he was back to his old tricks and sprayed his gas into an open window. There would be only one other report that the attacker tried to break into a house. The woman in this instance claimed that someone in dark clothing had tried to force open her front door. Was it really the Mad Gasser?

The attacks continued, and Mattoon residents began reporting fleeting glimpses of the Gasser, always describing him as a tall, thin man in dark clothes and wearing a tight black cap. Eventually the FBI was called in, but not even they could find the intruder, and the strange reports continued. Rumors began to circulate that the attacker was an escapee from an insane asylum or was an odd inventor testing a new apparatus.

Armed citizens took to the streets, organizing watches and patrols to thwart any further attacks, but several took place anyway. Now the attacker was leaving behind evidence like footprints and sliced window screens.

A group of citizens did manage to arrest one suspect, but after he passed a polygraph test, he was released. The Gasser was becoming more than a threat to public safety, he was becoming a blot on the image of the city.

By September 10, Mad Gasser paranoia had peaked. FBI agents were attempting to track down the type of gas being used, and the police force was trying not only to find the Gasser but also to keep the armed citizens off the streets. None of the law-enforcement officials were having much luck with any of these tasks. By Saturday night, several dozen well-armed farmers from the surrounding area had joined the patrols in Mattoon. Nevertheless, six more attacks took place.

This period seemed to mark a turning point in the case. In the words of Thomas V. Wright, the city's commissioner of public health: "There is no doubt that a

By September 10, Mad Gasser paranoia had peaked. FBI agents were trying to track down the type of gas being used, and the police force was trying . . . to keep the armed citizens off the streets.

gas maniac exists and has made a number of attacks. But many of the reported attacks are nothing more than hysteria. Fear of the gas man is entirely out of proportion to the menace of the relatively harmless gas he is spraying." At this point, newspaper accounts of the affair began to take on a more skeptical tone, and the police began to dismiss new reports of attacks, suggesting that residents were merely imagining things. They started to believe that if they ignored the problem, it would just go away.

The police chief issued what he felt was the final statement on the gas attacks on September 12. He stated that large quantities of carbon tetrachloride gas were used at the local Atlas Diesel Engine Company and that this gas must be causing the reported cases. It could be carried throughout the town on the wind and could have left the stains that were found on the rag at one of the homes. As for the Mad Gasser himself, well, he was simply a figment of their imaginations. Not surprisingly, a spokesman for the plant was quick to deny the allegations that his company had caused the situation in town, maintaining that the only use for that gas in the plant was in their fire extinguishers. Besides that, how exactly was this gas cutting the window screens on Mattoon homes before causing nausea and paralysis?

The official explanation also failed to cover just how

> **The last Gasser attack took place on September 13 and was possibly the strangest. It occurred at the home of Mrs. Bertha Bench and her son, Orville. They described the attacker as being a woman who was dressed in man's clothing and who sprayed gas into a bedroom window.**

so many identical descriptions of the "Gasser" had been reported to the police. It also neglected to explain how different witnesses managed to report seeing a man of the "Gasser's" description fleeing the scene of an attack, even when the witness had no idea that an attack had taken place!

The last Gasser attack took place on September 13 and was possibly the strangest. It occurred at the home of Mrs. Bertha Bench and her son, Orville. They described the attacker as being a woman who was dressed in man's clothing and who sprayed gas into a bedroom window. The next morning, footprints that appeared to have been made by a woman's high-heeled shoes were found in the dirt below the window.

After that night, the Mad Gasser of Mattoon was never seen or heard from again.

What really happened in Mattoon is still a mystery, though researchers today have their own theories. Could he have been an extraterrestrial visitor using some sort of paralyzing agent to further a hidden agenda? Or could the Gasser have been an agent of our government, who came to an obscure midwestern town to test some military gas that could be used in the war effort?

Interestingly, *Weird Illinois* was sent a letter in 2002 from a woman who said that her father grew up in Mattoon during the time the gas attacks were taking place. He told her that there had been two sisters living in town who had a brother who was allegedly insane. A number of people believed that he was the Gasser, so his sisters locked him in the basement until they could find a mental institution into which to put him. After they locked him away, her father told her, the gas attacks stopped.

Whoever, or whatever, he was, the Mad Gasser has vanished into time and, real or imagined, is only a memory in the world of the unknown.

Celebrity Bites

I have become an involuntary collector of partially eaten sandwiches that were bitten into by celebrities. It all started in September of 1960, when then Vice President Richard Nixon visited my hometown of Sullivan, IL (pop. 3,000 then) to give a political speech. I was a 14-year-old Boy Scout, stationed as "security" around his picnic table. He took a couple of bites out of his buffalo barbecue sandwich, made a nice comment, then excused himself to go to another area where he would make his speech. I noticed that he didn't finish his sandwich,

so I took it . . . paper plate and all. I ran home with it, and told Mom about it. She then put it in a plastic bag, inside a glass jar. A local newspaper ran my picture and a short story about that incident, and the story lay dormant for almost thirty years.

Then, during the political debates of 1988, a Decatur, IL newspaper columnist tracked me down to do a follow-up story. Her story was picked up by the wire services, and before I knew it, I was on all of the morning-drive radio talk shows. A rep from the Johnny Carson show read the story in *USA Today*, and to make a long story short, asked me to be on his show. I accepted, and "the rest is history."

Steve Martin, also a guest on that show in December of 1988, gave me something he had bitten in to, as did Johnny Carson. Then, I had the opportunity, because of this new celebrity status, to be in the company of Henny Youngman, Tiny Tim, pro golfers, etc., all of whom have contributed to my collection.

All half-eaten sandwiches are labeled and safely stored in my freezer here at home in Springfield. —*Steve Jenne*

Personalized Properties

Our state is filled with weird properties, from eccentric houses to peculiar places of business. The wide array of styles and personal visions may cause us to scratch our heads and wonder just what in the world the builders and designers were thinking. And not all of the places merely look weird—some of their strangeness may be hidden under the surface, lurking in the stories and the unusual minds of their creators.

In almost every case, the visionaries behind these unique dwellings seem to live outside the mainstream of so-called polite society. They are people who built elaborate tributes to dead wives, created Amish amusement parks, monuments to ancient Egypt, houses to keep ghosts from getting caught in the corners, and Moorish castles. The properties seem to be an extension of the owners' personalities, visions, and dreams—which also seem to be a little more off-center than those of the people around them.

Jubilee Rock Garden

The Jubilee Rock Garden can be found a few miles outside the small town of Brimfield. The garden is a perfect example of what one can accomplish with a lot of rocks, a few bags of concrete, lots of time, and a purpose in mind.

William Notzke began creating his rock garden in the 1930s on his dairy farm, the Jubilee Dairy. He designed it to entertain visitors, who could enjoy the terraced garden and its fountain while they ate the ice cream he sold.

In 1963, when Notzke's wife, Edith, died, the design of the garden changed—it started to grow and to contain simple mosaic images like clubs, diamonds, hearts, and spades, all fashioned from different-colored quartzes, mica, geodes, and other colorful rocks. The Jubilee Rock Garden became a vast monument to Ethel's memory, but Notzke was not yet done.

Later that same year he built a huge memorial arch, made from white and rose quartz, over his driveway entrance. Notzke would light the arch from the inside but only on Memorial Day and May 14, Ethel's birthday. It was one of his last constructions at the site.

These days the former Jubilee Dairy and its rock garden have new owners, and they request that visitors view the arch and the garden from the highway.

The House with No Square Corners

In the tiny community of Bull Valley, along a quiet and mostly deserted roadway, is the English-style country house that George and Sylvia Stickney built in the mid-1800s. They chose the isolated place for its peace and solitude and for their spiritualistic activities. Both were said to be accomplished mediums, and they wanted to host parties and séances for their friends.

As devout practitioners of spiritualism, the Stickneys insisted that the architect design no square corners in the house, since, as they explained it, spirits have a tendency to get stuck in these corners, which could have dire results.

According to legend, though, one corner of a room accidentally ended up with a ninety-degree angle. How this could have happened is a mystery. Perhaps the architect was unable to complete the room with anything but a right angle. Whatever the reason, it is thought that this single square corner brought misfortune to the Stickneys. Seven of their children died over a short

period of time, and while there are no records to explain the deaths, the couple eventually moved a short distance away, perhaps realizing that the one square corner had been their downfall after all.

No reports of strange goings-on in the house were recorded until the 1970s, when a man named Rodrick Smith moved in. He lived there for several years, but when he moved out, he claimed that he had often heard strange noises in the place and that his dogs were never comfortable there. He was certain that something was not right with the property and thought that the house had become "tainted" by a group of "devil worshippers" who lived in it during the 1960s. He was convinced that their "black magic rituals" conjured up something unpleasant that now inhabited the house.

It turned out that the so-called devil worshippers were actually a group of stoned-out hippies who painted the rooms in dark colors and built open fires on the floors of the house. When they departed, they left spray-painted messages and drug paraphernalia in their wake.

Since Smith was sure that they had changed the atmosphere of the mansion, he was certainly no help in getting the house sold, but neither was one of the real estate listings that came after his departure. A local antiques dealer claimed that he saw a real estate ad for the place, in which a woman in a wedding gown could be seen pulling aside a curtain and peering out. The photographer who took the picture said that no one was in the house at the time.

Today, the house is the Bull Valley Village Hall, and the local police department uses a portion of the building as their headquarters. They claim nothing out of the ordinary has occurred during their occupancy but confess that, thanks to the shortage of square corners in the place, it is one of the weirdest houses in the area.

The Shell-Encrusted House of Liverpool Landing

In 1997, archaeologists conducted an excavation at the Liverpool Landing Site in Fulton County. They recovered shell artifacts from an unusual twentieth-century boathouse (today known only from photographs) that was extensively decorated with large mussel shells attached to the exterior walls. Many of the shells were partially filled with mortar and nailed to the structure with their dark surfaces facing out. Others have their white inner surfaces showing.

The house was reportedly occupied from the 1920s to about 1950 by a man named Sam Meyers, who has been variously described as an eccentric beachcomber and/or bootlegger who shared his house with goats.

This photograph, taken during the 1943 flood, shows a small single-story house with a gently pitched roof, numerous windows, and an entryway covered by a small porch. The exterior is covered with dark- and light-colored objects, presumably shells—and perhaps some stones—which are clearly arranged in patterns. Light-colored shells cover the upper portion of the chimney, the eaves, the porch's support posts and some window frames. Light-colored shells also form a sequence of letters above the row of windows on the right-hand side of the photograph. They appear to spell out [S]AM[S] HOME.

Rockome Gardens

Rockome Gardens is a genuine Amish amusement park. If you think these two things are contradictory, just visit the place, and you'll soon learn that being Amish (at least for a day) can be its own kind of eccentric fun.

The history of Rockome Gardens dates back to 1939 when Albert Martin, a businessman from nearby Arthur, decided to turn the grounds of his country home into the biggest rock and flower garden in Douglas County. Martin became obsessed with the project, and it rapidly grew until it became the largest such garden in the country. People from all over central Illinois began traveling back and forth on the road in front of his property, amazed at his marvelous creations. They often called the place his Rock Home, and Martin eventually dropped the h, which explains the strange spelling of the park's name today.

In 1952, he gave the gardens to the Mennonite Board of Missions and Charities from Elkhart, Indiana, which was kind of strange. The garden was located in the heart of Illinois' Amish country, but Martin was neither Amish nor Mennonite. Rockome soon became a retirement home for Mennonite missionaries.

Unfortunately, the Mennonites did not share Martin's enthusiasm for the place, and in 1958 they sold the property to Elvan Yoder, a Mennonite raised in the Amish faith. Yoder originally planned to farm the land, but after

noticing the thousands of people who drove past the house each summer, he realized its tourist potential.

Yoder soon opened the place to the public, started giving buggy rides, and began adding on to the property, re-creating an Amish environment. When the Rockome Amish Home opened in 1963, visitors had a chance to learn about the Amish and their simple lifestyle.

Elvan's wife, Irene, started a small gift shop on the property, as well as a custard stand. Then the Yoders added a rock shop, an Indian trading post, and a cheese shop. In the 1970s, they opened a large family restaurant.

One of the most popular additions to the gardens was Old Bagdad Town, a set of restored buildings from a real settlement called Bagdad, which was started around 1800 on the nearby Kaskaskia River. The small town died around 1850 when the Illinois Central Railroad bypassed it. The old town's school, jail, quilt store, and blacksmith shop have become favorite places to visit on the grounds.

Visitors can also see a petting zoo, a horse-driven buzz saw, a "haunted" barn, antiques museums, and chickens and ducks that perform and almost inevitably beat their human opponents in games of electronic tic-tac-toe. Many Illinoisians who visited the place as children say that little has changed over the years.

While Rockome Gardens is an all-around unusual place, the main attraction for seekers of the weird is the unique stonework that has been crafted throughout the park. The Yoders spent years creating fences, archways, hearts, cups and saucers, birdhouses, giant mushrooms, fountains, and vintage houses. Concocted from concrete, stone, and old pop bottles, these one-of-a-kind structures can be found near the huge model train set and the "holy tree."

Even if you have become jaded by strange attractions on the road, you are likely to be surprised by what you will find at this place on the back roads of Illinois.

Gold Pyramid House

One of the world's great unsolved mysteries is just how the ancient Egyptians were able to create their spectacular pyramids without the aid of modern technology. We may never know the answer to that—but equally as mysterious is why someone would build a hundred-to-one scale reproduction of the Great Pyramid at Giza in northern Illinois.

Eccentric isn't quite enough to describe this weird home. It's the residence of the Onan family, complete with a replica of King Tut's tomb and a sixty-four-foot statue of the pharaoh Ramses standing on the front lawn. The piece is said to be the largest gold-plated object in the world and has inspired many legends about the creation of the site. It's said that mystical energy pervades the property.

According to the stories, strange occurrences began to occur at the Gold Pyramid House during construction when a bulldozer uncovered a large rock that turned out to be rich with high-grade gold ore. This is recorded as the only gold strike in the state of Illinois. As work on the site progressed, an underground spring was uncovered. Its water formed a natural moat around the pyramid structure and was so pure that the owners were able to bottle and sell it. Some stories say that the moat is often kept filled with sharks.

The Onan family continues to live in the house and to operate an Egyptian emporium from their website. At one time, the place was open to the public for tours, but today it is open only to private groups. A schedule of such gatherings remains erratic, but should you get the chance to go inside this place, don't miss out.

Reebie Storage & Moving

With the discovery of King Tut's tomb in 1922, Egyptian design and motifs became all the rage in America. Buildings, theaters, businesses, and even cemetery tombs were designed in what was called the Egyptian Revival style. The Reebie Storage & Moving building, located on North Clark Street in Chicago, is an excellent example of this unusual style.

Commissioned by John and William Reebie, twin brothers who used it for their storage and moving business, and designed by architect George Kingsley in 1922, the building has been added to the National Register of Historic Places and has been praised for its accurate use of ancient Egyptian imagery.

The interior lobby has decorative metalwork, art-glass windows, lotus-leaf columns, and plaster casts of ancient Egyptians moving grain on barges. The exterior is covered with brightly colored terra-cotta sculptures. The front doors, which open onto Clark Street, are guarded by two large pharaohs in full Egyptian attire. According to local legend, the faces of the pharaohs are those of the two Reebie brothers, pretending to be Ramses II. Above the door are Egyptian hieroglyphics by an unknown carver; they translate as a rather untraditional message: "I give protection to your furniture" and "Forever I work for all your regions in daylight and darkness." That's the kind of service anyone would like to get!

The building . . . has been praised for its accurate use of ancient Egyptian imagery.

House of Crosses

There is no way that seekers of the weird can miss this house as they turn onto West Chestnut Street, a narrow thoroughfare in Chicago. It's been called many things: the House of Crosses, the Cross House, the It's What I Do House. By the American Institute of Architects and by others it's been called downright strange. Whatever you want to call it, you have to see it to believe it.

For almost twenty-five years, the owners of the house have been covering their residence with hundreds of plaques, shields, and wooden crosses that are emblazoned with red, black, and silver. Many of the crosses are marked with famous names.

It began in the late 1970s, when a man named Mitch Szewczyk started making wooden crosses out of material that he found in the street. For some reason, he decided to nail them up all over the front of his house. This was not because he was fixated with death (or afraid of vampires) but because he wanted to create an artistic tribute to local politicians and to the movie stars of his youth. Many of the names that appear on the crosses are of people that are not dead, and many of them, like Tarzan and Jane and Zorro, never really lived at all.

As time passed, Szewczyk added more movie stars, movie characters, and even movie titles to what was rapidly becoming a strange and colorful place. Some of the dozens of names include Mickey Rooney, Sammy Davis Jr., Lancelot, Bing Crosby, Bette Davis, Zsa Zsa Gabor, Buckwheat, the Cisco Kid, and even former Chicago mayor Jane Byrne, who has a prominent spot.

Work continued on the house for years, but unfortunately, Szewczyk became bedridden in the early 1990s and was never able to complete his King Kong cross, which was going to be his biggest and best, he claimed.

Don't miss this famous spot and be sure to take plenty of photos from the sidewalk as you pass by. Szewczyk remains a beloved character in the neighborhood. While he might have dubbed his creation the Cross House, the locals just call it Mitch's Place.

Villa Kathrine

Those traveling along Illinois' Great River Road may be shocked when they reach the old town of Quincy and see what appears to be a small Moorish castle overlooking the Mississippi. The house is not a figment of their imagination but a real-life castle. It was created by an eccentric millionaire named George Metz, who abandoned the place after the death of his only companion—his dog, Bingo.

Villa Kathrine was built in 1900 as a setting for the exotic furnishings Metz collected

during his world travels. The son of a wealthy Quincy businessman, George was so rich that he never worked a day in his life, but traveled the world instead. His love for the world's wonders made Metz himself something of a wonder to folks in his hometown. Reporters wrote speculative tales about Villa Kathrine, which was named for his mother, and townspeople gossiped about the castle's mysterious owner.

According to legend, Metz's wanderings were motivated by his lifelong dream to find the perfect home. He found it in the centuries-old Villa Ben Ahben in Algiers. He once stated that he was struck by the golden color of the exterior and by its large domes, and he became obsessed with creating his own version of the place in Quincy. He claimed that he spent two years wandering North Africa, haggling with caravan trains of "secretive Moors." He bought thousands of items and pieces of furniture for the villa, including crescents for his domes, antique door knockers, divans, Egyptian lamps, and much more. During this time, he drew and sketched and discarded ideas for the house, and then he returned to Quincy to make his dreams come true.

Needless to say, he had a tough time finding a suitable architect in his hometown. But finally he found a young man named George Behrensmeyer, who took Villa Kathrine on as his first commission. Together they found a site for the house on a bluff above the Mississippi. Working from Metz's drawings, Behrensmeyer began designs for the dream castle. He scaled the place down so that it would rest securely on the bluff, and then in 1900, the brick and stucco walls of Villa Kathrine began to rise.

Locals whispered about the unusual house from the very beginning. According to legend, Metz built the house in mourning over a lost love. The stories had it that he met a "fair-haired, blue-eyed" woman in Germany, and together they had discovered the beauty of Villa Ben Ahben. Metz planned to bring his love home with him to his villa, but she refused to come to Quincy. Broken-hearted, Metz retired to a reclusive life.

His refusal to deny or confirm the story fueled the gossip, and speculation ran rampant. But all agree that the villa on the hill totally consumed the man.

The finished castle evoked images of Moorish homes in North Africa and Spain, but in fact, Villa Kathrine was a modest, two-story home. It was its one-story side wing, with two square towers, several porches, and numerous setbacks and projections, that gave it an exotic, castlelike outline. The villa's square south tower was decorated on all sides with a diamond pattern of inlaid, carved lattice woodwork. Another tower was topped by a Moslem minaret with swirling red-and-white stripes and a silver dome, which was a miniature replica of a dome on the famous Mosque of Thaïs in Tunisia. The north tower had a dome that was topped with a Muslim crescent that Metz found in an ancient ruin in northern Africa.

The building had an unusual variety of windows that included rounded and pointed arches, keyhole shapes, and diamonds. The larger windows were fitted with grilles in Moorish patterns. A terrace surrounded the front entrance, and visitors reached the door through a Moorish arch. Over the front door was a tile that held a relief cast of a woman's hand adorned with a wedding ring and holding a dove; some believe that it was the hand of Metz's lost love.

The interior of the house continued the Moorish theme. Heavy wooden beams crossed the ceiling, and keyhole niches were fitted into the walls. There were shelves of exotic pottery, carved chairs and tables, and numerous wall hangings and rugs. Inside the front door was the drawing room, and up a short flight of steps and through glass doors was the interior court, which was surrounded by a gallery that was supported by eight pointed arches embraced by spiral pillars. The pillars are copies of those in the Court of Dolls in Seville, Spain. Around the center court were small square rooms that bordered a central pool. The villa's atrium was open to the roof, where a winter glass cover would be replaced by a summer awning.

Metz lived at Villa Kathrine for twelve years, with his beloved dog, Bingo, as his only constant companion. Brought over from Denmark by Metz after one of his trips, Bingo was a 212-pound Great Dane that was rumored to be the largest dog in America. When Bingo died, a cloud descended over Metz's dream, plunging him into a terrible depression, and, on the urging of his relatives, he sold the villa and all its furnishings to a couple who professed great interest in the place. Metz was convinced he had sold it to ideal occupants. Little did he know that the buyers were actually agents for the Alton-Quincy Interurban Railroad, which planned to tear down the house and build a railroad yard on the site. Word got out, and vandals descended on the mysterious house, carrying off the decorations and the furniture, and turning the place into a ruin.

Metz returned in 1913 to find that the house was overrun with vermin and birds, the walls were stained, and what little furniture remained was shredded. He left it, vowing never to return. Nineteen years later, though, he did come back for one final visit. This time the villa was crumbling with decay. "I wish this place were mine again," he told a reporter. "I'd tear it down."

George Metz never lost his love for views of the Mississippi River. After leaving Villa Kathrine, he lived in a succession of apartments with a wide view of the river. He spent most of his spare time feeding the birds and squirrels in Quincy's parks. Poor health finally brought him to St. Vincent Hospital, where he died from pneumonia in 1937.

Villa Kathrine survived the treachery of the railroad, and it had many successive owners. It now is part of the Quincy Park District. After years of decay and vandalism, the castle has at last been saved and restored for generations of people to marvel over—and to wonder about.

Woodland Palace

Francis was a shy genius who retired at a young age and spent the rest of his life living in the woods with his wife, Jeanie. The house, dubbed Woodland Palace, became a showplace for his many talents and interests.

In a small park outside the city of Kewanee is a house built by a man named Fred Francis. Francis was a shy genius who retired at a young age and spent the rest of his life living in the woods with his wife, Jeanie. The house, dubbed Woodland Palace, became a showplace for Fred's many talents and interests. He was a mechanical engineer and mathematician, an inventor and builder, a poet and philosopher, an artist and lecturer — and a dyed-in-the-wool eccentric.

Fred Francis was born in January 1856 on his family farm, about four miles east of what would become Kewanee. Even at a young age, Fred demonstrated that he was gifted with a brilliant mind. In 1874, he became the first student from Kewanee to attend the Illinois Industrial University (which later became the University of Illinois) in Urbana.

Francis was in his element at the university. All of the school's resources, from books to facilities and professors, were available to him, and to pay his way through school, he designed custom steam engines. One semester, instead of paying tuition, Fred gave the university the rights to a patent that he had obtained for a particular engine.

While he may have excelled in his schoolwork, Fred was painfully shy with other students. He never attended any social functions, preferring to spend his time studying or in the shop. He graduated with a degree in mechanical engineering and took a job with the Elgin Watch Company in Elgin, where he designed and built tools to manufacture and assemble watches. While working there, he obtained several more patents, the most significant of which related to mainsprings and their installation in watches. Fred received royalties for this and other inventions, and the payments continued after he left the company in 1889. Eventually, he received so much money from the Elgin Watch Company that he wrote them a letter and told them they had already paid him enough for him to live the rest of his life comfortably. He asked that they discontinue the payments, and the company reluctantly agreed.

While Fred was living in Elgin, he met Jeanette Crowfoot, a widow with four grown children. They married in 1890 and never had any children of their own.

Fred was an atheist, but he believed in reincarnation and in Physical Culture, a philosophy developed in the latter part of the 1800s by Bernarr Macfadden. The main tenet of the belief was that a person should always be

The Coach Room, *which Fred modeled after the coach car on a passenger train.*

actively doing something, whether for the sake of work or just for exercise. The culture advocated daily exercise and long walks of between five and twenty miles. Preferably, these walks would occur in places where people could remove their shoes and socks, thus allowing minerals to be absorbed into their bare feet. Physical Culture also promoted nudism, which was referred to as taking an "air bath."

Fred would eat no meat, fearing that if he did, he might be eating one of his ancestors. He used no salt or other condiments to flavor his food. He believed that the body had a natural "sentinel" that determined when a person had eaten enough, but if someone used condiments or other flavoring, the "sentinel" could be fooled and that person would become overweight.

Kewanee area residents frequently saw Fred riding his bicycle into town. Normally, he wore no shirt, hat, or shoes, just light-colored pants, no matter what the weather was outside. He never shaved his beard and was said to look like a wild man.

Many wondered what attracted a delicate woman like Jeanie to an unusual character like Fred. Perhaps it was just his good nature and warm heart, but everyone agreed that she adored him.

The pair often traveled about on their bicycle, which was their only means of transportation. On the front of the handlebars, Fred had built a seat on which Jeanie would ride. He wore a rearview mirror on a wire loop that was placed on the top of his head so that he could keep an eye on traffic approaching him from behind.

Tragically, Jeanie contracted tuberculosis around 1910. She spent the last years of her life in a solarium that Fred added onto the house for her. He hung a bell outside the house and attached a string to Jeanie's chair so that she could summon him if he was outside in the yard. The love of Fred's life died on October 1, 1921, leaving him utterly alone in his magnificent house.

Fred had begun to build Woodland Palace in the autumn of 1889 on sixty acres of timberland. Using brick, stone, and wood that he cut from the land, he did all the labor himself. He followed no particular form of architecture; consequently, Woodland Palace possesses no real architectural style. Its bricks were purchased from a local brickyard, but Fred chipped each one of them by hand, removing the soft spots and giving them a striking appearance. He added stained glass windows to the building just because he liked the look and installed a dome that was made by a tinsmith in Sheffield. He placed it on a white limestone tower that made the house look like the palace it was named for.

On the south side of the structure were two screened porches that could be entered only from the interior of the house. The one on the west side was Jeanie's; the one on the east was Fred's. Among the many oddities of the house were the "missing bricks" openings, which could be found on all four sides of Woodland Palace. They were part of a system that Fred devised to provide heat to the floors and walls of the basement. He had a heat exchanger installed on the vent pipe for the furnace that heated the house. Heat from the furnace's exhaust warmed exterior air that was drawn into the structure by a windmill-driven fan at the base of an adjacent pipe. The warmed air was then directed under the floorboards in the basement via ducts in the walls and out through the "missing brick" ventilator openings. In this way, Fred was able to capture some of the wasted heat from the furnace and return it to the home to heat the floors and walls and to keep the basement dry.

Fred also had an air-cooling system that was run by the windmill. He achieved this by running a clay pipe underground from the lower level of the house and into the nearby woods. Air from the forest, cooled to about fifty-five degrees under the ground, was drawn into the pipe by a fan powered by the windmill.

The hot water heater was another invention ahead of its time. Under the stairs was a force pump that provided pressure to run water to the kitchen. The exhaust from the kitchen stove was routed into a pipe that surrounded the pressure pump and warmed the water in the pipe. There was a spigot to draw hot water from the pump, giving the house hot running water.

The coach room was so named because Fred designed and built it along the lines of railway coaches of the day. The area included an arched ceiling, slatted blinds, elongated narrow mirrors, and a three-tone green paint scheme. The wooden blinds disappeared into the ceiling when they were raised, as did the two glass doors that led out onto the screened porches.

The fireplace room was north of the coach room. The artwork on the copperplate of the fireplace was done by Fred, but the marble plaques under the mantel were made in Italy. He sent a picture of himself, draped only in a towel, bare-chested, right arm upraised and bicep flexed, to a marble cutter to have them made. Today, it looks as though the marble version of Fred is supporting the mantel on his upraised arm.

Fred designed and built a heat exchanger into the chimney of the fireplace. There were a series of metal tubes running from a fresh-air opening at the rear of the heat exchanger, through the chimney, and out into the room.

Just west of the fireplace room is the solarium addition that Fred built for Jeanie after she contracted tuberculosis. He designed it so that the air changed every sixty seconds to provide her with a constant supply of fresh air.

After Jeanie's death, Fred continued working on Woodland Palace, declaring that he would put the finishing touches on the house on his hundredth birthday. To alleviate his sorrow, he began inviting people to his home, where he gave lectures on his ideas, opinions, and philosophies. Sometimes he talked about plants, food, or wildlife; other times, he read poetry and sang.

He especially liked to entertain schoolchildren and built a merry-go-round for their enjoyment. He allowed people to visit the grounds of his home and use the woods for picnics and nature walks. He placed a sign at the entrance to the land that stated STOP, READ THIS—GROUNDS ARE FREE FOR ALL WHO DO RIGHT, AND ALL SUCH ARE WELCOME. THOSE WHO THROW PAPER AND RUBBISH ON THE GROUND, OR LETS KIDS DO SO ARE CORDIALLY INVITED TO STAY AWAY

As he aged, Fred arranged a signal with the mailman. If the flag on the mailbox was not up, he should check to see if Fred needed help or might be injured. On December 26, 1926, the flag was not raised. Worried, the mailman went to the house and peered into the back door, where he saw Fred lying on the floor in a pool of blood. Fred had died from a self-inflicted gunshot wound, leaving a note behind that said that the pain from a hernia could no longer be tolerated. Fred took his own life—and departed this world to spend eternity with Jeanie.

In his will, Fred wrote that he wanted to be cremated on his own land. He included instructions on how to build a funeral pyre and said that he wanted it to be left burning until all the mourners had left. Unfortunately for Fred, state law prohibited bodies to be burned in the open, and so he was taken to a crematory in Davenport, Iowa, and then returned to Kewanee, where he was buried in Pleasant View Cemetery.

Much to the dismay of his relatives, Fred left his entire estate to the city of Kewanee, and it has maintained Woodland Palace ever since. It remains today as a tribute to a remarkable and eccentric man.

African American Heritage Museum

In 1986, in the yard of his small home on the east side of Aurora at 126 South Kendall Street, Dr. Charles Smith began building his vision: a sculptural monument dedicated to the contributions and experiences of African Americans. Before his vision, Dr. Smith, a Vietnam veteran, had felt lost in pain and anger. Then he received his inspiration: "God told me, 'Use Art—I give you a weapon,' just like he gave Dr. King the Gandhi strategy." From that moment on and despite the fact that he had never received training in art, Dr. Smith started to fill his property with sculpted tributes to the leaders and martyrs of Black America: Harriet Tubman, Frederick Douglass, Emmett Till, and Martin Luther King Jr. among them. In addition, there are memorials to the four thousand Black Americans who died in Vietnam, to victims of the Rwanda tragedy, as well as to whites who helped with the Underground Railroad.

As scholar Lisa Stone writes, "The African-American Heritage Museum and Black Veterans Archives is equal parts memorial and mirror, commemorating and reflecting the complexity of late 20th Century life, and its elaborate, and at times bewildering, commingled histories."

In 2002, Dr. Smith moved from Illinois in order to start two new satellite museums in Hammond and New Orleans, Louisiana. (The New Orleans project, known as the Algiers Folk Art Zone, is a collaboration with artist Charles Gillam.) Before his departure, Dr. Smith organized a foundation to keep the original Aurora museum open to the public. Forever passionate, forever formidable, forever free, Dr. Charles Smith continues to spread his message of remembrance, hope, and vision.

—Larry Harris

OWNED & OPERATED by
The ED WALDMIRE family
Since 1949

COZY DRIVE IN
JUST AHEAD

OLD 66

LAND OF THE FREE
HOME OF THE BRAVE

Roadside Oddities

If you speed past Big Thunder Park as you drive through the city of Rockford, you'll have no idea that the place contains Illinois' very first roadside attraction. But indeed it does.

Big Thunder Park is named in honor of the Potawatomi Indian chief called Big Thunder, who died before the first white settlers arrived here in the 1830s. His method of burial followed Indian custom: He was placed in a seat, wearing his best attire and surrounded by food, tobacco, and all of the other necessary accoutrements for the afterlife. He was then encircled by a six-foot-tall wooden stockade and left to the elements. Early visitors, including travelers on the Chicago–Galena stagecoach line, were very curious to see the dead chief. Their curiosity led them to take souvenirs, and soon very little remained of Big Thunder. Undaunted, the locals began substituting bones of hogs and sheep as relics for the gullible tourists. And Illinois' first roadside oddity was born.

There are unusual places like this all over the state. Many of these sites have never been fully appreciated or documented, while others have become so familiar that we hardly notice them as we go by. And then there are those that will make your hair stand on end!

Hopefully, the sites we report on will convince you to slow down and perhaps even pull off along the side of the road for a closer look. And even better, to keep your eyes open for new additions to Illinois roadside culture—you just never know what may be waiting for you around the next bend in the road.

Roadside Food

World's Largest Catsup Bottle

Illinois is the proud home of the World's Largest Catsup Bottle, located along Route 159, just south of downtown Collinsville. This 170-foot-tall water tower was built by the W. E. Caldwell Company for the G. S. Suppiger catsup bottling plant—bottlers of Brooks Old Original Rich and Tangy Catsup.

Plans were started for the giant water tower in 1947 when the W. E. Caldwell Company of Louisville, Kentucky, was contracted to build the hundred-thousand-gallon structure. The water tower was needed for plant operations and to supply water to the new sprinkler system. Gerhart S. Suppiger, then president of the company, suggested that the tower be built in the distinctive tapered shape of their catsup bottles. Final drawings were approved in 1948, and the World's Largest Catsup Bottle was completed in October of 1949.

Big John the Grocery Clerk

Big Johns are friendly guys who carry automobile-size grocery bags in the parking lots of Big John food stores. Usually clad in button-down shirts, blue jeans, aprons, and giant black shoes, they grin amiably toward passing motorists from their thirty-foot height. You can find Big Johns at stores in Benton, Eldorado, West City, and Metropolis. The clerk is so friendly he even changes clothes and carries bags for competitors like Prairie Farms.

Big Weenies

The Big Weenies atop the Superdawg Drive-in are a well-known sight in Chicago. The uninitiated, however, are often surprised to be traveling along Milwaukee Avenue and look over to see two giant wieners perched on top of a drive-in restaurant.

Superdawg has been owned by Maurie Berman since 1948, and it's one of Illinois' last great drive-ins. The two trademark figures of Superdawg are best appreciated after dark, when their eyes glow a bright red that is a bit unsettling. The Tarzan Weenie is clad in a leopard skin and strikes a muscleman pose that is obviously meant to impress his topless Jane Weenie companion, who looks on adoringly in her miniskirt. If these eccentric figures are not enough to convince you to stop here for a dog and an order of fries, we can't think of what would be!

Hot Fish

Looking for a great fish sandwich? A stop at Hoot's Drive-In, located at a bend in the road called Grand Chain, just a few miles from the Ohio River, promises to be a uniquely fresh experience. Ever wonder how people eat fish or lobster in a restaurant where aquariums surround the room—allowing potential meals to stare at you as you devour their relatives? If you do, imagine how you would feel after coming out of Hoot's late at night to find this guy waiting for you in the parking lot. It might be enough to get you to swear off fish for good!

The Pork Chop Pig

It's a bit weird when eating establishments use the food items on the menu as colorful mascots to entice you to eat more. For example, have you seen dancing cows that advertise hamburgers or cute birds that beg you to eat fried chicken? In this case, it's a pig that flags down passing motorists to come into Moweaqua Foods, the "Home of the Jumbo Pork Chop Sandwich." It almost makes you feel sorry for the little guy, because he looks a bit nervous, but that feeling passes when you get a bite of the sandwich! Just be sure to look the other way when you leave the parking lot, and you'll have nothing to feel guilty about.

Roadside Lincoln

There is no greater figure in Illinois history than that of our most famous former resident, Abraham Lincoln. Scattered across the state are notable sites that have been dedicated to his memory, including Lincoln's former home, New Salem; the first state capitol building, in Vandalia; and dozens of small museums and historic sites. But in addition to these well-known sites are a number of places that are a little more off-center than one might imagine when it comes to honoring Honest Abe.

Lincoln's Lucky Nose

These days, the monument in Springfield that holds the tomb of Abraham Lincoln is a solemn place. However, it wasn't always this way. After the monument was rebuilt in 1901 (it was necessary to redesign the tomb because of shoddy workmanship), Lincoln's tomb became a popular tourist attraction and soon began to resemble a carnival sideshow. Caretakers were allowed to charge admission to supplement their meager salaries, and one caretaker, the creative and enterprising Herbert W. Fay, placed his thirty-thousand-piece collection of Lincoln memorabilia in the rotunda above Lincoln's burial place. Visitors could view a vial of Lincoln's blood (a small sign reads LINCOLN'S BLOOD, ASK HOW IT CAME HERE), admire bronze statues that for some reason had been painted, or ask a local schoolchild, who was there "on staff," to recite the Gettysburg Address for a quarter.

Several years ago some scientists put in a request to drill into Lincoln's coffin for tissue samples. They wanted to test his DNA for Marfan syndrome, a genetic disease that might have been responsible for his lanky frame. The request was denied. Conspiracy nuts theorized that scientists were really trying to get his tissue in order to clone him!

These days, though, the tomb is a quiet place, and thousands of people come here every year to pay their respects to the slain President. They also come with the hope that a little good luck will rub off on them, so to speak.

Near the tomb is a large bust that was sculpted by Gutzon Borglum, who also created Mount Rushmore. Tradition has it that visitors should rub Lincoln's nose for luck. How this got started, no one knows, but it has been going on for decades. Several years after the bust was placed, caretakers began to notice that Abe's nose had become a bright and shiny spot on his otherwise dark bronze face. In order to preserve the bust, they tried putting it on a pedestal that was out of the tourists' reach, but the public demanded that it be lowered again. The lucky nose was moved back down, and visitors today can easily reach up and get their own bit of good luck from the end of old Abe's nose.

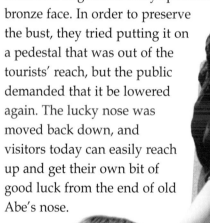

Skinny Lincoln

A clean-shaven statue of a young Abraham Lincoln stands in front of the Illinois exhibits building on the State Fairgrounds. It was constructed here back in 1968 apparently to intimidate the thousands of people who come to the fair each year. The statue, which stands about thirty feet tall and is very thin—in fact, too thin—is named the Rail Splitter, thanks to the axe that he holds in his hands. That's the official name for it anyway. It's more commonly known, perhaps because of its cadaverous appearance and menacing expression, as the Axe Murderer!

The Lincoln Watermelon Monument

Without a doubt, the weirdest monument to Abraham Lincoln in Illinois is not a statue of the President, but a statue of a slice of watermelon—located in Lincoln, the only city ever named for Abraham Lincoln with his personal consent. In fact, it was so named when Abe was just a well-known Illinois lawyer and long before he was elected to national office.

In 1853, Abe Lincoln was just a young lawyer who was called upon to draft the town's incorporation papers. The founders decided to name the place in his honor, and Lincoln responded to the suggestion with his usual humility: "I think you are making a mistake," he said. "I never knew of anything named Lincoln that ever amounted to much."

Lincoln then presided over the town's dedication on April 27—and the official story says that he poured out the juice from a watermelon to christen the ground, but other stories say that he actually spit out a mouthful of watermelon seeds as a christening.

In 1964, the statue was erected near the train station where it all took place.

Lincoln's Wagon

Located just off Old Route 66 near Divernon is a three-hundred-fifty-pound Abraham Lincoln who is inexplicably driving a wagon and reading a lawbook at the same time. The fact that it turns out to be the World's Largest Covered Wagon makes us forget about the President's unusual driving habits. The wagon itself weighs five tons and was hand-built from oak by David Bentley. It is twenty-four feet tall, twelve feet wide, and forty feet long. Apparently, it once had a covering over the bed of the wagon, but the cover is currently missing. Regardless, this is a nice (albeit weird) tribute to Roadside Lincoln.

Roadside Characters

Popeye the Sailor

The southern Illinois town of Chester has long been known as the "birthplace" of Popeye the Sailor, the famous cartoon character. In truth, though, Chester is the birthplace of Popeye's creator, Elzie Crisler Segar, who unveiled the beloved spinach-eating sailor in 1929 as a new character in his "Thimble Theater" comic strip. Popeye became a comic strip favorite and was soon known all over the world.

What is unknown to most readers outside southern Illinois, though, is that the fictional sailor and his menagerie of friends were inspired by real-life residents of Chester. Popeye was fashioned after Frank "Rocky" Fiegel, a one-eyed, pipe-smoking river man who had a penchant for getting into fistfights. Olive Oyl was modeled after a skinny shopkeeper named Dora Paskal, and Wimpy was based on William "Windy Bill" Schuchert, the proprietor of the Chester Opera House, where Segar once worked as a projectionist. Schuchert so loved hamburgers that he would send his employees out between performances to buy them for him. His roly-poly figure was a natural for the comic character's physique.

Even though Segar left Chester in the early 1920s, he was always considered a native son. When he died in 1938, his "Popeye" comic was appearing in more than five hundred newspapers. In Segar's honor, the Chester Sorority Ladies raised $10,000 in the mid-1970s to commission a sculpture of Popeye. The six-foot-tall, nine-hundred-pound bronze statue was unveiled in 1977 and stands today in Segar Memorial Park, which overlooks the Mississippi River. The statue has been vandalized three times (attacks likely orchestrated by Bluto!) over the years but remains today in its place of honor. Each year, it presides over the Popeye Picnic, which is held the weekend after Labor Day.

Superman

Metropolis is the self-proclaimed Hometown of Superman; its citizens have some fun with the situation and use the image of Superman to promote their town, celebrating its local hero every possible way it can.

The local bank is "Home of Super Financial Services." The town newspaper calls itself *The Planet,* and annual celebrations commemorate the comic book hero. Souvenirs and photo opportunities are available everywhere, from wooden cutouts (INSERT YOUR HEAD HERE!) at grocery stores to the famed Superman statue. At one time, the chamber of commerce even handed out free packets of Kryptonite to children. They had to stop when DC Comics protested and safety groups pointed out that the small chunks presented a choking hazard for the kids.

In 1972, the town made plans to build a thousand-acre Amazing World of Superman theme park at a cost of more than $50 million. As it turned out, the Arab oil embargo, not Kryptonite, brought the plan to its knees, and it took nearly a decade for the town to recover. In 1979, Superman came to the big screen in the form of Christopher Reeve, and once again the small town of Metropolis was besieged with calls and inquiries. Plans were made for festivals and of course, for a statue of Superman. By 1986, enough money was raised to erect a seven-foot Man of Steel (actually fiberglass), who quickly became a target for vandals who wanted to see if Superman really was faster than a speeding bullet. Guess what? He wasn't, and the statue began to look pretty shabby with all those holes in it. The efforts of Metropolis to honor their hero had been thwarted again.

In 1993, the perforated Superman vanished and enough money was raised to allow the town to erect an even larger, fifteen-foot version of the caped hero. The project, which cost around $120,000, was financed by engraved bricks that had been purchased by local residents

and businesses. The new statue was made from a harder, more bulletproof substance than fiberglass, and the Man of Steel officially became the Man of Bronze. The statue now stands proudly in Superman Square, near the Super Museum, which holds thousands of Superman artifacts like comic books, movies, television shows, and even props from all of them.

If you are a fan, you won't want to miss the annual Superman Festival, which is held each summer, when people from around the world descend on this small town. Superman himself flies in to sign autographs, and stars of the early series and other celebrity guests make occasional appearances.

Lauterbach Tire Man

In years past, the nation's highways were replete with hundreds of signs, murals, and other forms of roadside advertising aimed at motorists. Among the most famous were the giants created during the 1960s by International Fiberglass of Venice, California. Roughly one hundred and fifty of these signs were produced before the molds were broken and the concept discontinued.

Many of the fiberglass giants, known as Muffler Men, were designed to hold automobile mufflers and were originally placed in front of service stations as attention-getters. As many of these businesses closed or the giants were sold off, they were replaced by everything from lumberjacks to cowboys to spacemen and more.

The Lauterbach Tire Man in Springfield is just one of these retired Muffler Men who has now gone on to work for a tire company. His muffler was at some point replaced with an axe, turning him into a lumberjack, but now he proudly and patriotically holds an American flag.

The Lamb's Farm Giant

The Lamb's Farm Giant stands guard with his axe outside the miniature golf course and petting farm at Lamb's Farm, a working facility for people with mental disabilities in Libertyville. The giant is one of northern Illinois' better known former Muffler Men. His automobile part has long been replaced by an axe, and he is joined on security patrol by his friend the cow and a giant-sized bottle of milk.

Big Chief Blackhawk

Unlike most other roadside characters, which are works of art in their own way, Big Chief Blackhawk was created by a skilled artisan. Lorado Taft, one of the most famous sculptors of the early twentieth century, built the massive statue around 1911. The largest reinforced concrete statue in the world (as well as the world's second largest obelisk) overlooks the Rock River valley from a bluff in Lowden State Park, near Oregon. The statue weighs over one hundred tons and depicts a stoic Native American figure draped in a blanket. He was dubbed Chief Blackhawk when it was completed, but while it could be many Native Americans, he's not Blackhawk, who sported a Mohawk. Regardless, it's an amazing monument.

Onan Lumberman

Located on Grand Avenue in Gurnee, across the street from an abandoned home improvement store, is a giant who holds a house in one hand and a hammer in the other. Perched on top of a neon sign for Onan Enterprises, he stares out benignly toward the horizon. But who is he, and what does he advertise?

He is likely a refugee left behind by the home store when it went out of business. The giant actually stands in front of a questionable-looking "fantasy suites" hotel, but there doesn't seem to be much of a connection there. So, he's not a Muffler Man, not really a home improvement man—he's now just a big guy with a house under his arm!

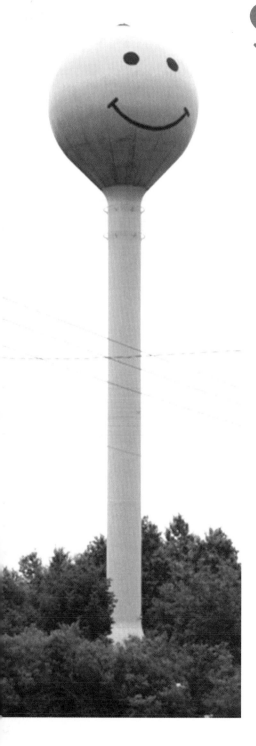

Smile! Your Face Is on a Water Tower!

Afraid of terrorism? Worried about the economy? Don't know where your kids are after dark? Well, stop worrying and be happy. We live in a happy place. The always optimistic icon from the 1960s—the smiley face—proves it by being alive and well and living in Illinois.

In small communities scattered around the state, water towers have been painted a bright yellow and adorned with a pair of dot eyes and a happy, upturned smile. The idea of turning spherical towers into smiling faces of joy began in the 1970s, when the smiley face was still a fresh idea. He was a counterculture symbol of the hippie era, but a safe and sunny one.

The first town in America to embrace the idea of highlighting the smiley face on water towers is believed to be Calumet City. The plan was inspired by a letter sent to the city council by eight-year-old resident Kim Fornero. She suggested that a smiley face would be much more fun to look at than a plain old water tower, and so in 1973 renovations began. Other towns soon began breaking out the yellow paint and spray guns to create their own smiley faces. Since 1973, Calumet City has added another tower to make a matching pair of "Mr. and Mrs. Water Towers."

Other towns with happy water towers include Atlanta, the little town of Makanda, home to Boomer the Dog and a thriving artists' colony, and Watseka.

Millennium Spire

Illinois' Millennium Spire is located at the National Shrine of Our Lady of the Snows near Belleville. The eighty-five-foot-tall stainless-steel sculpture rises from a room full of candles that is built into a hillside on the shrine's property. Strangely shaped, awesome to look at, and eerie to step inside of, the spire was created by the late William Severson, a nationally renowned sculptor. It was commissioned by the shrine as a symbol representing Pope John Paul II's vision of a new Pentecost.

But the spire is not just a piece of art—it is a radio tower that transmits prayer directly to God! During the day, the spire reflects the light of the sun, and it is continually illuminated with LED lights as a beacon to herald the third millennium (which arrived a couple of years ago). Prayer and petition requests that are sent to the Missionary Oblates of Mary Immaculate through their website are converted into binary language before they are symbolically sent upward to God on the network of lights built into the curve of the Millennium Spire.

Tallest Totem Pole . . .
. . . Well, East of the Rockies Anyway

On Abingdon's Main Street is the Tallest Totem Pole East of the Rocky Mountains. Although it was not built by Native Americans (it was built by towns-people in the 1970s and finished by an art student from Illinois State University), the totem pole is still pretty impressive. At the time it was built, it was supposed to be the tallest totem pole in the world. Unfortunately, a taller one was built in Canada not long after, so the designation was changed to the tallest pole in the east.

Purple Martin Capital of the World

If the memory of Alfred Hitchcock's *The Birds* still makes you shudder, you might want to avoid the small town of Griggsville. As you drive into town, you will see an alarming number of tall poles supporting multiple-dwelling birdhouses, seemingly on every corner. But they are nothing compared to the monstrous house that awaits you in the town center. This six-hundred-apartment birdhouse rises up on a sturdy pole that is visible for a long distance to both visitors and to the intended occupants of the house—purple martins.

This purple-black bird, which was once an endangered species, has made a huge comeback, thanks to protection by federal law, the promotion of towns like Griggsville, and its amazing talent of being able to eat as many as two thousand mosquitoes every day. This makes the bird especially popular here. Griggsville is located in the vicinity of the Illinois River, and during the humid summer months mosquitoes are a huge problem. And this is not a situation unique to Griggsville, as people in Missouri, Louisiana, Florida, and Arkansas can tell you. For just this reason, there are at least a dozen other towns that claimed to be the Purple Martin Capital of . . . well, wherever.

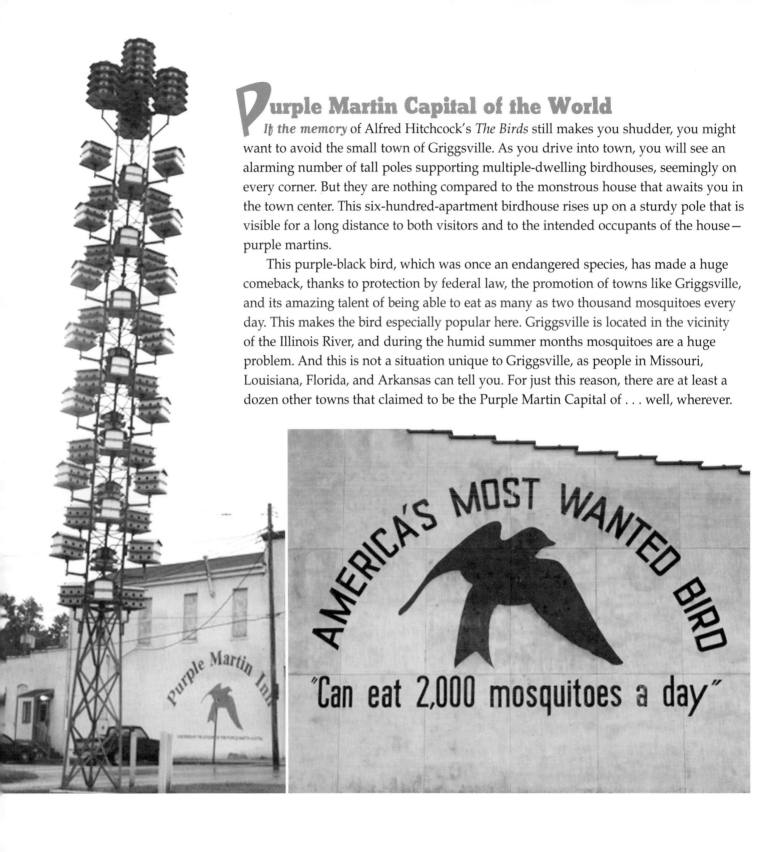

Purple Martin Inn

AMERICA'S MOST WANTED BIRD

"Can eat 2,000 mosquitoes a day"

America's Only Hippie Memorial

There are a number of places where you might expect to see a memorial to hippies, but Arcola is assuredly not one of them. Better known as a tourist spot for Illinois Amish Country, for its annual broomcorn festival, and as the birthplace of Johnny Gruelle, creator of Raggedy Ann and Andy, Arcola was also home to eccentric artist Bob Moomaw. Thanks to him, it has become home to America's only Hippie Memorial.

Moomaw, a local artist, constructed the sixty-two-foot metal sculpture that gives homage to the free-form soul of the 1960s. The sculptor divided his time between Arcola and Michigan, and the memorial was actually in Michigan when Moomaw died of a heart attack in 1998. After his death, the sculpture began to fall into disrepair, so his friend Gus Kelsey, an Arcola native who also lived in southwestern Michigan, decided to bring it to town.

Kelsey spent $8,000 to refurbish the memorial, and it was installed in 1998, adjacent to the town's historic Illinois Central Railroad Station. At the center of the monument's stucco wall is a sandblasted peace sign that reads DEDICATED TO HIPPIES AND HIPPIES AT HEART, PEACE & LOVE and bears Kelsey's and Moomaw's names. The crossbars of the welded scrap-metal sculpture are supposed to represent the progression of Moomaw's life. A vibrant peace symbol and flowers in the center represent the 1960s, which Moomaw felt was his best period of self-expression. Then, beginning with a rusted auto muffler, the memorial downsizes into a dull industrial look that Moomaw created to represent the 1980s.

The Norway Nosedive

Travelers who leave Interstate 80 and travel north along Route 71 might be startled as they motor toward the small town of Norway and see a crashed airplane on the side of the road. Don't worry—there's no need to call for help. This wreckage has been there for years, and it has nothing to do with airplanes. Instead, it's meant to conjure up the days of Farm-Aid and the white crosses that were planted in courthouse lawns to symbolize the family farms that were lost to bank foreclosures in years past.

The airplane was placed here by Melvin and Phyllis Eastwold of the Norwegian Implement Company as a silent protest. The sign that is out in front of the wreck says it all: DEDICATED TO THE FARMERS AND AG-RELATED BUSINESS FOLKS THAT LIVED THROUGH THE AGRICULTURAL CRASH OF THE 1980S.

Miniature Houses on the Prairie

While out on an excursion in search of other Illinois weirdness, we happened across this display of miniature houses at a place that has been dubbed Miles Prairie. According to a sign on the property, this was where the Miles Prairie Possum Gang originated in 1890. Who this gang may have been is anyone's guess, and we have yet to find any further information about them. We'll keep looking, though.

Cars on a Spike

Most people would not think that a shopping mall is a worthy location for an art display, and if you fall into this category, then you should visit the Cermak Plaza in Berwyn. A number of years ago the shopping center commissioned artists to decorate the plaza, but what they created has managed to upset the locals ever since. And to be honest, curious visitors usually go away scratching their heads in confusion as well.

Along the sidewalk are twenty visual and sound-related sculptures that are in various stages of disrepair. One of the weirdest is the Pinto Pelt, a smashed and flattened version of one of the flammable Fords. Another appears to be some sort of flying machine with what looks like a robot at the controls.

The largest piece is called *The Spindle.* The creator, Dustin Shuler, skewered eight automobiles on a huge nail in the center of the parking lot. It looks like a metal-eating giant's idea of a shish kabob! Critics howled in complaint when the sculpture appeared; they stated that it attracted pigeons. Things did quiet down, though, after the "artwork" appeared in the movie *Wayne's World,* and since that time, local residents have simply gotten used to it. No one is calling for it to be removed anymore, and in fact, if the Berwyn police have any say, the sculpture will never be removed. They use the shopping mall as a way to haze new recruits, sending the rookies out to the plaza to investigate an "eight car pileup"!

Leaning Tower of Niles

Thanks to the city of Niles, you no longer have to go to Europe to see the Tower of Pisa—you can see it right here! In 1933, the city constructed a half-scale replica of the famous leaning tower as a reservoir to supply water to the three swimming pools of industrialist Robert Ilg. Architect Albert Farr was criticized for what was considered a silly building—it was commonly called Farr's Folly—but it has become a popular attraction that just might outlast its namesake, which leans a little more every year. Farr's smaller version remains steadfastly at the angle at which it was placed. It is no longer filled with water, but a park has been built around its base, complete with reflecting pools and a European-style telephone booth.

Double-deck Outhouse

New York has the Statue of Liberty, and Chicago has the Sears Tower, but the tiny central Illinois town of Gays has the state's only two-story outhouse. The privy's history spans nearly a century and a half and is the greatest claim to fame for this town of two hundred and fifty residents. Not surprisingly, the very existence of the outhouse poses an interesting question: Who in their right mind would ever use the first floor of a two-story outhouse?

The outhouse's story starts when Civil War veteran Samuel Gamill built his general store in 1869 right across from the railroad depot on Front Street. There were apartments located above the store, and a short ramp offered the apartment dwellers access to the second floor of the outhouse. This allowed them to use the facilities without having to come downstairs and also offered them some privacy, since the store's customers used the lower-level privy. Both levels had two-seaters, one for a man and one for a woman, which was common at that time, so four people could be accommodated at once—in case of an emergency, I guess.

But how did it work? This was a well-kept secret for years, but eventually, it leaked out, so to speak. The seats on the top level were actually set farther back from the facilities below, and the contents dropped into a pit that was behind a false wall. Those who were downstairs didn't have to duck out of the way, but I can imagine that they tended to speed things up a little when they heard footsteps above their heads!

By 1984, the store had fallen into a state of disrepair and was torn down by the village, but the outhouse was preserved and restored by local volunteers. Since that time, the now padlocked privy has drawn many tourists, who stop to pose for a unique photo opportunity.

The Amboy Lurkers

Want to see something a little scary? Take a trip through the Amboy city park. It's an otherwise pleasant stretch of green on the edge of a nice northern Illinois town, but the unprepared might find it an unnerving place. Lurking in the trees and bushes of the park is a collection of carved wooden statues that appear to have been hewn from rough wood. Although they are not necessarily scary when confronted face to face, there is something creepy about seeing these stoic faces staring at you from behind a tree.

If you feel like someone is watching you here, it's because someone is!

Route 66

There is no greater highway in the history of America than Route 66—the "Mother Road"—and it had its start right here in Illinois. For millions of people, Route 66 brings back a treasure trove of memories and a link to the days of two-lane highways, cool convertibles, and cozy little diners advertising homemade cakes and pies. It conjures up images of souvenir shops, tourist traps, tiny motor courts, flickering neon signs, drive-in theaters, and cheesy roadside attractions. It's America, and our state's most famous highway—even though officially it no longer exists.

Although long stretches of Route 66 remain today, most of it is a hard-to-define mix of original roadbed, access roads, abandoned fragments, and lost highways. It has been reconfigured in so many ways that even diehard travelers can sometimes become lost and turned around as they try to follow the road's route. The remains of the road through Illinois are usually well marked but have seen many upgrades and realignments over the years.

Originally, the highway followed Illinois Route 4 southwesterly across the state, generally along the corridor that is now Interstate 55. If you drive along and begin to wonder if you are still on the old road, watch for abandoned stores, dead neon signs for businesses long since gone, and even creaky motor courts that sometimes still eke out a living from travelers that are now few and far between. The most obvious clue, though, is the road itself. Route 66 was first paved in concrete, two lanes wide, with distinctive rolled curbing in some spots.

Should you go, we've given you some weird sites to look out for.

Our state's section of Route 66 begins in the heart of downtown Chicago. The best-known site here is probably **Lou Mitchell's** place on West Jackson, which is famous for serving free Milk Duds instead of after-dinner mints. Most of the old highway has been lost in this area, but by driving along Ogden Avenue the traveler will end up in Cicero. In nearby Berwyn is **Henry's Hot Dogs.**

Atlanta's famous Hot Dog Muffler Man

Continuing south along the road, you will reach the town of La Grange, home of the historic **Wishing Well Motel.** The motor court, which was built by John Blackburn in 1941, still operates today. It started out with ten cabins, an office, and a small house out back that was the owner's residence. In 1958, Blackburn sold the motel to Emil and Zora Vidas, and they later connected the cabins to increase capacity and turned the small house into guest quarters. Emil Vidas passed away in 1985, and Zora has managed the place ever since.

Winding past Joliet, Route 66 curves through Wilmington, a small town split in half by the Kankakee River. Wilmington's most famous landmark is the **Gemini Giant,** which stands outside the **Launching Pad Restaurant.** It's an easy joke to say that the food here is out of this world, but in this case it's true. Watching over the small roadside diner is the twenty-eight-foot-tall giant with his silver space helmet and shiny green body suit. He holds a rocket ship in his hands as he looks out over Route 66. The giant was erected in 1965 after the diner's original owners, John and Bernice Korelc, saw the fiberglass statue at a restaurant trade show in Chicago. The country was heavily into the space program at the time, and the Korelcs came up with the idea of the Launching Pad to go along with it. In those days, their diner was known as the Dari Delite, specializing in hot dogs and ice cream, but with the arrival of the giant they changed the name and added hamburgers, chili, and fries to the menu. They have since become famous for their tasty meals—and of course for their giant spaceman.

Along the next stretch of road were once many of the first great landmarks of Route 66, including classic filling stations and motels. In Gardner was the famous **Riviera** roadhouse, which was established in 1928 at the height of Prohibition. In its heyday it offered a zoo, picnic grounds, and a swimming hole, as well as a restaurant that served

homemade Italian food, chicken, steak, and seafood. The lower part of the building was used as a tavern, and legend has it that Al Capone and his brother Ralph often stopped in for a drink. In 1972, Bob and Peggy Kraft purchased the Riviera and have carried on the tradition of good food and drink.

Traveling on south, the forgotten highway passes a number of fading locations. At Pontiac is the **Old Log Cabin Inn.** The restaurant was originally constructed by Joe and Victor Selotti in 1926 from cedar telephone poles. The path of Route 66 once ran on the eastern side of the restaurant next to the railroad tracks, but when it was realigned to the western side, the building was jacked up and rotated with horses so that the front door once again faced the road. The rotation was such a major event that half the town showed up to watch.

Past the larger towns of Bloomington and Normal, Route 66 travels on to the small community of **Funks Grove,** one of the region's first settlements. The 1865 Funks Grove Church and the Funks' home still remain today, as does the historic syrup factory, which gave the community its fame. The town is named for a stand of ancient maple trees, where the Funk family has been producing maple "sirup" since the early 1800s.

Continuing on south, the highway bends into the small, friendly town of **Atlanta.** Like the famous city that bears the same name in Georgia, the Illinois community suffered a devastating fire in 1865 that destroyed most of the town. Its structures were rebuilt mostly in brick and are remarkably preserved. Today the community boasts the historic Hawes grain elevator, a smiley face water tower, and the famous **Hot Dog**

Muffler Man that once stood outside Bunyon's Drive-in in Berwyn. In 1965, Hamlet Arthur Stephens purchased the giant fiberglass statue, swapped its original muffler for a hot dog, and placed it in front of his restaurant. Stephens purposely misspelled the name of his hot dog stand as Bunyon's in order to avoid a Paul Bunyan trademark infringement. Stephens, with the help of his family and longtime manager Agnes Abruzzo, operated Bunyon's until January 2003. When he closed his business he wondered what to do with the giant. The owner received offers for as much as $10,000, but in the end, he and his family decided to put the statue on permanent loan to the town of Atlanta as part of a Route 66 heritage exhibit. The Hot Dog Muffler Man was then refurbished and placed in a central location in downtown Atlanta, welcoming Route 66 visitors with a smile and a dog.

South of Atlanta, the town of Broadwell once drew large crowds of travelers who came to Ernie Edwards's **Pig-Hip Restaurant,** known up and down the highway for its barbeque. Edwards opened the place in 1937—when pork sandwiches could be bought for 15 cents—with just three tables, a bar, and $150 of borrowed money. He first called the place the Harbor Inn because of a great deal that he had gotten on wallpaper and glasses with a nautical theme. The name was short-lived. One day, a hungry farmer came into the diner and spotted a freshly baked ham on the stove. He pointed to the ham and said, "Give me a slice of that pig hip," and the rest, as they say, is history. Ernie finally hung up his carving knife in 1991 after fifty-four legendary years. Ernie's Pig-Hip Restaurant was transformed into a small museum in the spring of 2003 and stands today as a tribute to Ernie Edwards and his famous sandwich.

Route 66 continues to the town of Elkhart. It is named for **Elkhart Hill**, a raised, wooded hill that is one of the highest locations in this part of the state. Atop the hill is historic Elkhart Cemetery, a pleasant wooded burial ground that is the final resting place of Captain Adam Bogardus, expert marksman and performer in Buffalo Bill's Wild West Show; John Dean Gillette, a major cattle baron in the area; and former Illinois governor Richard Oglesby.

The highway then passes through Springfield, our state capital and, more importantly to fans of drive-in food, the true birthplace of the **Cozy Dog.** Ed Waldmire Jr. and his friend Don Strand developed the Cozy Dog while stationed in Amarillo, Texas, during World War II. To earn extra money, Ed sold a hot dog on a stick, which was dipped in a special batter and deep-fried, at the USO club and the base PX. First called the G.I. Hot Dog, it was officially dubbed the Crusty Cur by Waldmire. When he returned to Illinois, Ed introduced the dogs at the 1946 Illinois State Fair, and they were such a hit that he decided to sell his fast food in Springfield. The first stand was opened at the Lake Springfield beach house on June 16 to great success. At the insistence of Ed's wife, Virginia, who wondered who would eat anything called a Crusty Cur, he began kicking around ideas for a new name. After great thought, the name Cozy Dog was settled upon, and Ed opened a second eatery across town. By the start of the 1950s, customers were scarfing down so many of his dogs that he was inspired to open the Cozy Dog Drive-In on Route 66. The Cozy Dog moved to its current location in 1996 and sits partially on property that was once part of the former Lincoln Motel, another Route 66 landmark. You can still get the best Cozy Dogs in Illinois at the drive-in, but when you order one be sure not to call it a corn dog!

From Springfield to St. Louis, Route 66 is full of twists and turns. You can follow Route 4, the first alignment of Route 66, past Jerome and then through Chatham. Along this alignment, you'll find an unusual site dubbed **Snake Bridge.** The bridge can be found in an area that is now a wildlife preserve and a protected location for the Kirtland's Snake, a nonpoisonous reptile that is an endangered species.

The old alignment of Route 66 then travels south along Route 4 past Auburn, Virden, and on to Nilwood, where a section of the pavement is imprinted with turkey tracks. After the road was poured and just before the concrete hardened, a group of wild turkeys trooped across the road and left indelible marks on the highway.

The county seat of Macoupin County, Carlinville, lies south along the old route. The town is the home to the **Million Dollar Courthouse,** a massive structure that achieved both fame and notoriety when it was constructed in 1870, thanks to huge cost overruns and accusations of graft. Carlinville was also the original home of the Ariston Café, a Route 66 landmark. When the highway was reconfigured in 1940 and shifted east, the café was moved to nearby Litchfield. Hubert Humphrey once ate at the restaurant, as did band leader Tommy Dorsey.

Farther down the highway from Carlinville is the town of Benld, home to the famous **Coliseum Ballroom,** which brought Tommy Dorsey and scores of other entertainers, as well as gamblers and bootleggers, to downstate Illinois. Benld, which was founded by Ben L. Dorsey (hence the name Benld), was a rough mining community and seemed an unlikely place for a grand ballroom. In spite of this, local businessman Dominic Tarro opened the $50,000 dance hall here on Christmas Eve 1924. In those days, Benld was better known for the number of brothels and speakeasies it boasted than for big band entertainment, but regardless, it was an immediate success. Rumors say that the Coliseum soon became a frequent watering hole for Chicago gangsters who came to Benld to lay low when things got hot in Chicago. Among them was Al Capone, who owned several speakeasies and

whorehouses in the area. And there seems to have been some truth to the stories. In 1930, Dominic Tarro was indicted for bootlegging, and before he could sing to the authorities, he disappeared. His body was later found stripped and tied in the Sangamon River—a single bullet had been fired into the back of his head.

The Coliseum was later taken over by Joyce Tarro, Dominic's daughter, and she booked rock acts like Chuck Berry, Fats Domino, the Turtles, Fleetwood Mac, Tina Turner, Bob Seger, and many others. Then, in July 1976, Joyce Tarro was shot to death by intruders, leaving another violent mark on the Coliseum's history. It's no wonder that the place has a reputation of being haunted. The Coliseum remained open for many years but eventually began to fade into oblivion. It is open again as an antiques mall on the original Route 66, and it's well worth a stop for enthusiasts of the weird.

The old alignment continues on to the south through Staunton and, in Hamel, meets up with the newer version of Route 66, which left Springfield on a more easterly angle. Along this route are towns like Glenarm, Divernon, and Waggoner.

Just west of Raymond, travelers will find a marble statue of the Virgin Mary that has been affectionately dubbed **Our Lady of the Highways.** It's been there since 1959, watching over all who pass by.

South of Litchfield, Route 66 enters into coal mine country. In a burial ground here lie the remains of Mother Jones, a fiery union organizer who was once known as the most dangerous woman in America. Moving on, one comes to the small town of Hamel, which boasts a bright blue neon cross affixed to St. Paul's Lutheran Church, at the edge of town. It was placed here by the Brunworth family for a son who was killed at Anzio during World War II. Continuing south along Route 157, with a slight curve to the west, the highway passes through

Edwardsville and then drops down below the bluffs to travel along the old floodplain of the Mississippi.

From this point, Route 66 took three separate paths to St. Louis. The earliest went down Chain of Rocks Road, where it turned left near the **Luna Café** in Mitchell. The Luna Café was founded in the 1920s and is rumored to be yet another place where Al Capone hung out. Tales of the building's spacious second floor, which was allegedly used as a brothel, are connected to the Luna's famous neon sign, which bears the café's name and a martini glass that holds two red cherries. Legend has it that when the cherries were lit up, girls were available upstairs. The café has changed hands many times, and while it offers drink specials and free chicken-wing nights these days instead of illegal booze and ladies of the evening, it remains a little piece of history of Route 66.

After leaving the Luna Café, this first route jogged south along Route 203 and then west along Madison Avenue in Granite City. It continued on through Madison into Venice and then on to the **McKinley Bridge,** which crossed the Mississippi into St. Louis. The bridge has been closed for a number of years but is scheduled to be reopened some time in the future.

Another crossing to St. Louis was on the **Chain of Rocks Bridge.** It was closed down in 1968 but is open today as a footbridge that attracts bird-watchers, bicyclists, and Route 66 enthusiasts. It is considered to be the world's longest pedestrian bridge, stretching over a mile in length.

What is it about Route 66 that conjures up so many ghosts of days gone by? No one can say for sure, but few can deny that it's more than just some old roadway. It's a trip back in time to the weird, lonely, and magical side of Illinois. Turn your car off the mind-numbing modern interstate and follow the signs back to a time and place where you can still get your kicks—you won't be sorry that you did!

Roads Less Traveled

Have you ever run across a road that just seems to be bad? It might be a place that you really have no connection to or have much information about, and yet it just seems to be a spot in which you don't want to linger. We have always been intrigued by those stretches of roadway that manage to give travelers that always welcome creeping sensation at the back of the neck.

Some roads may have been the site of an unusually high number of accidents, or something happened there that no one can explain. Others are haunted by memories from the past—death, murder, and horrific events that can't quite seem to be forgotten by those who travel on the road.

Or are these events remembered by the roadway itself? Could this be why general weirdness seems to linger on such highways and back roads? Or could it be something else? Perhaps the roads and the events surrounding them are not scary at all, but serve as a doorway to our innermost fears and our darkest imaginations. Who among us has not, at some point in his or her life, climbed into an overcrowded car with a pack of friends to drive off into the night in search of some allegedly haunted place or mysterious spot? Such journeys become more frightening than they perhaps deserve to be, thanks to the retelling of the scary legends along the way. By the time the carload of night riders arrives at its destination, even the most innocent of happenings seem supernatural.

Does this mean that haunted highways are merely the figment of our collective imaginations? Perhaps—or perhaps not. Maybe such places really are an epicenter for strange activity, and maybe strange things happen along such roads for reasons that are much weirder than we can possibly imagine. But whatever the reason, it cannot be denied that many of the roads less traveled throughout Illinois have become a huge part of the state's strangest side.

Ghost Hollow Road

Ghost Hollow (located just south of Quincy), a secluded and wooded place by Ghost Hollow Road, has a dark presence that sends chills through the spines of the most hardened curiosity-seekers. The old road winds through woods and bluffs, and passes near an abandoned rail line from the Burlington Northern Railroad. No one knows how Ghost Hollow earned its ominous moniker, but we do know that there is a haunted cemetery there, where scores of would-be ghost hunters have had strange encounters over the years.

The eerie graveyard is supposedly surrounded by a high stone wall and is filled with crumbling stone crypts. In the center of the burial ground is a black tomb that bears a one-word inscription in Latin. Few seem to know the exact location of this cemetery, and *Weird Illinois'* inquiries into its whereabouts were met with either bad directions or silence. Those who did speak about it claimed that "you could hear the sound of whispers and singing" in the place at night.

Nearby are ancient Native American burial grounds over which houses have been built. Residents still find arrowheads on the property and sometimes spot the occasional ghost in the surrounding wooded area. People say that on some nights you can hear languages being chanted in the wind.

Another oddity on the road is the public grotto that is known as the Shrine of Our Lady of Lourdes of Ghost Hollow. In 1996, a Springfield man named Robert M. (Pete) Pohlman had a vision from the Virgin Mary that told him to build a shrine near Quincy—by an old cedar tree in the woods on a hillside that flowed with water. He and his wife, Janice, were already in the process of house hunting in that city, and just five days after the vision, they found a cedar tree on a property they visited, as well as a natural spring that flowed from the hillside.

On February 11, 1998, the 140th anniversary of the Blessed Virgin Mary apparition at Lourdes, France, Father John Carberry dedicated and blessed the grotto and spring on Ghost Hollow Road. Pohlman and his wife have opened the grotto to the public.

Walking After Midnight on Ghost Hollow Road

As a card-carrying insomniac and a well-known tempter of fates, I have often found myself alone in my car in the wee hours of the morning, exploring areas with legendary reputations, evil vibes, and dark legacies. One of my favorite nighttime sojourns is Ghost Hollow Road. With a name like that, I figured it had to be worth seeing.

I would often search the area, looking for signs of the legendary graveyard, always coming up with nothing. One night I had gotten out of the car and was doing a bit of walking, looking for clues as to the location of the crypts once again. My latest tip, like all the others, was a dead end—no pun intended.

I was headed back to my car, when I passed a woman in her twenties walking in the opposite direction on the other side of the road—maybe thirty feet across from me. I nodded at her and waved. She looked in my direction with the oddest look on her face. She was looking almost through me, not quite smiling, but more smirking. She was beautiful: blond hair, alabaster skin, sad, sunken eyes.

We passed each other, and I walked for about twenty more seconds, when it hit me. It was after three in the morning. I usually didn't see other cars out here at this time of night, let alone others walking on the road.

I spun around; she was nowhere to be found.

I ran back to my car, thoroughly creeped out. Maybe there's a rational explanation. Maybe I hallucinated the whole thing. Or maybe my gothic desires were fulfilled, and I had glimpsed the ghost of Ghost Hollow Road.–*Anthony Ford*

Beware of Goon Road

Near Fairview Heights and close to the bridge on Bunkum Road that crosses over Interstate 64 is a now abandoned roadway that is known as Goon Road. During the daylight hours, the place is not that unusual, but legend holds that at night, it becomes a terrifying place.

Some believe that the spot is haunted, cursed by bloody events that occurred here in the past. But others maintain that someone is still out there in these woods, waiting for the unfortunate and unsuspecting to come along. According to legend, a number of murders have been committed here that can be traced back to an inbred family that preyed on travelers. Some say that members of the family still prowl the forest.

They were said to live in an old ramshackle house in the woods, their property filled with broken-down cars and garbage. The parents had several children, who also had babies of their own, usually bred from one another. A pack of hound dogs was tied to trees near the house, and at night, the father would take them deep into the woods and hunt down trespassers. Stories circulated for years that a number of teenagers ventured into the woods near Goon Road one night and never returned.

The Inbred Goons of Goon Road

There is this road that's called Goon Road, because there was a family of goons who lived there that were supposed to be inbred and killed people a long time ago. Everybody says that it's haunted now, so my brother and I went out there one night to look around. When we got there, he was telling me that a lot of people have been killed and disappeared in the woods and that the goons had these wild dogs that they used to chase down anybody who came on their land. I don't know if it's true or not, but when we heard a bunch of dogs barking out in the dark, we got the hell out of there!
—*Joe O.*

Goon Spotting on Goon Road

In high school, my friends and I weren't the smartest or most creative people, but we did have a real sense of adventure and often drank mass quantities of liquid courage. One of our favorite ways to waste a couple of hours on a weekend was to make our way out to Goon Road. We had heard from some older guys in the area that there was a compound where a whole bunch of inbred freaks, all related in one way or another, lived in the woods along this road. These goons laid in wait, hoping to capture and kill anyone who wandered into their woods.

We used to love pulling up alongside the area where they supposedly lived and shouting taunts aimed at getting them to try to drag us into the woods, where they would presumably murder us. We always wanted to see if they were really deformed from the generations of inbreeding. We had some tried-and-true phrases aimed at baiting them out to the roadside, such as "Hey, goons!" and "Yo, where you at, goons?" Like I said, we weren't the most creative bunch.

One night I was driving, and my friend Pete was hanging halfway out the passenger-side window, yelling at the goons. Suddenly he leaped back into the car, completely freaked out and totally pale and shaking. He told me to gun it—so I did.

When we reached a safer area, he calmed down a bit and told me that while he was yelling into the woods, he saw the silhouette of something emerge from behind one tree and run toward another. He had a hard time making it out, but he saw that it moved quickly, with a lurching, limping type of run. He still claims to have seen a bona fide goon, out looking for victims.

I had always assumed that the goons of Goon Road were just a legend, but now I'm not so sure. Who knows, maybe there is a freaky family out there looking for blood!—*James P.*

Phantom Horses of Kean Avenue

Kean Avenue is in the southwest Chicago suburb of Palos Hills, at the far edge of the Cook County Forest Preserve. Along the roadway, there have been many reports of motorists seeing phantom animals that suddenly appear in their headlights and then vanish. The majority of these animals are horses, perhaps because of the riding trails that are found nearby. All the witnesses report the same thing: The horses look absolutely real, and they suddenly appear in the middle of the road. A few moments later they disappear, never having moved at all. For many years, this was a dangerous road for riders to cross, plagued by a lack of streetlights, speeding cars, and patches of low-lying fog. It is thought that perhaps the ghostly horses that appear here are the phantoms of animals and riders who were struck and killed in the past.

Phantom Automobiles Ride the Midlothian Turnpike

Close to Chicago's most haunted cemetery, Bachelor's Grove, is the Midlothian Turnpike, and it too is reputed to be haunted. Could there be such a taint to the cemetery that even the surrounding area is affected?

The turnpike is said to be the scene of vanishing "ghost cars" and phantom automobile accidents. No historical events can provide a clue as to why this might be, but the unexplained vehicles have been reported numerous times in recent years. The stories are all remarkably the same. People who are traveling west on the turnpike see the brake lights of the car in front of them go on and the car slows as if to turn off the road. However, as the following auto pulls up, the first vehicle simply vanishes. Other drivers have reported passing these autos, only to see the car disappear in their rearview mirrors.

One young couple even claimed to have had a collision with one of these phantom cars in 1978. They had just stopped at the intersection of Central Avenue and the Midlothian Turnpike. The driver looked both ways, saw that the road was clear, and pulled out. Suddenly a brown sedan appeared from nowhere, racing in the direction of the cemetery and crashed into the couple's car. There was a shuddering impact and the sound of screeching metal and breaking glass. But to make the horrible event even more traumatic, the couple was then shocked to see the brown sedan literally fade away! They climbed out of their car and saw to their amazement that it had not been damaged at all. They had distinctly heard the sound of the torn metal and broken glass and had felt the crush of the two cars coming together, but somehow it had never physically happened!

It remains a mystery as to where these phantom cars come from, and where they vanish to.

German Church Road

On German Church Road in Chicago, shadows hang long and low and a chill always seems to be in the air. The atmosphere is fitting, since it was along this road that the victims of a horrific, still unsolved crime were found.

On December 28, 1956, Patricia Grimes, thirteen, and Barbara Grimes, fifteen, left their home at 3624 South Damen Avenue and headed for the Brighton Theater, only a mile away. The girls were both avid fans of Elvis Presley and had gone to see his film *Love Me Tender* for the eleventh time. They were recognized in the popcorn line at nine thirty p.m. and then seen on an eastbound Archer Avenue bus at eleven p.m.

The girls' mother, Loretta Grimes, expected the girls home by eleven forty-five. At midnight, she sent her daughter Theresa, seventeen, and her son Joey, fourteen, to the bus stop to watch for them. After three buses had stopped and failed to discharge their sisters, Theresa and Joey returned home.

When the police were notified that the girls were missing, they theorized at first that they had run away, but they eventually initiated the greatest missing persons hunt in Chicago police history.

As the search went on, reports of sightings of the girls began to come in. Two of their classmates said they spotted them at Angelo's Restaurant at 3551 South Archer Avenue, more than twenty-four hours after their reported disappearance. Other accounts included those of a railroad conductor who said he saw them on a train near the Great Lakes Naval Training Center in Glenview and a security guard who claimed he saw them on the morning of December 29. On January 1, the girls were reported to be passengers on a CTA bus on Damen Avenue, and the following week George Pope, a night clerk at the Unity Hotel in Englewood, said he refused them a room because of their ages. Three employees at Kresge believed they saw the girls listening to Elvis Presley songs at the record counter on January 3. And speaking of Presley, in a statement issued from Graceland he asked the girls to come home and ease their mother's worries. The plea went unanswered.

Then there were the two telephone calls received by Wallace and Ann Tollstan on January 14. Their daughter, Sandra, was a classmate of Patricia Grimes's at the St. Maurice School. The first call jolted Mr. Tollstan out of his sleep, but when he picked up the receiver, the person on the other end of the line did not speak. Fifteen minutes later, the phone rang again, and this time Ann Tollstan answered it. The voice on the other end of the line asked, "Is that you, Sandra? Is Sandra there?" But before Mrs. Tollstan could bring her daughter to the phone, the caller had clicked off the line. Ann Tollstan was convinced that the frightened voice on the telephone had belonged to Patricia Grimes.

Another strange event occurred on January 15, when a police switchboard operator

received a call from a man who said the girls' bodies would be found in a park at Eighty-first and Wolf. He claimed that this revelation had come to him in a dream, and he hung up. The call was traced to Walter Kranz, a fifty-three-year-old steam fitter. According to a *Chicago Sun-Times* article, he was taken into custody after the bodies were found—less than a mile from the park that Kranz said he dreamed of! He became one of the numerous people who were questioned by the police and released.

The search for the Grimes sisters ended on January 22, 1957, when construction worker Leonard Prescott spotted what appeared to be two mannequins lying next to a guardrail on German Church Road. He drove to the local police station, and investigators soon discovered that the mannequins were actually the Grimes sisters.

Officials surmised that the bodies had been lying there for several days, perhaps as far back as January 9. This had been the date of the last heavy snowfall, and the frigid temperatures that followed the storm had preserved the bodies.

They were taken to the Cook County Morgue, where they were stored until they thawed out and an autopsy became possible. Before they were removed, though, police investigators noted bruises and marks on the bodies. According to a newspaper article, there were three wounds in Patricia's abdomen, and the left side of her face had been battered. Barbara's head had also been bruised, and there were punctures in her chest from an ice pick.

Once the autopsies were performed, hope that the examinations would provide evidence or leads was quickly dashed. Pathologists stated that the girls had died from shock and exposure but were able to reach this

conclusion only by eliminating other causes. They also determined that the girls had died on December 28, the night they had disappeared. If so, how could the sightings that took place after that date be explained? And if the bodies had been exposed to the elements since that time, then why hadn't anyone else seen them?

As there is no statute of limitations for murder, the case officially remains open, but there seems little chance that it will ever be solved. Loretta Grimes passed away in December 1989, a tragic and broken woman. Some believe that perhaps in death Mrs. Grimes found the answers that she was looking for and could finally rest in peace.

Those with an interest in the case will sometimes travel down German Church Road, in the southern suburb of Willow Springs, and wind up at the "haunted highway" where the bodies were discovered. A short distance from the site, its entrance now blocked with a chain, is a narrow drive that once led to a house that was nestled in the trees. Mysteriously, the house was abandoned by the young family who lived there soon after the girls' bodies were discovered. Many belongings were left in the building, and toys lay scattered about the yard for years. At some point, vandals set fire to the house, and the owner had to demolish what was left. And while the owner never lived there again, people would occasionally see a tall, gaunt man roaming about the property in the spring and fall. It was assumed that he had once occupied the place, but those who saw him were afraid to ask.

Why the family abandoned the home remains a mystery. Some believe the owner may have been questioned about the crime and simply felt too embarrassed to stay. Or perhaps the family saw something the night the bodies were dumped and were too frightened to remain.

Others claim that the house became haunted. And perhaps this is not as far-fetched as you might first think. Since the discovery of the bodies, the police have received reports from people who hear a car pulling up to the location where the bodies were found. They say they hear a car door open, followed by the sound of something being dumped alongside the road. The door slams shut, and the car drives away. They hear these things, and yet there is no car in sight!

You may believe in hauntings or not—but should you ever travel along German Church Road, I defy you to stop along the roadway where the bodies of Barbara and Patricia were found and to say that you are not moved by the tragedy that occurred here.

I think you will agree that, without a doubt, this is a dark and haunted place.

A Ghost and His Car on Stone Church Road

There is a road about ten to fifteen miles from me, in Bartonville. It's called Stone Church Road. I had always heard it was haunted and that some old guy lived behind the church on this road and would shoot at drivers going by his house. Now, I didn't believe the shooting thing, because he would get arrested. But I do believe in ghosts.

Rumor has it that a man died on that road and his spirit was stuck there with his car. The road runs right off the road that I take to get to my girlfriend's. Every time I go by that road, I would see car lights just sitting there. They were not white, but yellow. One night me and my friends got the guts to check it out. We turned down the road and just started driving. We got about twenty seconds down the road, when we saw a car parked on the side and a man in the street. So we slowed down. We couldn't turn around, so we had to keep going to get off the road, but the guy wouldn't move.

My friend Donnie got out and asked the guy what his problem was. But the guy just looked at him without saying a word. Donnie was getting mad that the guy wouldn't answer him, so he kept yelling. I started getting chills and so did my other friend. I knew something was wrong. I told Donnie to get back in the truck and let's get out of there. He listened and got in the truck.

We kept staring at the guy, and he didn't move. I turned around for a second to turn on the radio, and when I turned back to look again, the guy was gone—along with the car. I knew it was the ghost. To this day I get chills whenever I drive past that road.—*Chris B.*

Bringin' Out His Chicken

I live in central Illinois and know of both the stories of Old Stone Church and Bartonville Hospital. The stone church has always been a creepy hangout for teenagers. I checked it out one afternoon with some friends. This was about 1986, and, yes, there is a nasty farmer who carries a rifle and was fixing the barricades. I got out and, brave soul I am, approached him. I made up some story about a paper for school. I mentioned the ghost, and his defenses went up.

"Tell your teacher there is nothing to see and stay the hell away if you know what's best," was his response. There were rumors in the '80s about satanic cults doing animal sacrifices. I never saw anything like that, nor did I hear any chants.

As far as the state hospital, you couldn't get me to set foot in that place. That's where my chicken comes out. Maybe in the daytime, but after dark, the place takes on its own personality.—*Anonymous*

Bodies in the Woods Along Hop Hollow Road

Illinois' first penitentiary was opened in Alton in 1833. Conditions were bad right from the beginning, and the prison became known as a grim and horrific place, plagued by rats, vermin, and disease. The health of the prisoners was completely broken while they were incarcerated, and many of the men died within months of their release.

By the 1850s, conditions were so bad that Dorothea Dix, a social reformer, began a crusade to close the Alton prison. Her complaints brought about a legislative investigation that eventually led to the construction of a new prison near Joliet. In May 1859, Alton prisoners began to be transferred to Joliet, and the Alton penitentiary was finally abandoned in 1860.

Abandoned for civilian prisoners, that is. Soon the prison was fixed up enough to pass military inspection, and it reopened in 1862 as a military facility to hold Confederate prisoners.

Within three days of the arrival of the first Confederate soldiers, the penitentiary was already overcrowded. While the maximum capacity of the institution was eight hundred, throughout most of the war it held between one

thousand and fifteen hundred prisoners and often more. Just as it was in former times, the prison was plagued by lice, rats, and countless diseases, including a smallpox epidemic that claimed a great many lives.

When a prisoner died, soldiers observed the same procedure as the penitentiary guards had followed. The men on burial detail loaded the body onto a raft and floated it up the Missouri to a ferry landing not far from the prison. The body was then placed in the back of a wagon and transported along a wooded trail known as Hop Hollow Road. The path wound through the forest, around the bluffs, and through Hop Hollow itself. Eventually, it ended in an area in North Alton that had been turned into a cemetery by the original prison officials. The body was placed in a shallow grave, and a numbered stake was placed over it. An undertaker recorded what information existed about the man, and he became the next line in the ledger book—until another prisoner died and the process was repeated all over again.

Or at least that was supposed to be how it worked. Stories have long circulated that the soldiers attached to burial detail would never actually make the entire trip up Hop Hollow Road to the burial ground. Rather, they would stop the wagon along the roadway somewhere and dump the corpses in the woods. A bottle would be broken out, and the soldiers would play cards and drink for the amount of time it would have taken to transport and bury the bodies.

I admit that I was skeptical when I first heard this story, but one thing I've learned over the years is that at the heart of every legend lies a kernel of truth, no matter how small. Hop Hollow Road is no exception.

One day, about six months after hearing this story for the first time, I spoke with an Alton police officer who had once answered a call about a body found near what was

once Hop Hollow Road. Today, the largest part of this road no longer exists. A faint trail leading away from the highway is all that can be found. It curves into a heavily wooded area (which is private property) and comes to an end at Holland Street. Beyond it, the remains of the road become Rozier Street, which passes by the Confederate Cemetery. This police officer was told that a body had been discovered in the woods near the crossing of Holland and Rozier. When he arrived, he found a collection of old bones that, apparently, had been there since sometime around the Civil War. Could this have been the remains of one of the Confederate prisoners?

As it happened, bodies being left in the woods was not the only fantastic portion of the story about the duty-shirking Union soldiers. In fact, it was only the beginning.

The legend went on to say that the ghosts of these improperly buried Confederates refused to rest in peace and that they returned to haunt Hop Hollow Road. Over the years, their apparitions had been seen along the roadway. As time passed, the tale was expanded to include the fact that these ghosts not only walked the road near where their bodies had been left but that they signaled passing vehicles in hopes of getting a ride! A ride to where? To the cemetery where their bodies were supposed to have been laid to rest, of course. Those luckless drivers who did pick up one of these passengers were always shocked when the hitchhiker simply vanished without a trace from the seat beside them. At that point, so the story goes, they realized that they had picked up a ghost.

Could such a story be true? I'll leave that up to you, but if you do happen to be driving along the street off Hop Hollow Road some night and you see someone near the edge of the woods, waving his arms and looking for a ride . . . drive on.

Chains of the Dead Still Heard on Hop Hollow Road

I don't go out looking for the unusual. If anything, I've always been a skeptic. In fact, I still am, despite what happened to me one night many years ago along a road in Alton. Did I encounter something supernatural? Some may say yes, others no. I myself am still not sure.

This incident occurred about ten years ago. I was working the midnight shift at a convenience store near Alton. I'd often be the only one on the road as I made my way home early in the morning. I was driving a 1982 Monte Carlo that was falling apart at the seams. Many nights I found myself cursing as I made makeshift repairs to the car alone on some roadside. This was one of those nights. I had gotten a flat tire and pulled off next to a patch of woods. It was no big deal at all really; by this point, I had become a master at changing flats—it wouldn't take me more than ten minutes. Those ten minutes, though, gave me a story that I still tell today.

I began to hear a sound emanating from the woods as I worked with the tire. "Chink . . . chink . . . chink . . ." It was methodical, and sounded like chains banging together. They freaked me out. They got progressively louder and closer to me. I have never worked faster at changing a tire than I did that night. I wrapped up, threw my tools into the trunk, and got in the car. Just as I did, I heard a low moaning noise accompanying the clanking of the chains, which now seemed to be just at the edge of the tree line. I got out of there fast. I've never been more scared in my life.

I tried to think of a rational explanation for the noises, but couldn't come up with any. I did some research and found out that those woods lie along what was once known as Hop Hollow, an area where many Confederate soldiers had their bodies dumped after they died in a nearby prison. Many friends have told me that the only explanation for what I heard was that a ghost, bound in chains, was approaching me for help.

Despite my experience, I would say that I still generally don't believe in ghosts. However, when it comes to Hop Hollow, I'll never travel that road again without AAA!—*Andy D.*

Ghostly Monks, Weeping Women, and Spook Lights

The famous story of Archer Avenue's Resurrection Mary is only one of many connected to this south Chicago roadway. The tales from this mysterious road range from vanishing hitchhikers to phantom monks, eerie ghost lights, and even an appearance by the devil himself.

What makes Archer Avenue so haunted? No one knows, but maybe it goes back to the early days of Chicago, when the road was an Indian trail that stretched from Fort Dearborn and the old mouth of the Chicago River to today's southwest suburbs. Some have suggested that the original inhabitants created a path here because of some mystical magnetic force that connected it to the next world. They say that paranormal energies would also be attracted to this magnetism, and this would explain the hauntings in the area.

Whether there is a magnetic force or not, it is true that for many years, Indians used the area as a burial ground. When the French arrived in the 1600s, a mission and then a signal post were built there. Finally, the Irish settled in the area, and in 1833 they constructed a church, St. James-Sag, right next to the old burial grounds.

The first church they built was a simple log cabin that stood on the highest point of a ridge. In 1850, it was replaced by the limestone building that is still in use today. The pale yellow building and the newer rectory near it stand watch over the hundreds of graves scattered about on the hills below. It is an idyllic scene and could easily be part of the Irish countryside, rather than a landscape from the southwest side of Chicago.

Legend has it that an early rector of St. James-Sag placed a curse on the community when its residents failed to attend church regularly. This may have been the cause of the supernatural events that began being reported at the church in 1847. It was then that sightings of the "phantom monks" took place. These stories continued for decades, and there were many reliable witnesses to the strange activity. One witness was a former rector who admitted on his deathbed that he had seen ghosts roaming the cemetery grounds for many years.

One cold night in November 1977, a Cook County police officer was passing the cemetery and happened to turn his spotlight up past the cemetery gates. He claimed to see nine hooded figures floating toward the rectory. Knowing that no one was supposed to be in the cemetery, he stopped and yelled out his car window for them to come back. If they did not, they would be arrested for trespassing. The figures ignored him and continued up the road.

The officer grabbed his shotgun, got out of his car and ran into the graveyard. He pursued what he first thought were pranksters, but while he stumbled and fell over the uneven ground and tombstones, the monklike figures eerily glided past without effort. He later reported that he nearly caught up with them when "they vanished without a trace." Unable to believe what had just happened, he searched the area for any sign of the figures but found no one. Finally, he returned to his squad car to write up his report. The paperwork that he filed merely stated that he had chased some trespassers through the cemetery, but he always maintained that what he had seen was beyond this world.

Another legend of St. James-Sag is probably what gave the burial ground its ghostly reputation in the first place. This story concerns a phantom hearse that has also been seen on Kean Road and at nearby Archer Woods Cemetery. The description of the vehicle is always the same, from the black horses to the glowing coffin of a child, and was first reported back in 1897. According to a report in the *Chicago Tribune,* two musicians spent the night in a recreation hall that is located at the bottom of the hill below the St. James-Sag rectory. They were awakened in the early morning hours by the sound of a carriage on the stones outside. They looked out and saw the macabre hearse. They were the first to report seeing the vehicle, but not the last.

The eerie stories about Archer Avenue include one that stars the devil himself. Apparently, the devil came to dance at a ballroom many years ago. Tradition says that this supernatural event occurred at Kaiser Hall, just west of Loomis Street on Archer Avenue.

The story is told that a young woman became entranced one night with a handsome and dashing stranger that she met on the dance floor. As they danced

the night away, she glanced down at her partner's feet—and let out a horrified scream! Assuming that the stranger had made an inappropriate advance toward the girl, other men at the dance angrily pursued the man, who quickly fled from the room. He managed to get himself cornered near a second-story window. Suddenly he leaped out of the window, and when the crowd rushed to see what had happened to him, they saw him running away.

The folks from the neighborhood followed the man outside (wisely using the staircase) and were amazed to see the real reason for the young woman's scream. Pressed into the concrete, just where the stranger had landed, they found the unmistakable mark of a cloven-hoof print!

Then there is the woman in white who haunts Archer Woods Cemetery. For years, she has been spotted by drivers passing by the place at night. When they stop for a closer look, they see a woman in a white gown wandering near the edge of the graveyard, weeping and crying and covering her face with her hands. She is normally seen for only a matter of seconds before disappearing.

Spook lights are another part of the mystery of the Archer Avenue area. They have been spotted close to Maple Lake, a tranquil reservoir located at the swampy north end of the Sag Ridge. The setting at the lake is quiet and picturesque and offers much to outdoor enthusiasts during the daylight hours. At night, though, things look different. The towering trees that are so awe-inspiring during the daytime become foreboding and ominous in the darkness. The vast expanse of the lake, clear and crystal blue in the sunlight, becomes a sea of blackness after the sun sets.

And thanks to the forest preserve that surrounds the area, Maple Lake has become home to both rumors and dark events. For many years, the forest preserves have been plagued by stories of black magic rituals and devil worshippers, and unfortunately they have hosted some very real tragedies as well. In April 1991, the body of a seventeen-year-old girl was found floating in the lake. Her killer was quickly apprehended, but the event cast a dark pall over the area for some time afterward.

But it's not incidents like this that have made Maple Lake so enticing to those with an interest in the unknown. What attracts so many nocturnal visitors to the lake are the accounts of the ghost light that is said to shine there. This light appears out over the water between 95th and 107th streets and can most often be seen along the northern edge of the water, across from the Maple Lake Overlook. Here visitors have reported seeing a red light that moves slowly along the edge of the water on the far side of the lake. The light is round and burns a brilliant red. It is often so bright that it casts a glare down onto the water in front of it.

No one knows for sure what this anomaly may be, but some claim that a Native American was beheaded near the lake, and is now seen as the ghost light, searching for his missing head. A variation of the story claims that the headless ghost is that of an early settler who was attacked and killed by Indians. The strange light is his lantern as he wanders the shoreline in search of his head. Another explanation is that the light is that of a man killed while digging the nearby Illinois-Michigan canal, or of the victim of gangland violence of the 1920s whose body was dumped nearby.

What is it about this strange and haunted place called Archer Avenue? Is it really connected to the world beyond, or is there a natural explanation for the ghost sightings linked to the region? Are they truth or legend? We at *Weird Illinois* wish we knew.

Cuba Road

A secluded roadway near Barrington, called Cuba Road, has an eerie reputation. Along the road is a small graveyard called White Cemetery, which dates back to the 1820s. For many years, the cemetery has been said to be haunted by eerie white globes of light that hover and float among the tombstones. Witnesses have gone to the local police and have described not only the glowing lights but also hazy figures. The lights are said to sometimes float along through the cemetery, drift over the fence, and then glide out over the road. The hazy humanlike figures tend to appear and then vanish at will. No explanation has ever been given for the visions.

Most of the stories involve Cuba Road itself. There are reports of a phantom black automobile that appears near the cemetery as well as of an old house that is seen and then vanishes. The house is believed to have actually existed many years ago, and legends say that it burned down under mysterious circumstances. It has been spotted repeatedly, often by people who have no idea that the house once really existed. Other sightings involve a spectral old woman who walks along the road, carrying a lantern and flagging down passing motorists. When someone stops and tries to help her, she disappears along the edge of the roadway.

Other stories say that the ghostly image of a cigar-chewing gangster sometimes appears in the rearview mirror of drivers who pass along this road. Since Chicago gangsters did live in the area during the Prohibition era, could this be the ghost of one of them? And could this also be the explanation for the mysterious black cars?

Just off Cuba Road is another narrow and wooded roadway called Rainbow Road. There is a closed-off gravel track here that leads to an old abandoned place. Legend has it that the place was once an insane asylum and that it is haunted. There have been dozens of reports over the years that tell of ghostly lights burning in the windows of the empty place, strange figures, and moaning and crying sounds that cannot be explained.

How much truth there is to these stories is anyone's guess, but when they are combined with all the other tales of the area, it's hard to deny that weird things happen along Cuba Road.

Emotions Run High on Cuba Road

Nothing particularly strange had ever happened to my friends and me on our trips to Cuba Road, although for some reason we found ourselves drawn back to it time and time again.

Here's what you have to understand about those of us who were out there one particular night. It was the summer after our senior year of high school, and Laura, Donna, and I were as close as three girls could be.

We made our way down Cuba Road, telling stories about ghosts. We were laughing it all off—we were so used to the road that it had become a joke to us. All of that changed as we approached the White Cemetery. As our car passed the edge of the

Feeling the Pressure on Cuba Road

I had my own particularly strange incident on Cuba Road one night nearly twenty years ago. There was a group of friends, and some of them had gone by the White Cemetery. One guy in particular, Mike, was doing the tough guy act. He kept saying, "There's nothing there. There's no such thing as ghosts," and so on. I'm sure you know the type. A couple of us didn't feel like going and stayed at my girlfriend's house in town. A while later, maybe forty-five minutes or so, we got to feeling like maybe something was wrong, so my friend Bryant and I drove out to the cemetery to check up on our friends. We turned off Route 59 and headed west on Cuba Road toward the cemetery. Maybe fifty feet down Cuba, Bryant and I both just stopped talking. I was feeling decidedly weird and unable to talk. It was difficult breathing. We didn't see our friends and kept driving, past the cemetery, to the next street to turn around. As we passed the cemetery, the feeling subsided and Bryant started breathing again at pretty much the same time as I did.

I think of myself as being skeptically open-minded. While I don't dismiss the possibility of ghostly encounters, I tend to take people's descriptions of those encounters with many grains of salt. But I knew what I had felt, and I thought about it for a minute before I said anything to Bryant. I didn't want to give him any suggestions of what I had felt, so I asked him if he had felt anything. Bryant said that he had, and he described exactly the same feeling that I had, coming on and dissipating at exactly the same time.

Basically, what we both felt was this: As we approached White Cemetery, we both felt a strong upward pressure on our diaphragms, making it difficult and painful to breathe. It felt very much like a fist had materialized in our bellies and was pushing straight up on our diaphragms.

After we had turned around and headed back toward the cemetery, we found that our friends had parked in a little side street across from the cemetery and were getting up the nerve to walk around inside. Bryant and I joined them, and the rest of the evening was much what you might expect of a group of high school kids hanging around a cemetery in the middle of the night. There were several spots in there that felt cold, a couple that felt sad, and one, a stone with two little pines next to it, that felt downright angry. Most of our feelings inside the cemetery, I attribute to the power of suggestion, but that feeling in my chest earlier that night was very real. *–Letter via e-mail*

graveyard, I felt an intense wave of sadness wash over me. Tears began pouring down my face almost instantaneously. Laura was crying as well. Donna, in the back seat, was having an entirely different reaction. She was angry and began shouting at us, calling us horrible names, punching and slapping the back of Laura's seat.

Just as suddenly as it started, this behavior stopped when we reached the center of the cemetery. At that moment a bright light appeared and began bouncing in the direction of our car. As it did, we all screamed, and it screamed back, letting out an inhuman snarl before disappearing. We got out of there, didn't speak for about half an hour, and when we did, we swore never to test Cuba Road's powers again. *–Danielle Ramos*

Ghost Stories and Local Haunts

Who can really say for sure that ghosts are not real? Are you totally convinced that restless spirits do not wander the lonely fields and forests of Illinois? Or that undead souls don't inhabit that lonely old house on the hill? Is the moaning you hear at midnight really just the wind in the eaves, or could it be the voices of the undead, crying for eternal rest? Is the creak of a door just the sound of an old house settling, or does it mark the passage of an ephemeral figure, moving through rooms that exist in another time and place?

If you really think about it, perhaps you'll realize that you really aren't sure that ghosts are just figments of the imagination—fanciful tales told by fools and drunks. You may have had too many strange experiences that can't be explained, or maybe you've heard tales from friends that made your skin crawl and your disbelief falter.

Our modern world may be bright and clean, but there are still dark corners that resist exploration and strange, ghostly stories that defy explanation. Coincidence or not, you can find a lot of those stories lurking in the shadows of Illinois. And if they can't make you second-guess your belief that ghosts don't exist, maybe nothing will.

Resurrection Mary

It is a cold night in late December on the south side of Chicago. A taxicab travels along Archer Avenue as rain and sleet pelt the windshield. The driver reaches over to crank the heater up one more notch. It is the kind of night that makes one's bones ache.

As the car rolls past the Willow-Brook Ballroom, a pale figure, blurry through the rain-slicked windshield, appears along the roadside. The driver cranes his neck and sees a young woman walking alone. She is oddly dressed for such a cold, wet night, wearing only a white cocktail dress and a thin shawl over her shoulders. She stumbles along the uneven shoulder of the road, and the cabby pulls over and stops the car. He rolls down the window, and the girl approaches the taxi. She is beautiful, he sees, despite her disheveled appearance. Her blond hair is damp and plastered to her forehead. Her light blue eyes are the color of ice on a winter lake.

He invites her into the cab, and she opens the back door and slides across the seat. The cabby looks into the rearview mirror and asks her where she wants to go. He offers her a free ride—it's the least that he can do in this weather, he tells her. The girl simply says to keep driving down Archer Avenue, so the cabby puts the car into gear and pulls back onto the road. He notices that the girl is shivering, so he turns up the heater again. He comments on the weather, trying to make conversation, but she doesn't answer at first. He wonders if she might be a little drunk. Finally she answers him, although her voice wavers and she sounds almost fearful. The driver is unsure whether her whispered words are directed at him or whether she is speaking to herself. "The snow came early this year," she murmurs, and then is silent once more.

The cabby agrees with her and attempts to make more small talk, but he eventually realizes that she is not interested in conversation. Then suddenly she shouts at him to pull over to the side of the road. This is where she needs to get out!

The startled driver jerks the steering wheel and pulls off the road in front of two large metal gates. He looks up and realizes where they have stopped. "You can't get out here," he says to the young woman. "This is a cemetery!" When he looks into the rearview mirror, he realizes that the girl is no longer in the back seat. He never heard the door open or close, but the beautiful girl has simply disappeared.

This is the account of just one man's encounter with the girl who would become known as Resurrection Mary, one of the most enigmatic and sought-after ghosts in the Chicago area. Chicago is a city filled with ghosts, from haunted houses to eerie graveyards, but the tale of Resurrection Mary rises above all the others. It has all of the elements of the supernatural, including actual eyewitness accounts of a beautiful female spirit that have yet to be debunked.

Mary's tale begins in the 1930s. Around this time, drivers along Archer Avenue started reporting strange encounters with a young woman in a white dress. As they passed by Resurrection Cemetery, she would attempt to jump onto the running boards of their automobiles. She always appeared to be real—until she inexplicably vanished.

Soon the strange encounters began to move down the road, away from the graveyard and closer to the O'Henry Ballroom (now known as the Willow-Brook Ballroom). The white figure was reported on the roadway outside and, sometimes, inside the ballroom itself. On many occasions, young men would meet a girl at the ballroom, dance with her, and then offer her a ride home at the end of the evening. She always accepted and gave vague directions that led north on Archer Avenue. When the car reached the gates of Resurrection Cemetery, the young woman always vanished.

More common were the claims of motorists who would see the girl walking along the road. They would offer her a ride; she would accept and then would vanish from their cars. These drivers could describe the girl in detail, and nearly every description precisely matched the previous accounts. She was said to have light blond hair, blue eyes, and to wear a white party dress. More attentive witnesses would sometimes add that she wore a thin shawl or dancing shoes, or that she had a small clutch purse.

Others had more harrowing experiences, claiming to have actually run her down in the street. A woman in a white dress would bolt in front of their car near the cemetery, and there would be a sickening thud as she was struck by the front of the car. When they stopped to go to her aid, she would be gone. Some even said that the automobile passed directly through the girl. At that point, she would turn and disappear through the cemetery gates.

Bewildered and shaken drivers began to appear almost routinely at the nearby police station. They told strange and frightening stories that helped create the rich legend of the vanishing girl.

It has never been known who the earthy counterpart of Mary might have been. Some say she was a young girl from Chicago's Polish immigrant community who got into a fight with her boyfriend at the O'Henry Ballroom in 1934. When she tried to hitchhike home, she was struck and killed by a passing driver. Others say it was Mary Miskowski, a young woman who was killed crossing the street while going to a costume party. And some say it could have been Anna Mary Norkus, who convinced her

father to take her to the O'Henry Ballroom for her thirteenth birthday. On the way home, their car overturned and she was killed.

Others have speculated that she never really existed at all. They have scoffed at the search for her identity, believing that she is nothing more than an urban legend—Chicago's version of the "vanishing hitchhiker." But while the story of Resurrection Mary does bear some resemblance to that tale, her story has certain details that many versions of the hitchhiker stories do not: credible eyewitness accounts with places, times, and dates. And to top it off, Mary is one of the few ghosts to ever leave physical evidence behind!

Aside from the motorists who encountered Mary along Archer Avenue, one of the first people who met her face-to-face was a young man named Jerry Palus. His experience with Mary took place in 1939 but left such an impression that the tale was still with him when he died in 1992. Jerry remained an unshakable witness and appeared on a

Soon the strange encounters began to move down the road, away from the graveyard and closer to the O'Henry Ballroom (now known as the Willow-Brook Ballroom).

number of television shows to discuss his night with Resurrection Mary. He never once doubted that he had spent an evening with a ghost.

Jerry met Mary at the Liberty Grove and Hall, a dance hall on 47th Street and Mozart, in the vicinity of Archer Avenue. He had seen her there on several occasions. He noted in later interviews that he did not recall ever actually seeing her come into the dance hall—she just seemed to suddenly appear. Jerry asked the young woman to dance. She accepted, and they spent several hours dancing. She seemed a little distant, and Jerry noticed that her skin was strangely cold, almost icy to the touch. When he later kissed her, he found her lips were also cold and clammy.

At the end of the evening, the young woman asked Jerry for a ride home, and when they got to his automobile,

she directed him to drive down Archer Avenue. Jerry was confused. Earlier in the evening the woman had told him her address—in the Bridgeport area of Chicago—and he knew that it would be far out of the way for them to travel there via Archer. When he asked her about it, she simply told him again that she wanted to go down Archer Avenue.

As they drove down the street, they approached the gates to Resurrection Cemetery, and she asked him to pull over. She had to get out here, she told him. Jerry was confused, but agreed that he would let her out, but only if she allowed him to walk her across the street. This she would not allow. "This is where I have to get out," she said softly, "but where I'm going, you can't follow."

Jerry was bewildered, but before he could respond, the girl got out of the car and ran toward the cemetery gates. She vanished before she reached them—right before Jerry's eyes! That was when he suspected that he had danced with a specter.

Determined to get to the bottom of the strange meeting, on the following day Jerry visited the address the girl had given him. The woman who answered the door told him that he couldn't possibly have been with her daughter the night before because she had been dead for several years. However, Jerry was able to correctly identify the girl from a family portrait in the other room.

From that point on, Mary's ghost began making more regular appearances on Archer Avenue. Stories like Jerry's have become commonplace over the years, but his account remains the most convincing.

During the mid-'70s, the number of Mary sightings began to increase steadily. People from many different walks of life, from cab drivers to ministers, claimed they had picked her up and had given her rides. During this period, Resurrection Cemetery was undergoing some major renovations; perhaps this was what caused her restlessness?

In 1973, Mary was said to have shown up at least twice at a nightclub called Harlow's on Cicero on the southwest side, where she danced alone in a faded white dress. Despite the fact that bouncers checked the IDs of everyone who came through the door, no one ever saw the girl enter or leave. Later that same year an annoyed cab driver walked into Chet's Melody Lounge, located across from the gates to Resurrection Cemetery, looking for a fare that had skipped off without paying. The young blond woman that he reportedly picked up was nowhere to be seen. The manager explained that no blond woman had entered the bar.

On August 12, 1976, Cook County police officers investigated an emergency call about an apparent hit-and-run victim near the intersection of 76th Street and Roberts Road. The officers found a young female motorist in tears at the scene, and they asked her where the body was that she had allegedly discovered beside the road. She pointed to a wet, grassy area, and the policemen could plainly see a depression in the grass that matched the shape of a human body. The girl said that just as the police car approached the scene, the body had vanished!

In May 1978, a young couple was driving down Archer when a girl suddenly darted out in front of their car. The driver hit the brakes but knew it was too late. As the couple braced for the impact, the car passed right through the girl. She then turned and ran into Resurrection Cemetery, melting past the bars in the gate.

In that same year, a man was on his way to work in the early-morning hours and spotted the body of a young girl lying directly in front of the cemetery gates. He stopped his truck and got out, quickly discovering that the woman was badly injured but still alive. He jumped into his truck and sped to the nearby police station, where he summoned an ambulance and then hurried back to the cemetery. When he got there, he found that the body was gone. However, the outline of her body was still visible on the dew-covered pavement.

Perhaps the strangest encounter from that period was one that occurred on the night of August 10, 1976. On this occasion, Mary did not just fade away in the night. She left evidence behind!

A driver was passing by the cemetery around ten thirty that night when he saw a girl standing on the other side of the gates. He said that when he saw her, she was wearing a white dress and grasping the iron bars of the gates. The driver was considerate enough to stop down the street at the Justice police station and alert them to the fact that someone had been accidentally locked in the cemetery at closing time. Two officers responded to the call, but when they arrived at the cemetery gates, no one was there.

However, when they inspected the gates where the girl had supposedly been standing, they found something so unusual it chilled both of them to the bone. Two of the bars had been pulled apart and bent at sharp angles. To make things worse, there were blackened scorch marks on the green-colored bronze where the bars had been pried apart. Within the marks, handprints, clearly showing the pattern of skin texture, had been seared into the metal with incredible heat.

The marks of the small hands made big news, and curiosity-seekers came from all over the area to see them. In an effort to discourage the crowds, cemetery officials cut off the bars and installed a wire fence.

The cemetery denied the supernatural version of what

had happened to the bars. They claimed that a truck backed into the gates while doing sewer work at the cemetery and that grounds workers tried to fix the bars by heating them with a blowtorch and bending them. The imprint in the metal, they said, was from a workman trying to push the bars together again. While this explanation was convenient, it did not explain why the marks of small fingers were clearly visible in the metal.

Two of the bars had been pulled apart and bent at sharp angles . . . there were blackened scorch marks on the green-colored bronze where the bars had been pried apart. Within the marks, handprints . . . had been seared into the metal with incredible heat.

People soon began asking why the bars had been taken out. What did the cemetery have to hide? The events allegedly embarrassed local officials, who demanded that the bars be put back. Once they were returned, they were straightened and painted over with green paint. But the scorched areas continued to defy all attempts to cover them, and the twisted parts where the handprints had been impressed were obvious. Recently the bars were finally removed for good.

This era of regular sightings reached its peak on the last weekend in August 1980. Mary was seen by dozens of people, including the deacon of the Greek church on Archer Avenue. Many witnesses contacted the police department about what they saw, and squad cars were dispatched, but by the time the cars arrived, the mysterious young woman was always gone.

During the 1990s, reports of Mary slacked off, but they have never really stopped altogether. Then in July 2001, a witness named Paul contacted *Weird Illinois*. He stated that one night he and his girlfriend had spotted Mary near Resurrection Cemetery.

She was wearing a white gown that fluttered in the wind. When he realized who was in front of his eyes, Paul called his sister on his cell phone, marking the exact time of the sighting. After he explained to his date who Resurrection Mary was, she insisted that they go back for another look. Paul turned around and headed south, keeping his eyes peeled for a ghostly young girl walking toward them. But there was no sign of the girl in the white dress.

Then they spotted her again, standing along the shoulder of the road. Her white gown was faded and discolored, and she was carrying a bouquet of dead flowers. "She wasn't looking at us," Paul recalled. "She was just staring down the road. She looked somewhat young and had the blankest expression that I have ever seen on a face."

There are still drivers who stop to pick up the forlorn figure of Resurrection Mary. Curiosity-seekers still come to see the gates to see where the twisted and burned bars were once located, and some even roam the graveyard, hoping to stumble across the plot where the real Mary was laid to rest.

Perhaps we will never know for sure why Mary haunts this particular stretch of roadway. As soon as people think she is gone for good, she appears again, as reliable as the seasons, the mysterious, beautiful, and romantic ghost of the Windy City.

The Old Slave House

High on a windswept rise in southern Illinois, in a region better known as Little Egypt, stands one of the state's most famous haunted houses: Hickory Hill. Over the years, Hickory Hill has been many things: a plantation house, a tourist attraction, and a chamber of horrors for the slaves who were once brought here in chains. Because of this dark blight on its history, Hickory Hill is more familiarly known as the Old Slave House.

For decades, people have come from all over the state and beyond to visit this mysterious and forbidding place. The secrets of the slaves who were tortured here are now well known, but dark whispers about the place persist, insisting that the dead of Hickory Hill do not rest in peace.

John Hart Crenshaw built Hickory Hill in the mid-1800s. Crenshaw was a powerful man in southern Illinois who amassed a fortune through his business interests, but despite his successes, he is best remembered today for building Hickory Hill and for his ties to illegal slave trafficking in Illinois.

Although the law did provide some protection for free blacks, it did nothing to discourage bands of men, called night riders, from kidnapping them and their children and selling them into slavery down south. They also kidnapped escaped slaves and ransomed them back to their owners.

Crenshaw was a respected member of his community and a pillar of his church, so at the time no one suspected that he was involved in these despicable slave kidnappings.

Hickory Hill, a classic Greek-revival plantation house, was the perfect headquarters for this illegal operation. Located near the town of Equality, the house is just a short horseback ride away from the border of Kentucky, a slave state. Crenshaw stationed his slave catchers here at night to capture slaves trying to flee over the border.

The house stands on a hill overlooking the Saline River. Legend has it that the river was once connected to Hickory Hill's basement by a tunnel through which slaves were loaded and unloaded at night. In addition, a passageway large enough to contain a wagon was built into the rear of the building, allowing wagons to enter it and unload slaves unseen.

The infamous third floor of Hickory Hill houses the attic, which is reached by a flight of narrow stairs that exit into a wide hallway surrounded by a dozen tiny cell-like rooms with barred windows and flat wooden bunks facing the corridor. Originally the cells were even smaller and there were more of them, but at some time they were enlarged. An average-sized person can scarcely turn around in the ones that remain.

The slaves were secured in their cells with chains and heavy metal rings, which left scars still visible on the wooden walls and floors. Chains and heavy balls are kept on display, as are two whipping posts, where slaves who disobeyed orders were flogged.

Stories have long been told about the many cruelties that Crenshaw inflicted on the slaves, from beatings to disfigurement. By 1846, his business holdings were in decline, and to make matters worse, Crenshaw was attacked by one of his slaves, who reportedly severed one of Crenshaw's legs.

During the Civil War, Crenshaw sold Hickory Hill and moved to a new farmhouse, where he lived until his death in 1871. Whether he rests in peace is unknown, but the tales that abound in Little Egypt suggest that his former captives certainly do not. According to many accounts from over the years, at Hickory Hill "mysterious voices can be heard in that attic, sometimes moaning, sometimes singing the spirituals that comfort heavy hearts."

And that's just the beginning.

Weird Illinois has visited the Old Slave House more than a dozen times, and each time we climbed that old staircase to the third floor, we felt the hair rise on our arms. Something is just *not right* there. Although we have yet to encounter the spirits of Hickory Hill, others have some spine-tingling stories to tell about ghostly faces. Could it be that the tormented souls of the slaves are still trapped in the attic after more than a century?

Over the years, countless visitors have had strange experiences that have only deepened the house's mystery. Beginning in the 1920s, people would come to the door—at any hour—and ask to look around. Living there at the time was the Sisk family, the last family to own Hickory Hill, and they began offering tours.

Thanks to a savvy advertising campaign, by the 1930s the house had become a popular destination for out-of-town visitors. The owners charged admission; for just a dime (a nickel if you were a child), you could tour the place where "Slavery Existed in Illinois," as the road signs stated. Soon Hickory Hill was one of the most frequently visited sites in Little Egypt. And it would quickly gain a reputation for being the most haunted one.

Shortly after the house became a tourist attraction, visitors began reporting that strange things were happening there. They told of odd noises in the attic, including cries, whimpers, and even rattling chains. Many visitors felt cold chills or had the sensation that invisible hands were touching them. Others felt unseen figures brush by them.

Such stories did little to dampen the flow of visitors. One legend arose that no one could spend the entire night in the attic. The story got its start in the late 1920s after Hickman Whittington, a ghost chaser from Benton, paid the house a visit to investigate stories about cries coming from a whipping post.

Whatever happened to Whittington that night apparently scared the life right out of him. One of his descendants told *Weird Illinois* that Whittington left the Old Slave House, arrived home, sat down to dinner, and abruptly fell over dead into his plate of mashed potatoes.

When *Weird Illinois* asked George Sisk, the elderly owner of the house, about this story, he mused, "I wouldn't want to be the one to say, but it could have been the same thing that scared those two marines who tried to stay in the attic overnight in 1966."

According to the tale, these marines had scoffed when told that no one had ever been able to spend a full night in the attic. They were sure they could. Just as they were about to go to sleep, their kerosene lantern began to flicker, even though there were no drafts, and the light began to dim. Then an agonized moan seemed to emanate from all the walls, followed by voices. Finally, just before the lantern blew itself out, the marines claimed they saw "swirling forms" coming out of the shadows. George recalls, "They came flying down the stairs at about one thirty in the morning. They tore out of here in a hurry."

Over the years, many others tried to spend the night up in the eaves of Hickory Hill, but no one ever made it until daybreak. That is, until David Rodgers came along.

In 1978, Rodgers spent a night in the attic as a Halloween stunt for a local television station. He later admitted that he felt "queasy" going into the house. "I heard a lot of strange noises," he said the next morning. "I was actually shaking. The place is so spooky. The tape recorder was picking up sounds that I wasn't hearing." Although he was proud of his accomplishment, he confessed that he "didn't want to make the venture an annual event."

Out of nearly one hundred fifty challengers over the years, Rodgers had become the first person ever to stay the whole night in the slave quarters.

In 1996, the Old Slave House was finally closed down, due to the declining health of Mr. and Mrs. Sisk. Although it appeared that the house might never reopen, it was purchased by the state of Illinois in 1999, and plans are in the works to turn it into a state historic site.

What will become of the ghosts or at least the ghost stories? Unfortunately, local legends and lore don't often hold up well at official locations. Regardless, if you get the chance, pay a visit to the historic—and possibly haunted— Hickory Hill. If you climb those stairs to the attic, you might feel your stomach drop just a little. And we can guarantee that you will find yourself speaking softly in the gloomy third-floor corridor in deference to the nameless people who suffered there.

The Cold Chill of the Old Slave House Attic

I just wanted to tell you that my husband and I visited the Old Slave House when it was still open, and when we were up in the attic in one of the cells, I felt the hair on my arms stand on end. I called my husband over, and he felt a cold chill pass over him when he walked through the door. I have never been so scared in my life! –Donna M.

Ghostly Face in the Attic Window

I was passing through southern Illinois in the late 1970s on my way back to Chicago, where I teach at a university, and decided to stop and see the Old Slave House. I was the only visitor there that day, and I took my time going through the house, except for when it came to the attic. The whole time I was up there, I was sure that someone was there with me. I was constantly turning around to see who was behind me, but there was never anyone there. Finally I became so unnerved that I left the house and walked out to my car. It was parked in the gravel lot directly in front, and when I reached it, I looked up at the attic window. I clearly saw a face looking out at me, even though I knew no one had been in the house! I was so shaken up that I went back in and asked the owner if someone else had come inside. He said that no one had. I still have no explanation for what happened. I never believed in ghosts before that, and while I'm still not sure that I do, I just have no explanation for what I saw in that window. –David A.

Ghostly Scent of a Woman

I was just shopping one day at the Mineral Springs stores, and I had no idea the place was supposed to be haunted. I wouldn't find out until later that everybody knew about the ghosts but me. As I passed the bottom of the staircase, I caught this sickening flowery scent, but I had no idea that it meant there was supposed to be a ghost around. Just after I smelled the perfume, I felt this cold chill, almost like a breeze blowing. Then I looked up. There are these signs that hang out in front of some of the stores down the hallway, and all of the ones close to me start swinging back and forth. I left after that. I have been back there since, and nothing else has happened, but I'll never forget that.

—*Christy T.*

Ghosts of the Mineral Springs Hotel in Alton

If you ask ghost hunters to name the most likely places to be haunted, hotels will be near the top of their lists. Most believe that old buildings can soak up and hang on to the energy of the past, replaying bygone events like an old recording. It's also been said that ghosts are essentially a little piece of ourselves that we leave behind in places where we have suffered tragedy and grief. The anonymous setting of a hotel encourages both death and despair at times, and perhaps for this reason, ghosts are said to linger in some of them.

The Mineral Springs Hotel in Alton is just such a place. Even though it was turned into a unique collection of shops some years ago, you almost expect to see guests strolling through the lobby, and when you walk inside, you will still find traces of the old hotel, which was built in 1914. At the Mineral Springs, many guests checked in—but some never really checked out.

The ghost stories of the Mineral Springs Hotel date back to the early 1930s. *Weird Illinois* spoke to a woman who worked there as a desk clerk in the 1950s; she said staff members were talking about the hotel's most famous ghost long before she ever started working there.

According to her, the legendary Jasmine Lady has haunted the hotel's staircase for decades. Jasmine Lady and her husband were once guests who had come to the hotel to take in the healing waters of the nearby springs. While they were there, she became romantically involved with another guest. One evening while her husband was away, she took the other man up to her room—with disastrous results. Her husband returned unexpectedly and caught the adulterous couple in the act. He was enraged, and in the course of their violent encounter, she ran away from him and started down the staircase.

What happened next remains a mystery; either she tripped and fell on the stairs or her angry spouse pushed her down them. Whatever the story, she broke her neck and died instantly. Her husband was not charged, and her death was ruled an accident.

Over the years, many staff members and visitors have claimed to have witnessed this woman's tragic tumble down the stairs as her apparition replays the terrible event over and over again. Stranger still, they have also caught whiffs of her pungent jasmine

perfume near the staircase and in other spots throughout the hotel. Even former hotel owner Bob Love, whom *Weird Illinois* spoke to back in 1998, has puzzled over the presence of this strong scent. "I have to say I'm not a believer [in ghosts]," Mr. Love said, "but one morning I walked in the Alton Street entrance, and I smelled a strong, almost putrid, jasmine scent. It was strange."

Another spot said to be haunted is the hotel's old, empty swimming pool in the basement. In the 1950s, staff members frequently reported unexplained sounds coming from this room, such as music playing, glasses tinkling, voices, and laughter—as if one of the parties frequently held there during the hotel's heyday was still going on.

One staff member recently told *Weird Illinois* that he heard water running in the pool area one afternoon and went in to see if perhaps a pipe had broken. He discovered that the pool was still dry, but then he saw something that made his heart stop—on the side of the pool was a set of wet footprints that led away in a line across the tile floor.

The Jasmine Lady and the ghosts of the old swimming pool may be the most famous hauntings at the Mineral Springs Hotel, but they are definitely not the only ones. Strange encounters abound, and those who come here seeking ghosts rarely go away disappointed. If you are ever in Alton and looking for ghosts, be sure to include the Mineral Springs on your list of places to visit. You just never know who you might run into!

Ghosts Still Checking In at Mineral Springs

I had just started working at the Mineral Springs, and I had heard some of the ghost stories about the place. I wasn't sure that I believed them, until one day when I was working in my office, which was just off the old hotel lobby. The building was empty that day because we are closed on Mondays, and no one else was there but me. I was sitting at my desk when I heard someone ringing a bell just outside my office. I had no idea who it was, but I got up to look. There was no one out there, and I couldn't see any bells anywhere. I sat back down, and a few minutes later, it happened again. This time I realized that it sounded like one of those handbells that you put on a desk and ring when you want service. Later I found out that the hotel's front desk used to be right outside my office—and that they used to keep one of those bells on the desk. That really gave me the creeps!—*J.B.*

The Phantom July Fourth Funeral Procession

Near the sleepy southern town of Prairie du Rocher, whenever Independence Day falls on a Friday, the heartland's most famous phantom funeral procession is said to walk the land, moving silently down an old road to the local cemetery.

The ghostly procession begins at Fort de Chartres, a place with a rich and violent history. The fort, Illinois' earliest military post, was built in the early 1700s to protect French settlers who had established trading posts in the area. After France was defeated in the French and Indian War in 1763, Illinois territory was ceded to the British. They eventually took over Fort de Chartres, but under British command, the fort declined and fell into ruin.

However, time never completely forgot Fort de Chartres, and at least one event from its violent past replays itself over and over. According to the legend, if three people stand somewhere along the road from Fort de Chartres to a small cemetery in Prairie du Rocher, they will be able to witness a spectral funeral procession between the hours of eleven and midnight—but only when July 4 falls on a Friday.

The legend began to take shape with a strange occurrence in July 1889 near the old fort. Around midnight a local woman named Mrs. Chris was sitting on her front porch with her neighbor. The two women were talking quietly and enjoying the cool night air.

Suddenly one of the women noticed a large group of people and wagons coming toward them on the road from the ruins of Fort de Chartres. She pointed it out to her friend, and they both puzzled over why a procession would be on the road at such an odd hour. As the entourage drew closer, they counted more than forty wagons full of men and women, led by horsemen and soldiers on foot, all looking eerie in the pale light of the moon. They had no idea what the

procession was all about until a low wagon holding a casket finally rolled into view.

Mrs. Chris and her friend finally realized they were staring at a funeral procession—but for whom? And where was it going so late at night? It was then that the women noticed something else very peculiar about the grim parade: Despite the size of the group, the procession made no sound at all.

The only things the two women could hear were the rustling of the trees in the breeze and the incessant barking of the family dog, which sensed that something was not right. The barking awakened the neighbor's husband, who looked out his window and also witnessed the strange entourage on the road. As they all watched, the procession passed by and vanished down the road in the direction of a small cemetery just outside town. The two women waited for the mourners to return, but they never did.

These three people were the only witnesses to what has since become one of the most enduring mysteries of the Mississippi River region. It would be years before they learned the grisly story behind the murder that led to the procession. A murder that had happened more than a hundred years earlier and had replayed itself in front of their eyes on that hot July night.

The story behind the procession took place during the French occupation of Fort de Chartres, when a prominent local man got into a violent disagreement with one of the officers of the garrison. The two men exchanged heated words, and the local merchant was accidentally killed. Unsure of how to handle the affair, the fort's commander sent a delegation to the government offices in nearby Kaskaskia. They advised keeping the incident under wraps and ordered the local man to be buried at midnight in the small cemetery outside Prairie du Rocher. A procession of soldiers and horsemen led the way—the very procession glimpsed by Mrs. Chris, her neighbor,

and her neighbor's husband a century later.

Since that night in 1889, other eyewitness accounts of the phantom procession have been collected, but as with most ghost stories, no actual proof has ever materialized.

In more recent times, July 4 fell once again on a Friday in 1997 and 2003. And while no one actually saw the procession in 1997—perhaps because of the crowds that gathered and drove back and forth along the four-mile stretch of road between the fort and the cemetery all evening—one odd event did take place. A staff member at the historically preserved fort reported to *Weird Illinois* that precisely at midnight all the coyotes in the area began to howl in unison. It only lasted for a minute or two, but what a strange coincidence it was. Or was it?

Intrigued by the tale? You will have the chance to search for the phantom funeral procession yourself when July 4 falls again on a Friday in 2008, 2014, and 2025. If you are feeling brave, take along two friends and stake out the old road that leads to Fort de Chartres. You might just be in the right place at the right time when the dead procession walks the road once more.

Felt the Phantom Funeral with My Family

My family and I went down to Prairie du Rocher in 2003 to be there when the Fourth of July fell on Friday night. There were lots of people waiting to see if they would see anything near the old fort, so my son and I decided to go and wait at the cemetery instead. I can't swear to you that I saw anything, because it was more like I "sensed" it, but at just about midnight, I felt like there was a huge group of people moving toward us from up the road. I sort of feel like I saw their shadows in the moonlight, and I definitely got a sense that they were there, even right down to the type of uniforms the men were wearing, but that is all that I can say for sure. When I went home, I drew their uniforms as I remembered them, and my son later told me that they were very close to what the French soldiers of the period wore. I don't know, I never believed in any of this stuff before. Now I'm not so sure.—*Ed B.*

The Saint Valentine's Day Massacre started a wave of reform that would eventually break the stranglehold of Capone's South Side gang. It also started a wave of spooky stories involving the blood-drenched site.

Ghosts of the St. Valentine's Day Massacre

There are few periods of American history as fascinating as the gangster era of the '20s and '30s. During this period, organized crime gained a foothold in America's larger cities and gangsters became celebrities. With Prohibition the law of the land, the mob came into its own, giving people the liquor they craved and then diversifying into other criminal pursuits.

In Chicago, no event defined the bloody era of the Roaring Twenties like the Saint Valentine's Day Massacre. And while it did not put an end to organized crime in the city, it did mark the end of the so-called glory days of Al Capone's Chicago mob. Few gangland murders have inspired as much interest and speculation, and fewer still have inspired as many gangland ghost stories.

The most spectacular mob hit in gangland history took place on February 14, 1929, in a red brick warehouse at 2122 North Clark Street, home to the SMC Garage.

At the time, Al Capone was the reigning king of the Italian South Side mob and the supplier of liquor and vice to that side of the city. Bugs Moran was the head of the Irish North Side mob. Trouble had been brewing between the two gangs since 1927, and early in 1929, Moran reportedly gunned down Pasquilino Lolordo, one of Capone's men.

Capone, who was living outside Miami at the time, put in a call to his crew in Chicago. He had a very special valentine to deliver to Moran: He vowed he would have him wiped out on February 14.

On that morning, a group of Moran's men had gathered inside the Clark Street garage. One of them was Johnny May, an ex-safecracker who had been hired by Moran as an auto mechanic. He was working on a truck that morning, with his dog, Highball, tied to the bumper. While he worked, six other men were waiting for a truck of hijacked whiskey to arrive, as well as for Bugs Moran, who was running late.

While the seven men waited, a police car pulled up outside. Five men got out of the car, entered the building, and a few moments later, the rat-a-tat of machine gun fire broke the stillness of the snowy morning. Soon after, five figures emerged and drove away. Inside the warehouse, Highball began barking and howling.

The landlady in the next building was bothered by the barking and sent one of her boarders over to investigate. He came outside two minutes later, face pale, and ran frantically upstairs to beg the landlady to call the police. The garage was full of dead men!

When they got to the garage, the police were stunned by the carnage. Moran's men had been lined up against the rear wall and sprayed by machine guns. The death toll stood at seven, but the killers had missed Moran, who had probably spotted the car when he arrived and quickly taken cover.

The Saint Valentine's Day Massacre started a wave of reform that would eventually break the stranglehold of Capone's South Side gang. It also started a wave of spooky stories involving the blood-drenched site.

Fast-forward to 1967, when city officials slated the building for demolition. A savvy Canadian businessman purchased the bullet-ridden bricks from the rear wall. Eventually he began selling them for $1000 each. But to his amazement the bricks began being returned to him. It seemed that anyone who bought one was suddenly stricken with bad luck: illness, financial ruin, divorce, and even death. Apparently, the bricks themselves had become infested with the powerful negative energy of the massacre.

And then there is the old warehouse site itself. Even recently, people who have passed by 2122 North Clark Street have reported the sound of screams and machine guns. Other passersby have heard weeping. Skeptics have laughed this off, saying that the sounds are the product of the overactive imaginations of those who already know about the bloodbath that occurred there. However, many of these reports were made by people who had no knowledge of the history of the place.

Even after all these years, it appears that the violent events of the city's gangster past are still reverberating through time, and the inexplicable sounds continue today. Al Capone left an indelible mark on Chicago. And it appears that the events of the Saint Valentine's Day Massacre did too.

Cemetery Safari

Everyone has contemplated the mystery of death at one time or another. No matter what we believe in, we all wonder what will happen to us after we leave this world. Will our spirits pass on to a heavenly realm or remain behind as ghosts? Our curiosity about such things may be why every society has developed elaborate rituals and practices surrounding death. Honored and feared since the beginning of time, death is also the main theme in our darkest and most frightening legends and lore.

In Western society, grave markers and tombstones immortalize and pay tribute to our dearly departed, but they have also given rise to innumerable tales of hauntings and strange occurrences. And cemeteries—those silent cities of the dead—are peaceful sanctuaries where the living can visit loved ones who have passed on, but they are also grim and stark reminders of our mortality.

Such places can be disturbing, to say the least, and the graveyards of Illinois are certainly no exception. The vast majority are tranquil, lush, and landscaped urban burial grounds or small rural graveyards nestled between cornfields on dusty back roads. But then there are the others: Cemeteries with a reputation for spectral sightings and unexplained mysteries. In these places, the famous, the infamous, and the eccentric dead continue to make history—and make spines tingle—even after their deaths, reinforcing Illinois' reputation for just plain weirdness.

Curious? Read on to discover why our graveyards are some of the most historically fascinating—and superbly strange—sites in the state.

Bachelor's Grove Cemetery: The Most Haunted Spot in Chicago

Rubio Woods Forest Preserve is an island of trees and shadows in the southwest suburb of Midlothian. The rambling refuge is so large it seems to be truly secluded from the urban sprawl that threatens its borders. Perhaps it is.

On the edge of the forest is a small graveyard that many believe is the most haunted place in the Chicago area. Called Bachelor's Grove, this ramshackle burial ground has yielded more than one hundred documented reports of paranormal phenomena, from apparitions to glowing balls of light. There have been no new burials here for many years, so most people have forgotten about this isolated place, but if you ask any ghost hunter where to find a haunting, Bachelor's Grove is usually the first place they mention.

Isolated and cut off from the nearby Midlothian Turnpike, Bachelor's Grove began to show signs of vandalism and decay in the 1960s. Pranksters knocked over, destroyed, spray-painted, and even stole gravestones. Many stones have turned up at other grave sites, giving birth to rumors that they move about under their own power. Vandals also dug trenches and pits next to some graves as they tried to make off with souvenirs of the dead. Worst of all, in 1964, 1975, and 1978, hooligans opened graves and removed caskets, and caretakers found bones strewn about the cemetery. Even today, graves continue to be desecrated.

All of this only adds to the cemetery's spooky atmosphere, so it's no real surprise that people believe the place is haunted and report numerous chilling occurrences. Although some contest just how much paranormal activity takes place on the grounds, few deny that strange things have been happening here for more than three decades.

Officers patrolling the woods at night and visitors to the cemetery have reportedly found evidence of black magic and occult rituals here, such as the remains of chickens and other small animals that have been slaughtered and mutilated in a ritualistic fashion. Inscriptions and elaborate writings have been carved in and painted on trees and grave markers.

Just beyond the rear boundary of the cemetery is a small stagnant pond that can be seen by motorists passing by on 143rd Street. Although the pond is outside the graveyard, it too is touched by the horror of the place. One night in the late 1970s, two Cook County forest rangers were stunned to see what looked like the apparition of a horse emerge from the waters of the pond. The animal seemed to be pulling a plow steered by the ghost of an old man. As the vision crossed the road in front of the rangers' vehicle, it was framed for a moment in the glare of the headlights. Then it vanished into the forest. The men simply stared after it in shock, then looked at one another to confirm that both had seen the same thing. They reported the incident, and since that time, many others have also witnessed this spooky sight.

It's said that during Prohibition, gangsters dumped their murder victims into the pond and the spirits of those unfortunates are said to haunt its dark waters.

But the most bizarre tales of the site are not about the restless spirits of gangland execution victims. One particularly gruesome one comes from an elderly couple who claimed to see movement near the bridge at the edge of the pond. They stopped for a closer look and were understandably terrified to see a huge two-headed man emerge from under the bridge and cross the road in front of their headlights! The creature, whatever it was, quickly vanished into the woods.

Many ghosts and apparitions have been sighted in Bachelor's Grove Cemetery itself. The two most frequently seen are the "phantom monks" and the so-called Madonna of Bachelor's Grove. Sightings of the monklike ghosts, clothed in the flowing robes and cowls of an obscure monastic order, have also been reported in other places in the Chicago area. There are no records to indicate that a monastery ever existed near any of the locations where the monks have been seen, making them one of the area's greatest enigmas.

The Madonna of Bachelor's Grove is known by a variety of names, including the White Lady and the affectionate moniker, Mrs. Rogers. Legend has it that she

Many ghosts and apparitions have been sighted in Bachelor's Grove Cemetery itself.

is the ghost of a woman who was buried in the cemetery next to the grave of her young child. On nights when the moon is full, visitors have seen her wandering there with an infant wrapped in her arms. She walks aimlessly, completely unaware of the people who encounter her.

Bachelor's Grove is home to other spirits as well, such as a ghostly child who has been seen running across the bridge at the pond, a glowing yellow man, and a black carriage that travels along the old road through the woods.

Dale Kaczmarek of the Ghost Research Society and his investigators have turned up many pieces of evidence that seem to corroborate the mysteries of Bachelor's Grove. For example, a series of photos taken by the group in 1979 near the cemetery fence shows a figure wearing a hooded robe and holding a baby in its arms. Oddly, this was three years before the Ghost Research Society came across any accounts of the White Lady.

Researchers took perhaps the most stunning photograph from Bachelor's Grove in August 1991 during a full-fledged investigation of the cemetery. While they noticed nothing when taking the photographs, once the film was developed, the investigators were shocked to see that something mysterious had apparently been there. One photo, taken by Mari Huff, shows the semitransparent form of a woman seated on the remains of a tombstone. Was she one of the ghosts of Bachelor's Grove? Skeptics immediately rejected this idea, claiming that the apparition was the result of a double exposure—or an outright hoax.

Curious, *Weird Illinois* requested a copy of the photograph and had it examined by several photographers. They all ruled out the double exposure theory or the suggestion that the figure in the photo was an actual woman made to appear to be a ghost.

Clearly, there is something very strange going on at the cemetery. But is it as haunted as we have been led to believe? We'll leave that up to you to decide.

Saw the Ghosts of Bachelor's Grove

One time my friend went to Bachelor's Grove at night and had a big shock. He was just walking around and came to one of the tombstones, where he saw this beautiful teenage girl in a white dress. She smiled at him, and my friend wanted a picture. Luckily, he had come there for scares and had brought a camera. He took a picture of the girl, and then she wandered off into the cemetery. He sat down to rest and to think about what had just happened. Then a man wearing a top hat and nice suit came up to him and cursed at him in an angry tone. The man's eyes were glowing red—"swear on a stack of holy Bibles," my friend said. In moments the girl reappeared and ran to the man in the top hat. She was worried and tried to hit the man, but he slapped her and she faded away. Well, my friend ran out of the cemetery and the next day got the pictures developed. The girl in the photo was just a mist of black orbs.—*Hannah*

Ghost Lights and the Weeping Woman of Greenwood Cemetery

The origins of Greenwood Cemetery in Decatur have remained a mystery for more than one hundred and fifty years. There is no record of when the first burials took place in the area of land that would someday become Greenwood, although early Native Americans did use it as a burial site. It's believed that during the 1820s local settlers used this as a graveyard, and legend has it that a few captured runaway slaves were interred there under cover of night. The only trace these early folks left behind were numerous unmarked graves scattered around the present-day grounds.

In March 1857, the Greenwood Cemetery Association was organized and the cemetery was incorporated into the city of Decatur. By 1900, Greenwood had become Decatur's most fashionable place to be buried. By the 1920s, however, the cemetery had fallen into disrepair. The roads became covered in mud and so deeply rutted that they were no longer passable. Time, the elements, and vandals had wreaked havoc on Greenwood's grave markers too. Many stones were tilted, and others were damaged beyond repair.

By the time Decatur took over operation of the cemetery in 1957, the place had become neglected, remembered only as a spooky novelty.

The stories and legends that have haunted Greenwood for years took root in the deteriorated condition of the oldest section of the graveyard, where people have seen wandering spirits and glowing apparitions.

On a small hill at the edge of the forest that makes up Greenwood's northwest corner sits an old burial plot that belongs to the Barrackman family. If you approach it from the east, you will find a set of stone steps that lead to the top of the grassy hill. Four rounded stones mark the burial sites of the family.

According to dozens of accounts, visitors who remain in the cemetery as the sun sets may be treated to an eerie sight. As dusk falls, a diaphanous woman in a long dress appears on the steps leading up to the graves. She sits on the staircase with her head bowed and appears to weep, although no one has ever heard her make a sound. Those who have spotted her never see her for long—she vanishes as the sun dips below the horizon. She has never been seen in the daylight hours and never after dark—only at sunset.

Of all the ghostly events that have occurred here, however, the strangest mystery of the cemetery is likely the oldest. The story involves ghost lights that appear on the south side of the burial grounds. These small globes of light have been reported here for decades.

It's said that many years ago, during one particularly wet spring, the Sangamon River, just south of the cemetery, overflowed its banks and washed into the lower sections of the burial grounds. The surging water knocked over tombstones and washed away layers of sod and dirt, forcing buried caskets to the surface. Many of them went careering downstream on the swollen river.

Once the waters receded, it took many days to find the battered remains of the coffins, and many were never found. For some time after, farmers and fishermen were startled to find caskets and even corpses washed up on riverbanks several miles away. The identities of these bodies were a mystery, so they were reburied in unmarked common graves in the southern hills of Greenwood.

Since that time, spook lights have appeared there. Dozens of trustworthy witnesses have seen them moving in and out among the old, weathered stones. Whether natural or supernatural in origin, the mysterious lights have confounded everyone.

Want to see the lights for yourself? Some night go to the gravel parking lot across the road from the cemetery fence, where you can sit and observe the hills. You need a lot of patience and may even have to make more than one trip, but eventually you should be lucky enough to see the ghost lights.

Weird Illinois first started seeking out the lights in the late 1980s, and it took several years before our persistence paid off. One night in 1991 we drove down to the cemetery to look for the lights. We sat on the hood of the car and waited for about two hours. It was a cloudy night, but just enough of the moon seeped through the clouds to softly illuminate the stones of the cemetery in the distance. Our friend Larry spotted the first light as it moved quickly from the bottom of the hill to the top. A second later it vanished, almost as if it had been switched off. We then began to see more lights darting and zipping among the trees and stones, some shooting upward and others speeding off into the darkness and fading away. The light show lasted for about fifteen minutes.

We have since seen them on other occasions. The lights, about the size of softballs, are white tinged with a faint blue. They have an electric glare, almost like lightbulbs, and surge with energy. So what are they? Supernatural beacons from the otherworld or simply natural phenomena?

Many researchers say the lights are balls of electric friction caused by railroad tracks, power lines, or sources of water. The area has all three: The lights are seen on a hillside that is only a few yards away from the Illinois Central rail line, power lines run next to the tracks, and both the railroad tracks and the power lines cross the Sangamon River. Given this, it's possible that the Greenwood lights are of this world, rather than the next one.

But if you're sitting out on the south side of the cemetery in the dark and happen to catch a glimpse of the famous Greenwood spook lights, an eerie feeling will make you believe that they are ghostly in nature, and all the researchers in the world cannot explain them away.

Encounter with the Hollow-Eyed Spook

I was in Greenwood Cemetery one night back in 1977 and had decided to wait until after dark to climb the back fence and get inside. I walked out into the tombstones by moonlight. I didn't bring a flashlight with me because I didn't want to chance being spotted by a caretaker or a police car, but I saw something that night that has kept me from returning to the cemetery to this day! I crossed the road and started up a hill, and then I saw someone standing among the stones. I froze, sure that I was about to be caught. The cemetery closed at sunset, and I knew that I could be arrested for trespassing. So I ducked behind the largest stone that I could find and figured I would stay there until the other person—whom I figured was a caretaker—walked away. After a few minutes, I looked to see if he was still there, and he was. He was staring at something, not moving, but was not staring at me. I saw that he was tall and ordinary-looking, but it was really too dark to get a good look at him. He was just standing there, staring out toward the fence. I couldn't figure out what he was looking at. Then the man turned slowly around, facing in my direction—but he really didn't turn, it was almost like he rotated. Then I saw his eyes, which looked empty! They were like black holes, but they sort of glowed a little, like the moon was shining through the back of his head. I took off running then, and I don't have any idea if the man chased me, but he wouldn't have caught me anyway at the speed I was going! I have never been back to Greenwood Cemetery since.–*Jack G.*

Chased by the Unknown on a Snowy Winter Night

One winter's night I was cutting through Greenwood Cemetery on my way to a friend's house. I was walking along a cemetery road when I heard the distinctive sound of hard-soled shoes behind me. I looked back several times but couldn't see anyone, because it was too dark. Finally, unnerved by the sound, I veered from the paved road and set off across the cemetery grounds. But the sound followed me! I still couldn't see anyone, but I could hear his footsteps behind me, sinking through the hard crust of the snow. The footsteps got closer and closer . . . and that was when I took off running. Finally I arrived at my friend's house, breathless and pretty damned scared. It wasn't long, though, before my friend managed to calm me down and made me realize that the so-called chase had been all in my mind. To prove his point, he accompanied me to the cemetery the next morning. We soon found the place where I had left the road, and we got quite a surprise when we examined the surface of the snow. We easily found my footprints, but behind them was a second set of tracks that followed my tracks to the edge of the cemetery—then abruptly disappeared!–*David T.*

Dorothy's Really Not in Kansas Anymore

Somewhere over the rainbow—or at least in a lonesome corner of the Evergreen Memorial Cemetery in Bloomington—lies the worn and weather-beaten grave of a little girl named Dorothy Louise Gage. She was born on June 11, 1898, to Sophie Jewel and Thomas Clarkson Gage, the brother of Maud Gage Baum. Maud was the wife of novelist L. Frank Baum, famous for his wonderful series of books about a magical place named Oz.

Maud and her husband had four sons but had always longed for a little girl, so she was thrilled when her niece Dorothy was born, and doted on her lovingly. She often traveled from Chicago, where she and her family lived, to Bloomington to see the baby. Tragically, on November 11, five months to the day after she was born, Dorothy died. Cemetery records state that the cause of her death was "congestion of the brain." When Maud received the news, she traveled back to Bloomington to attend the baby's funeral. She was so overcome with grief that, when she returned home, she required medical attention. "Dorothy was a beautiful baby," Maud wrote to her sister. "I could have taken her for my very own and loved her devotedly."

At the time of the little girl's death, L. Frank Baum was putting the finishing touches on the tale that his wife had been urging him to put to paper for so long, *The Wonderful Wizard of Oz*. Legend has it that the story evolved as Baum wove it together for his children and their friends. Seeing his wife so distraught after the funeral of her niece and not knowing how to comfort her, he decided to name the heroine of his story after little Dorothy, forever immortalizing the child as "Dorothy Gale," rather than "Gage."

A new facet was added to the story in the fall of 1996, when Dr. Sally Roesch Wagner, doing research on Maud's mother, Matilda Joslyn Gage (a suffragist who worked closely with Susan B. Anthony), located Dorothy's grave. The stone was so faded with age that the inscription was nearly indecipherable, but newspaper stories about her discovery brought much attention to the site. Sadly, however, it looked as though the gravestone would not last much longer.

After hearing of this, Mickey Carroll, who had played one of the munchkins in the original MGM film, decided to help out. Carroll had operated his family business, the Standard Monument Company, in St. Louis, for nearly sixty years. He immediately contacted Evergreen Memorial Cemetery and made plans to go to Bloomington to visit the grave. An expert stone craftsman, Carroll decided to create and donate a new marker for Dorothy, and he received permission from the cemetery caretakers to do so. The new stone was installed next to the original, which was restored as much as possible. In addition, cemetery officials added a children's section to the graveyard and named it the Dorothy Gage Memorial Garden. The new section and the stone were both dedicated in October 1997.

Because of Carroll's selfless act, the grave of Dorothy—namesake for one of the most beloved characters in literature and film—is now easy to find. Just look for section 7 of the cemetery.

Oak Hill's Mysterious Spinning Sphere

In the Oak Hill Cemetery of Taylorville, there is a grave marker that seems to have a life of its own. The marker was constructed around 1910 and bears the family names Richardson and Adams. It is not an unusual monument; there are many like it in cemeteries across America. Consisting of a large marble ball set on top of a granite pedestal at the center of a family plot, it is so nondescript that it was a forgotten ornament in this cemetery for many years. That is, until local people began to notice that it moved on its own.

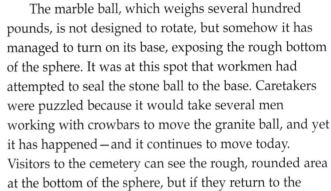

The marble ball, which weighs several hundred pounds, is not designed to rotate, but somehow it has managed to turn on its base, exposing the rough bottom of the sphere. It was at this spot that workmen had attempted to seal the stone ball to the base. Caretakers were puzzled because it would take several men working with crowbars to move the granite ball, and yet it has happened—and it continues to move today. Visitors to the cemetery can see the rough, rounded area at the bottom of the sphere, but if they return to the cemetery on another occasion, they will see the rough spot facing in another direction.

There are abundant theories regarding the huge sphere's mysterious movements. One geologist has suggested that the phenomenon is caused by the unequal expansion of the stone as one side faces the sun and the other is in shade. Some believe that weather might be the culprit. If moisture on the stone freezes at night and thaws in the daytime, the ball might shift slightly as the dampness lubricates it. While this theory may hold up in the winter months, what about in the summer, when the stone is also reported to move?

The mystery remains unsolved.

The Circus Train Tragedy of Showmen's Rest

In the summer of 1918, the Hagenbeck-Wallace Circus was touring the Midwest. Although this era was the heyday of the traveling circus, these were not good days for the company. World War I was under way, and government restrictions on the use of railroads made moving three special trains filled with equipment, 22 tents, 1,000 employees, and almost 400 animals a logistical nightmare. However, the show must go on, so routes were mapped out, and the trains somehow managed to get from place to place, arriving in time to put on a memorable show.

That July the circus was touring Indiana. After performing in Michigan City on July 21, the troupe packed up for its next stop, in Hammond. Exhausted performers caught up on their sleep as the train roared along through the night. Their plans were to mark their arrival in Hammond with a grand parade through town.

But there would be no circus parade in Hammond the next day. Just a few minutes before four a.m., on the edge of town, a speeding troop train slammed into the circus train from behind. The circus train had been stopped on the tracks due to a mechanical problem, and although red lights were displayed and a flagman was sent out, the troop train didn't stop in time, because its engineer, A. K. Sargent, had fallen asleep at the throttle. At his manslaughter trial, his defense was that he had been taking prescription medicine to combat the overwork and fatigue

caused by the war effort. The trial ended with a hung jury.

The impact destroyed a portion of the Hagenbeck-Wallace train that consisted mostly of the sleeping berths. As cars were crushed together or thrown from the tracks, the train burst into flames. Many of the sleeping passengers never woke up, and those who survived the crash were knocked unconscious by debris. Many awoke to find themselves trapped under splintered wood and twisted steel. Broken gas lanterns caused the fire to spread rapidly, and many performers were burned alive.

Although the Hammond Historical Society, which carefully researched the disaster, believes the most accurate death toll is eighty-six, there was never a complete count of how many died in the horrific crash. The problem was that no accurate lists were kept of those who traveled with the circus, and many of the workers' names were not recorded at all. The last sleeping car contained the roustabouts, temporary employees hired for day labor, many of whom were drifters and used assumed names or nicknames to identify themselves. The wreckage compounded the problem: Many bodies were simply torn to pieces or burned beyond recognition. The wreck is still remembered as one of the greatest disasters in American circus history.

On July 27, just five days after the accident, a large plot at Woodlawn Cemetery in Forest

Park was used as a final resting place for the circus performers. The Showmen's League of America, an organization founded by Buffalo Bill Cody, had purchased the plot earlier that year and donated it for the burial of fifty-six of those killed in the wreck. Tragically, only thirteen of the bodies could be positively identified. However, all were buried with dignity in separate graves with individual headstones. Most of the stones were marked unknown, but others included inscriptions of clowns and names like Baldy and 4 Horse Driver.

Since those first burials, hundreds of other circus and carnival showmen have been buried here. Five stone elephants with their trunks lowered in mourning pay tribute to those who lost their lives in the 1918 disaster and to the legion of other performers who have followed them to the grave.

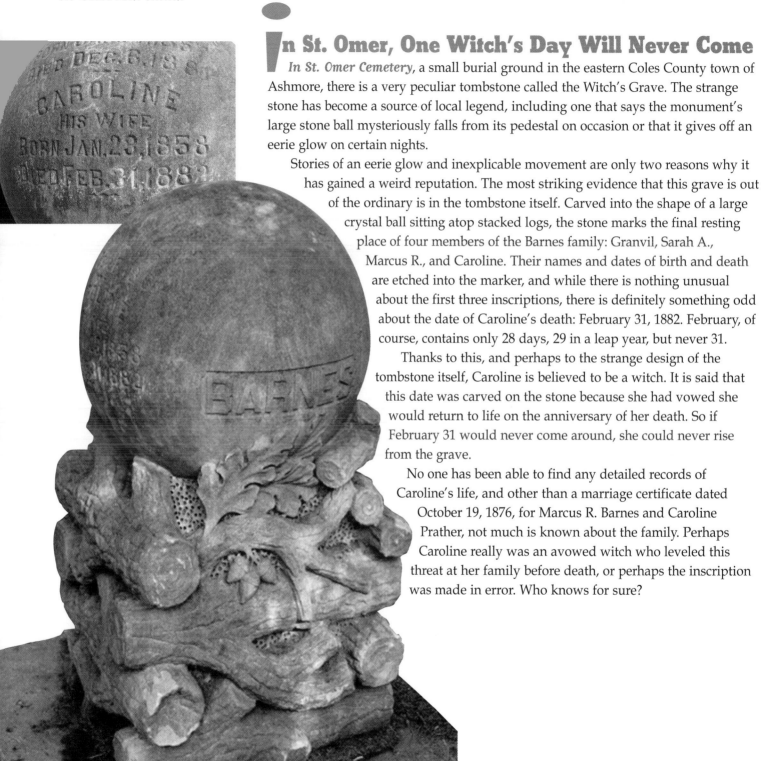

In St. Omer, One Witch's Day Will Never Come

In St. Omer Cemetery, a small burial ground in the eastern Coles County town of Ashmore, there is a very peculiar tombstone called the Witch's Grave. The strange stone has become a source of local legend, including one that says the monument's large stone ball mysteriously falls from its pedestal on occasion or that it gives off an eerie glow on certain nights.

Stories of an eerie glow and inexplicable movement are only two reasons why it has gained a weird reputation. The most striking evidence that this grave is out of the ordinary is in the tombstone itself. Carved into the shape of a large crystal ball sitting atop stacked logs, the stone marks the final resting place of four members of the Barnes family: Granvil, Sarah A., Marcus R., and Caroline. Their names and dates of birth and death are etched into the marker, and while there is nothing unusual about the first three inscriptions, there is definitely something odd about the date of Caroline's death: February 31, 1882. February, of course, contains only 28 days, 29 in a leap year, but never 31.

Thanks to this, and perhaps to the strange design of the tombstone itself, Caroline is believed to be a witch. It is said that this date was carved on the stone because she had vowed she would return to life on the anniversary of her death. So if February 31 would never come around, she could never rise from the grave.

No one has been able to find any detailed records of Caroline's life, and other than a marriage certificate dated October 19, 1876, for Marcus R. Barnes and Caroline Prather, not much is known about the family. Perhaps Caroline really was an avowed witch who leveled this threat at her family before death, or perhaps the inscription was made in error. Who knows for sure?

Bride Buried Alive in Mount Carmel

In Hillside, just outside Chicago, is Mount Carmel Cemetery. In addition to being the final resting place of Al Capone, Dion O'Banion, and other great Chicago mobsters, the cemetery is also the burial place of a woman named Julia Buccola Petta, better known as the Italian Bride. Julia's grave is marked today by a life-sized statue of the unfortunate woman in her wedding dress, modeled after the wedding photo mounted on the front of her monument. It is said that Julia's apparition appears at the statue; not surprisingly, her ghost is clad in a glowing white bridal gown.

Julia Buccola grew up on the West Side of Chicago, and when she and her husband married, they moved to a more upscale Italian neighborhood. Eventually, she became pregnant, but complications set in and she died giving birth to a stillborn child in 1921. Julia's mother, Filomena, angrily blamed her daughter's husband for the young woman's death. She claimed the body and had her buried with the Buccolas at Mount Carmel Cemetery. According to Italian tradition, a woman who dies in childbirth is a type of martyr. Filomena wanted to bury Julia in white, the martyr's color, so her wedding dress became her burial gown. Her dead infant was tucked into her arms, and the two of them were laid to rest in a single coffin.

Shortly after Julia was buried, Filomena began to have strange and terrifying dreams every night. In these nightmares, Julia told her that she was still alive and needed her help. Filomena was plagued by these dreams for the next several years, and she began trying, without success, to have her daughter's grave opened and her body exhumed. She was unable to explain why she needed to do this; she only knew that she must. Finally, due to Filomena's sheer persistence, a sympathetic judge granted her request and ordered Julia's exhumation.

In 1927, six years after Julia's death, the casket was removed from the grave. When it was opened, Filomena and other onlookers were shocked to see that Julia's body had not decayed at all. In fact, her flesh was still as soft and dewy as it had been when she was alive. At the time of the exhumation a photograph was taken of Julia's incorruptible body in the casket. It shows a young woman with fresh-looking skin who appears to be merely sleeping; there are no visible discolorations on her body, even after six years. But her coffin looks rotted and decayed, proving that it had been underground for some time. Her family considered her preserved body to be a sign from God. After collecting money from relatives and neighbors, they created the impressive monument that stands at her grave today.

The Spirited Statuary of Graceland Cemetery

Graceland Cemetery, located far away from Chicago proper along North Clark Street, was established in 1860 by real estate developer Thomas B. Bryan. Over the years, a number of different architects have worked to preserve the natural setting of its one hundred and twenty acres. Two of the men largely responsible for the beauty of the place were architects William Le Baron Jenney and Ossian Cole Simonds. Simonds became so fascinated with the site that he ended up turning his entire business over to landscape design. In addition to the natural setting, the cemetery boasts a number of wonderful monuments and buildings, including the cemetery chapel, which holds the city's oldest crematorium, built in 1893.

Graceland is home to several supernatural stories. One continues to puzzle both cemetery buffs and ghost hunters alike. It is centered around an underground vault, belonging to a man named Ludwig Wolff, which was excavated in the side of a mildly sloping hill at the south end of the cemetery. Apparently, a ghostly green-eyed dog guards the tomb and howls at the moon on some nights. Some believe the creature is a supernatural entity, while others dismiss it as nothing more than a legend that arose due to the last name of the man buried in the crypt.

Two other stories are connected to monuments in Graceland.

The first concerns the statue that was placed over the resting place of a man named Dexter Graves. He was a hotel owner and businessman who brought a group of settlers to the Chicago area in 1831. When he passed away, he was buried elsewhere, but his body was moved to Graceland in 1909. Famed sculptor Lorado Taft created a statue that was placed on the new grave. Taft christened the statue Eternal Silence, but the brooding and menacing

figure has become more popularly known as the Statue of Death.

The figure was once black, but over the years the black has mostly worn away, exposing the green, weathered metal beneath. Only one portion of it remains darkened—the face—which is hidden in the deepest folds of the figure's hood. It cloaks the ominous face in shadow, and it is said that anyone who looks directly at the face will get a glimpse of his or her own death.

Without a doubt, the most famous sculpture (and most enduring ghost) of Graceland is that of Inez Clarke. Inez died in 1880, at the tender age of six. It's said that she was killed during a lightning storm while on a family picnic. Her parents, stunned by the tragic loss, commissioned a life-sized statue of the girl to be placed on her grave. It was completed a year later and, like many Chicago-area grave sculptures, was placed in a glass box to protect it from the elements. The statue remains in nearly perfect condition today. Even in death, Inez manages to charm cemetery visitors, who discover the little girl perched on a small stool, wearing her favorite dress and holding a tiny parasol. Her perfectly formed face has just the hint of a smile. It is not uncommon to find flowers and toys placed at the foot of her grave. The site has become one of the most popular places in the cemetery, admired by graveyard buffs and curiosity-seekers alike.

Despite the statue's charming appeal, some say that Inez's grave is haunted. Not only are eerie sounds heard nearby, but the statue supposedly moves under its own power. It is reported that during violent thunderstorms Inez will sometimes vanish from inside her glass box and roam the cemetery grounds. Recent visitors to Graceland have also spotted a spectral child who sometimes appears and disappears in the vicinity of the monument.

Inez Just Won't Stay Put

There is a statue at Graceland Cemetery of a little girl named Inez Clarke. There is a glass box on her grave to protect the statue from the weather. It's not hard to find, because people leave flowers and toys for her there all the time. There's a story that says that sometimes the statue disappears from the box and walks around the cemetery. I don't know if this is true or not, but supposedly it happened one night and was seen by a Pinkerton guard who was on duty at the cemetery. He was making his rounds and found the box empty. He had heard the stories, and this scared him so bad that he quit. They say that other guards have seen it over the years too.—*Christy C.*

Legions of the Restless Dead at Rosehill Cemetery

Chicago's Rosehill Cemetery, established in 1859, is the oldest and the largest graveyard in the city. It serves as the final resting place of more than 1,500 notable Chicagoans, including a number of Civil War generals, mayors, millionaires, local celebrities, and early founders of the city. Infamous graves here include the one belonging to Reinhart Schwimmer, the unlucky eye doctor and gangster hanger-on who was killed during the St. Valentine's Day Massacre. Another grave site belongs to young Bobby Franks, the victim of thrill killers Nathan Leopold and Richard Loeb. After his death, Bobby Franks was buried at Rosehill with the understanding that his lot number would never be given out to the curious. To this day, it remains a secret, although, by accident, visitors will sometimes stumble across it among the tens of thousands of graves here.

It is said that a number of these deceased Chicagoans do not rest here peacefully, giving the cemetery a reputation for hauntings and strange happenings. Perhaps the most famous ghostly site is the tomb of Charles Hopkinson, a real estate tycoon in the mid-1800s. On the anniversary of his death, visitors have heard a horrible moaning coming from the tomb, followed by the sound of rattling chains.

Ghost lore is filled with stories of the dead returning from the grave to protest wrongs that were done to them in their lifetime or to continue rivalries they started when they were among the living. Rosehill's community mausoleum is the site of one such tale.

In 1912, cemetery officials proposed building the Rosehill Cemetery Community Mausoleum and appealed to the elite businessmen of the city for funds to begin construction. A massive multilevel structure was built, with marble passageways and row upon row of deceased Chicago notables from the world of business. It even houses the mausoleum's architect, Sidney Lovell.

Two famous men who are entombed there, Aaron Montgomery Ward and his bitter business rival, Richard Warren Sears, apparently do not find the setting very restful. It would be a wonder if either of these men could rest in peace with the other in the same structure, and many believe that the rivalry that plagued them in life still lives on in death. In fact, the ghost of Sears has been seen walking through the halls at night; visitors have spotted him, wearing a top hat and tails, heading to Ward's tomb.

The Demonic Masonic Lodge

Of the plethora of odd monuments and unusual stories connected to Rosehill Cemetery, one concerns the monument erected for the Lincoln Park Masonic Lodge. The Grand Lodge of Joliet revoked the group's charter when allegations were made that the Lincoln Park masons were dabbling in the black arts. The defunct lodge's monument features a large sphere affixed to its pinnacle. Although it weighs several tons, the sphere reportedly falls from the monument about once every decade, as if signifying that the stories told about the lodge are true.

The Two Faces of Mary Shedden

Mary Shedden was allegedly poisoned by her husband in 1931. Those who find her gravestone may have to use their imaginations a little, but they will likely see two startling visions within it. One is the young and happy face of Mary Shedden; the other is her grinning and cadaverous skull! Skeptics dismiss the tale, saying that the illusion of the faces is nothing more than a trick on the eye caused by the stone's material. Others are not so sure.

The Scent of Flowers in Winter

Lulu Fellows died at age sixteen in 1833. Visitors to her grave, above, often leave behind coins, toys, and tokens for the girl whose monument bears the words Many Hopes Lie Buried Here. A number of visitors claim to have smelled fresh flowers around her monument—even in the winter, when no fresh flowers are present.

A Mysterious Mist

The striking monument at the grave of Frances Pearce, above right, was moved from the old Chicago City Cemetery to Rosehill many years ago. It features a life-sized stone statue of Frances reclining with her infant daughter. The figures are encased inside a glass box. Apparently, on the anniversary of their deaths, a glowing white haze fills the interior of the glass box as mother and daughter reach out from beyond the grave for the husband and father they left behind.

Pining for a Lost Love

The specter of another doomed soul belongs to Elizabeth Archer, an attractive young woman who committed suicide after her high school sweetheart, Arnold Fischel, was killed in an accident in the 1950s. They had been students together at Senn High School on the North Side, and their deep devotion was obvious. Grief-stricken by the death of his daughter, Elizabeth's father erected the Archer-Fischel Monument, where Elizabeth is sometimes seen lurking on cold nights in the month of November.

The Little Girl at the Gate

Philomena Boyington was the granddaughter of William W. Boyington, the architect who designed Rosehill's gothic gates. According to lore, people who pass by the cemetery at night may see Philomena peering out at them from the window to the left and just below the bell tower of the Ravenswood gates. It is said that the young girl often played near the site when the gates were being constructed back in 1864. She was buried at the cemetery after she died of pneumonia not long after the gates were completed, and she has haunted the site ever since.

A Friend of the Wickedest Man in the World

Gerhardt Foreman was a contemporary of the notorious British occultist, Alistair Crowley. For several years, Foreman studied in England with the so-called wickedest man in the world, and after returning to America, he was instrumental in spreading the word of the Golden Dawn throughout the country. He also helped found the Ancient and Mystical Order of the Rosicrucians. Foreman's mausoleum in Rosehill is chained shut—some say to keep his ghost from wandering about.

The Curse of the Pharaoh Lives On

Darius Miller had a keen interest in ancient Egypt, and it is readily apparent in his mausoleum, a replica of the Egyptian Temple of Anubis. Miller's death—and the stories that surround his marvelous tomb—have long been of keen interest to enthusiasts of the supernatural.

Darius Miller was the curator of Egyptology at Chicago's Field Museum of Natural History. He was in Egypt in November 1922 when Howard Carter and Lord Carnarvon opened the tomb of Pharaoh Tutankhamen in the Valley of the Kings. While this must have been the experience of a lifetime for Miller, it also made him susceptible to the Curse of the Pharaoh, which says that anyone who witnessed the opening of the tomb would soon die. True to the curse, he died mysteriously the following spring.

Whatever caused Darius Miller's death, tales persist that his tomb in Rosehill is haunted, and it is said that every May 1, during the early-morning hours, a blue light emanates from the tomb. To this day, no one has offered a satisfactory explanation for this, and some supernatural buffs insist that the light is Miller's spirit calling out from the other side more than eight decades after his death.

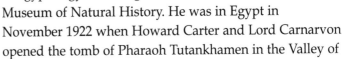

Lincoln's Restless History at Oak Ridge

Oak Ridge Cemetery, on the edge of the town of Springfield, seems innocuous enough for a graveyard. Established in the 1860s, this remote rural burial ground is dotted with thick stands of trees. But this cemetery, as well as the grand monument here that marks the tomb of former president Abraham Lincoln, has long been a vortex of mystery, intrigue, and bizarre speculation about the real location of Lincoln's body.

A native of Springfield, Lincoln himself chose Oak Ridge as his final resting place. After he was assassinated, in April 1865, Mary Todd Lincoln remained true to her husband's wishes and requested that he be buried there, despite city leaders' insistence that his grave should be somewhere more central.

After traveling west from Washington along a circuitous route so that people could pay their respects, Lincoln's body arrived at Oak Ridge on May 4. The body of his son Willie, who had died during Lincoln's presidency, had accompanied him from Washington, while the body of his son Eddie, who had died many years earlier, was exhumed and brought over from another cemetery.

Once reunited, all three were placed in a receiving vault while workers began building a temporary tomb to house them until a permanent monument could be built. Seven months later, on December 21, the temporary tomb was finished. Six of Lincoln's friends wanted to be sure his body was still in the coffin before he was interred, so they asked a plumber's assistant, Leon P. Hopkins, to cut an opening in the lead box for them to peer inside. All was well, a square was soldered over the hole, and Lincoln and his sons were laid to rest. In a newspaper story published soon after, Hopkins stated that he was "the last man to look upon the face of Abraham Lincoln," but at that moment, he had no idea just how many more times he would look upon the President's face.

Construction of the permanent tomb took more than five years, and it was during this period that people began reporting strange occurrences in the vicinity of Lincoln's resting place. Springfield residents and curiosity-seekers began relating tales of a spectral Lincoln wandering near the temporary vault. Occasionally the shadowy figure was accompanied by the sound of weeping. The reports appeared in local newspapers and were the first ghost stories about Lincoln—but many more would follow. Sobbing noises and footsteps were also heard after the bodies were moved to the finished monument, but this was just one part of the strange story surrounding Lincoln's final tomb.

On September 19, 1871, the caskets of Lincoln and his sons were removed from the temporary vault and taken to the catacomb—a finished section inside the monument where the bodies would remain until the whole monument was completed. During the move, friends noticed that Lincoln's mahogany outer coffin was beginning to deteriorate, so they bought a new one of iron. But before transferring his inner lead coffin into it, they again had Hopkins cut a small hole in the inner coffin, and the same six friends peered at the President's face. Satisfied, they laid Lincoln to rest for another three years. At last, on October 9, 1874, the monument was completed, and Lincoln's coffin was put into the

BIRTH PLACE of ABRAHAM LINCOLN, ELISABETHTOWN, HARDENS Co. KY.

ABRAHAM LINCOLN'S RESIDENCE AT SPRINGFIELD ILL.

THE LINCOLN MONUMENT AT SPRINGFIELD, ILLINOIS, DEDICATED THURSDAY, OCTOBER 15TH.—PHOTOGRAPHED BY J. Q. A. TRESIZE.—SEE PAGE 110.

permanent marble sarcophagus at the center of the semicircular catacomb.

But then a new threat arose that no one could have predicted. In November 1876, a band of thieves broke into the tomb and lifted the casket partway out. Their plan was to hold the body for ransom. The plot failed only because one of the men in their ranks was a spy for the Secret Service. The would-be grave robbers fled, empty-handed.

Hundreds of people flocked to Lincoln's burial site, and many asked about the robbery attempt. Custodian John C. Power gave evasive answers. He was terrified of one question in particular, and it seemed to be the one asked most often: Was he sure that Lincoln's body was in the sarcophagus? Power was afraid of that question for one good reason: At that time, Lincoln's grave was completely empty!

Back on the November morning when John T. Stuart of

the Lincoln National Monument Association had learned about the attempted robbery, he had rushed out to the site. Fearing the return of the grave robbers, he made a decision: He told the custodian that they must hide Lincoln's body elsewhere in the building. Together, they decided the best place for it would be in the maze of passages between the catacomb and the monument's Memorial Hall.

That afternoon a Springfield marble worker and some of his assistants lifted Lincoln's casket from the sarcophagus, then cemented the lid back into place. Later that night Johnson, Power, and three members of the Monument Association sneaked out to the monument and carried the five-hundred-pound coffin into the dark labyrinth, placing it near some leftover construction materials. The following day Johnson built a new outer coffin while Power set to work digging a grave in the dirt floor. It was slow going because it had to be done between visitors to the site, and Power also had a problem with water seeping into the hole. Finally he gave up and simply covered the coffin with some leftover boards.

As Lincoln lay beneath a pile of debris in the labyrinth, visitors from all over the world wept and mourned over the sarcophagus at the other end of the monument. They continued to ask questions about the theft attempt—questions full of suspicion, as if they knew something they really had no way of knowing.

Then, in the summer and fall of 1877, the tale took another strange turn. Workmen arrived at the monument to erect statuary depicting naval and infantry groups on the monument's upper deck. Their work would take them into the labyrinth, where Power feared they would discover the coffin. The scandal would be incredible, so Power quickly called the workmen together and, swearing them to secrecy, showed them where the coffin was. They promised to keep the secret, but within days everyone in Springfield seemed to know that Lincoln's body was not where it was supposed to be. Soon the story was spreading all over the country.

Power was now in a panic. The body had to be more securely hidden, and to do this, he needed more help. He explained the situation to two of his friends, Major Gustavas Dana and General Jasper Reece, and they brought three other Springfield men to meet with Power.

On the night of November 18, the six men began digging a grave for Lincoln at the far end of the labyrinth. Cramped, cold, and stifled by stale air, they gave up around midnight. The coffin was just barely covered, and traces of their activity were very evident, but Power promised to finish the work the next day. These six men, along with three others they had brought in to help, were sobered by the responsibility they had taken on and decided to form a brotherhood to guard the secret of the tomb. They called themselves the Lincoln Guard of Honor and had badges made for their lapels. Eventually the Guard finished its work, and things were quiet . . . but for only a few years.

When Mary Todd Lincoln died five years later, in 1882, she was at first laid to rest in the catacomb. But Robert, the only Lincoln son who had survived into adulthood, told John T. Stuart he wanted his mother's body placed next to his father's spot. So, late on the night of July 21, Stuart and the Guard slipped into the monument and buried Mary's double-leaded casket in the labyrinth next to Lincoln's.

Visitors to the tomb increased as the years went by, all of them paying their respects to the two empty crypts in the catacomb, but also asking Power questions about Lincoln's real grave. With all of the foot traffic, the crypt became worn, and in 1886, the Lincoln National Monument Association decided to replace it with a new and stronger crypt of brick and mortar.

The press was kept outside as the Guard and others

who shared the secret of the tomb brought the Lincoln caskets out of the labyrinth. Eighteen people who had known Lincoln in life filed past the casket, peering into the again uncovered hole that Leon P. Hopkins had cut into the lead coffin years earlier. Strangely, Lincoln had changed very little. His face had darkened a little after twenty-two years, but he still had the same sad, familiar features. The last man to identify the body was Hopkins, who then soldered the square back over the hole, perhaps again thinking that he would be the last person to ever look upon the face of Abraham Lincoln.

The Guard of Honor took Lincoln's and Mary's coffins into the catacomb and lowered them into the new brick-and-mortar crypt, where they were supposed to rest for all time. But all time lasted only another thirteen years. The monument had settled unevenly over time, cracking in places, so in 1899, Illinois legislators decided to tear down the whole thing and build a new one on the old foundation.

There was once again the question of what to do with the bodies of the Lincoln family. The remaining members of the Guard of Honor came up with a clever plan. During the fifteen-month construction period, the Lincolns would be buried secretly in a multiple grave a few feet away from the foundations of the monument. As the old structure was torn down, tons of stone and dirt would be heaped onto the grave site—both to disguise and protect it. As the new monument was built, the grave would gradually be uncovered.

When the new building was completed, the bodies were exhumed once again. Lincoln's coffin, which had been buried beneath the others and so safely hidden that the side of the temporary vault had to be battered away to reach it, was the last to be removed. It was close to sunset when it was finally hoisted up out of the ground. After the protective outer box was removed, six construction workers carried the coffin on their shoulders into the catacomb, then dispersed after switching on the new electric burglar alarm. This device connected the monument to the caretaker's house, a few hundred feet away.

As up-to-date as this device was, it still did not calm the fears of Robert Lincoln, who was sure that someone would try again to snatch his father's body. On his next trip to Springfield, he brought with him his own set of security plans and gave officials explicit directions: He wanted the construction company to break a hole in the tile floor of the monument and place his father's casket at a depth of ten feet. The coffin would then be encased in a cage of steel bars, and the hole would be filled with concrete, turning the President's final resting place into a solid block of stone.

On September 26, 1901, a group assembled to make the final arrangements for Lincoln's last burial. The discussion quickly turned into a heated debate. Should the coffin be opened and the body viewed one last time? Most felt this would be wise, especially given the ongoing rumors about Lincoln's missing body. The Guard of Honor was all for laying the tales to rest, but Robert was against any further invasion of his father's privacy by opening the casket again.

In the end, practicality won out and Leon P. Hopkins was brought in to chisel out an opening in the lead coffin. The casket was placed on two sawhorses in the still unfinished Memorial Hall. The room was described as hot and poorly lit, as newspapers had been pasted over the windows to keep out the stares of the curious.

Hopkins cut a small hole in the coffin and lifted the piece away. According to diaries, a "strong and reeking odor" filled the room, but the group pressed close to the opening anyway. The face of the President was still covered with a fine powder of white chalk, which an

upon the face of Lincoln. The casket was then lowered down into the cage of steel, and two tons of cement was poured over it, forever encasing the President's body in stone.

That should have been the end of it, but as with all lingering mysteries, a few questions remain.

undertaker had applied in 1865 when Lincoln's face turned inexplicably black as his body traveled around the country for mourners to view.

Lincoln's features were said to be completely recognizable. The casket's headrest had fallen away, and his head was thrown back slightly, revealing his still perfectly trimmed beard. His small black tie and dark hair were as they had been in life, although his eyebrows had vanished. The broadcloth suit that he had worn to his second inauguration was covered with small patches of yellow mold, and the American flag he clutched in his lifeless hands was now in tatters.

According to those present, there was no question that this was Abraham Lincoln. The casket was sealed back up again by Hopkins, making his claim from many years ago finally true: He really would be the last person to look

Does the body of Abraham Lincoln really lie encased in concrete in the catacomb? Or was Robert Lincoln's plan part of some elaborate ruse to throw off any further attempts to steal the President's body? Did Robert simply arrange with the Guard of Honor to have his father's body hidden in a different location altogether?

Most historians would agree that Lincoln's body is safely encased in the crypt, but consider this with a conspiratorial eye for a moment. Whose word do we have that Lincoln's body is where they say it is? We have only the statement of Lincoln's son Robert, his friends, and of course, the Guard of Honor. But weren't these the same individuals who let visitors to the monument grieve before an empty sarcophagus while the President was actually hidden in the labyrinth beneath a few inches of dirt?

Sort of makes you wonder, doesn't it?

Abandoned in Illinois

More years ago than I would care to admit to now, I happened upon an old, abandoned house in the woods. Such unusual finds were not uncommon for me. I grew up on a farm in a rural part of Illinois, and during the summer months I would often explore the back roads, cemeteries, and stretches of forest near my parents' home. However, this particular house turned out to be a little more unusual than most.

The old house was located in a dark stand of woods, and it did not appear that anyone had lived in it for many years. There was no path left through the woods that would have provided access to the surrounding roadways. Only a shallow track remained, and it had long since been covered with brush and decades of fallen leaves. Remarkably,

though, the structure looked to be in fairly good condition. I crossed the sagging porch, pushed open the leaning front door, and entered the shadowy interior.

Strangely, all the furniture had been left. There were even photographs on the walls and coats hanging in a closet. Although there was evidence of animals passing through and the weathering of years passing by, all in all the place had been eerily preserved.

This was all strange enough, but it was the kitchen that would unsettle me the most. There were still plates and silverware on the table and pots and pans sitting on the stove. It was as if the family that had once lived here had suddenly simply gotten up and walked away—never to return.

What could have happened to cause people to just leave a house and everything they owned and to disappear?

The house has long since been destroyed, and the mystery has never been solved. I returned many times to that house over the next several years, and though I eventually moved away, I never forgot this place. I searched many times for some clue as to where the former occupants had gone, but I never found anything.

From the moment I walked into that house, my interest in abandoned sites began, and I have ever since been on the lookout for weird and empty places, crumbling buildings, decaying structures. There is

nothing that will make me turn off the highway faster than seeing a long forgotten farm, church, or house.

Sadly, places like this have become harder and harder to find. "Progress" and urban renewal have wiped out many historic places, as well as the otherwise ordinary buildings and homes that were once hidden in the fields and woods of Illinois. So whenever I get a lead on an abandoned place, I attempt to track it down—which is what once led me to make a trip to a small town in the southern part of the state.

An old friend of mine had told me of a place that he remembered when he was growing up. Located in the town of Colp was a joint that was once called Ma Hatchet's. This fabled brothel was known all over the region and reputedly was noted for the number of beautiful girls that Ma Hatchet kept in her employ. Ma Hatchet's was a legendary place and, according to my friend, now sat abandoned, silently crumbling and forgotten.

After hearing this story, I became determined to find the former brothel and to resurrect its stories. This was a tale that desperately needed to be told— a little piece of unusual history that only a handful of people would still remember but that would fascinate many.

Some readers can likely guess the end of this story. I traveled to Colp but soon learned that the old building had been torn down several years earlier; another piece of local history had been lost.

This is why the places in this chapter are important. If nothing else, they will serve to preserve a bit of Illinois history. And I hope they will inspire you to seek out these sites on your own.

This is a weird and spooky place, and even those who do not believe in ghosts or hauntings will admit that the cemetery has a very mysterious air.

The Mausoleum on Eagle Cliff

One of the eeriest landmarks of southwestern Illinois is an abandoned mausoleum that looks out from the edge of Eagle Cliff toward the distant Mississippi. The mausoleum is in a cemetery located about eight miles north of the small town of Valmeyer. The site was once a grand estate, built by an accomplished violinist named Stephen Miles, who moved to Illinois from New York. Miles was a veteran of the War of 1812, for which he received land in Monroe County, Illinois; he arrived to settle the land in 1819. After establishing a home near Eagle Cliff, Miles began to prosper and soon owned several thousand acres of fertile farmland—much of which he bought at the government office in Kaskaskia, but he also purchased the claims of other settlers. Legend has it that after these settlers had transferred their claims to Miles, they would disappear, sometimes mysteriously.

Today, only the abandoned mausoleum remains to remind us of the glory of the Miles estate. An inscription on the large marble panel to the right of the doorway informs the visitor that it was built in 1858 by Stephen W. Miles, Esquire, the son of the elder Miles, as a memorial to the Miles family and their descendants. It states that the mausoleum was to be cared for by the eldest son of each generation to hold it "through this succession in trust for the above family." However, the bankruptcy of the younger Miles brought this plan to an end. The vault, which had been built to hold fifty-six bodies, housed only eleven—those of Miles, his two wives, and other descendants. Some say that Miles's mistress and some servants were buried in the tomb.

In the early 1960s, curiosity-seekers who managed to find the mausoleum found that vandals had already wrecked the place years before; the vaults inside the crypt were torn apart, and marble and broken wood from the caskets were scattered over the floor. Visitors found numerous bones with pieces of dried flesh still clinging to them, cloth from burial shrouds, bits of glass from the coffins, and other assorted debris. There were stories of grave robbers who stole jewelry from bodies that had been in the vaults.

Things got even worse in the late 1960s, when a cult group broke into the mausoleum and pulled the remaining bodies from the crypt. Attempting to "raise the dead," they burned the corpses of Miles and his descendants, desecrating the area forever. Is it any wonder that the mausoleum is said to be haunted?

Since that time, members of the Miles Cemetery Association have thoroughly cleaned up the mausoleum and the cemetery on the cliff and have worked hard to preserve the site. But despite a dusk-to-dawn curfew, problems still occur: The interior of the tomb is often marred by spray paint and by obscure messages that mean nothing to anyone other than those who left them.

This is a weird and spooky place, and even those who do not believe in ghosts or hauntings will admit that the cemetery has a very mysterious air.

McPike Mansion

The infamous McPike Mansion, located on Alby Street in Alton, is well known throughout southwestern Illinois. It was built in 1869 for Henry Guest McPike, who was active in the business and political community of Alton; he eventually served as mayor of the town and became the president of the oldest horticultural society in Illinois. During the Civil War, he had held a management position in the War Department.

McPike's Italianate-Victorian mansion, still one of the more elaborate homes in Alton, has sixteen rooms and a vaulted wine cellar. It stood on fifteen acres—which McPike called Mount Lookout—that, thanks to his interest in all things horticultural, were planted with rare trees and shrubs, orchards, flowers, and extensive vineyards.

The McPike family lived at the estate for some time after Henry died in 1910. Some reports say that they stayed in the house until 1936, while others say that Paul A. Laichinger purchased the place in 1925 and lived there until his death in 1945. Laichinger reportedly died from an illness caused by his heavy smoking. The house then may have become a rooming house, but that must have failed, since the place was silent and empty for years. Finally it was sold to a developer who planned to demolish it and turn the site into a shopping center. Those plans were scrapped, and the condition of the house went rapidly downhill.

Thieves and vandals descended on the place and stole everything that was not nailed down and many things that were, including marble fireplace mantels, banisters, chandeliers, and plumbing fixtures. It was destruction for the sheer thrill of it.

In the 1980s, the gutters failed and water began to seep into the house. The roof started to deteriorate and leak, and since all the windows were broken, the damaged interior was left to the elements. The days of Mount Lookout seemed numbered.

Fortunately, in 1994, Sharyn and George Luedke purchased the house at auction. They had always wanted to fix up an old house, and this purchase seemed a dream come true—but the restoration has been an uphill battle. Contrary to assurances they received on the day of the auction, they discovered that no grant money was available for restoring the house from any federal, state, or local agencies. However, they continue with their plans, determined to ensure that the McPike Mansion remains a part of the city's present and future—and not just its past.

Throughout much of its history, Mount Lookout has had a reputation for being haunted. Ghost stories abound, including many firsthand accounts from reliable people with absolutely no reason to lie. Almost from the beginning, Sharyn Luedke believed the house was haunted by the ghost of Paul Laichinger. Even today it is not uncommon for visitors to smell strong whiffs of cigarette smoke—even though no smoking has been permitted in the structure in decades. Sharyn told *Weird Illinois* that on one occasion a group of people at the house not only smelled the smoke but actually saw a cloud of it appear above their heads.

Sharyn says that she had her first encounter with the ghost about six weeks after she bought the house. She was watering some plants in the garden when she noticed a man standing in the window, looking out at her. A chill came over her. She had enough presence of mind to note that the man, who quickly vanished, was wearing a striped shirt and a tie. Sharyn later obtained a photograph of Laichinger, and he was wearing identical attire. She now believes that it was his presence that she witnessed.

As time has passed, many unresolved mysteries have arisen about the McPike Mansion. Hundreds of stories have been told by ordinary people who never expected to find anything out of the ordinary in this crumbling old house. It is an eerie yet wonderful place—a part of our haunted history that we hope to enjoy for years to come.

Old Stone House

Along the Illinois River near the small communities of Eldred and Hillview is one of the most famous places in this region: the Old Stone House. It is the site of murder, mystery, lost treasure, and perhaps even a ghost or two.

The Old Stone House was built in 1848 by a wealthy cattleman named Azariah Sweetin, who had come to America from England, where he had been a stonemason. When he arrived in Illinois, he decided to build a magnificent mansion from the native stone that could be found on his new property. The lime was burned in kilns, and limestone was then hewn into large blocks, creating three-foot-thick walls for the house. All of the woodwork was walnut, and the mansion was cooled by a large tank that ran with natural spring water, an early form of air-conditioning. The third floor held a large ballroom where special dances were held on July 4, Christmas, and New Year's. That floor had two west windows, which were kept lighted as a signal for passing steamboats.

There are a number of legends concerning the mansion and the lost treasure that is said to be hidden there. The most famous story, altered and embellished over the years, concerns a murder that took place at a dance held at the house in 1862. The party was being given for men who would soon be departing for Civil War battlefields.

During the party, the sons of two local farmers began arguing, and the disagreement soon turned heated. Tired of bickering, one of the young men threw up his hands in disgust and walked away. When he turned, the other man took a large knife from his belt and stabbed him in the back. The wounded soldier cried out in pain and then crumpled onto a fireplace hearth; he lay bleeding on the rough stone until he died a few hours later.

This story has been passed down for decades because an image of the young man's body appeared on the hearth soon after his body was removed. The blood that he spilled had seeped into the stone in the perfect outline of the corpse and the stain could not be removed, no matter how much scrubbing was done. For many years, stories were told about the bloodstains on the hearth, and some people say the outline remains there today—if you know where to look among the ruins of the house.

But this is not the only strange tale of the Old Stone House. There is a lingering mystery that involves the lost treasure of Azariah Sweetin. Legend has it that the old man made a fortune trading cattle before the Civil War, but during the fighting, he lost faith in banks and began hiding gold coins all around his property. Some claimed that the coins were hidden in coffee cans; others said he put them in wooden chests or perhaps beneath the floorboards or secreted within the masonry of the fireplaces.

No one knew for sure—including Azariah Sweetin himself, because, the story goes, one day he was thrown from his horse and hit his head; he was never the same again and could not remember where he had hidden his money. Although his family searched for it, they never discovered the hiding place.

Eventually, the mansion fell into ruin. Once it was abandoned, local youths, treasure hunters, and curiosity-seekers tore the house apart in a search for the lost gold. The mansion was nearly destroyed by the looting, but the gold was never found—leading many to believe that it was never hidden there, but rather in one of the caves in the bluff behind the house.

But beware. Searching for the treasure is hazardous: The caves are hiding places for rattlesnakes, whose telltale rattling sounds have frightened off many gold-seekers.

The snakes are not, according to the legend, the only guardians of the gold. Some say the ghost of Azariah Sweetin lingers there too, watching over his treasure, having found in death what he lost in life.

The Hartford Castle

Hartford Castle, a magnificent house once located near the small town of Hartford, is long gone; its ruins — crumbling foundations, some broken statuary, a decaying stone gazebo, and a murky, water-filled moat — remain, hidden in the woods along New Poag Road. But in addition to the abandoned ruins, stories of the legendary place remain as well, stories of tragic death, bootleggers, and ghosts.

Lakeview, as the castlelike house was officially known, was constructed by a French immigrant named Benjamin Biszant in 1897 and was incredibly expensive. The source of Biszant's wealth is unknown. He may have been an insurance executive, a contractor, or an investor of some sort, but whatever his profession, he was able to purchase a large section of land and begin construction on what was to be a dream house for his English bride.

Teams of workers with horses were brought in to excavate a moat around what would be the homesite; the soil removed to create the moat formed a rise on which Lakeview was built. When the house was completed, it boasted fourteen rooms and red-capped turrets that loomed high above the surrounding countryside. The castle's floors were made of imported cypress wood, and the ceilings were supported by hand-carved columns. Crystal chandeliers hung from the ceiling in the mirror lined main hall, and music could often be heard drifting out over the fields in the evening.

The landscaped gardens were decorated with gazebos and statuary, and Biszant filled the grounds with his own concrete creations of animals and cannons. A stone bridge was built to reach an island in the middle of one of the small lakes on the property. Biszant stocked the lakes with goldfish; once when high waters brought crappie into the lakes, they mated with the goldfish. Locals remembered some strange-looking fish in the water after that.

Tragically, Biszant's wife died in the early 1900s, and he returned her body to England. He then lost interest in the castle, sold it, and moved to California. Soon thereafter, ghost stories about the place told of a lingering spirit of the Frenchman's wife, who was haunting the place that she had loved most in life.

The castle had several owners after Biszant and was reported to have been a boys' military school and later a school for unwed mothers. In the early 1920s, it was turned into a resort and may have been operated for a time as a speakeasy.

Later the castle was purchased by a couple from Wood River, who soon began to have problems with intruders and trespassers. The place seemed to be viewed by the public as community property or a park, and the owners stated that people would often just roam through the thirty-five acres at all hours of the day and night. Some even broke into the occupied house and wandered from room to room as if on a tour. Hoping to counteract this invasion of privacy, the family opened the grounds to the public on weekends for several years, but eventually, this practice ended and the property was again closed down.

In 1964, the owner died, and his wife moved back to Wood River. The house soon began crumbling into ruin, and the lawn became thick and overgrown. In 1972 intruders gutted the residence, ripped mantels from the fireplaces, broke windows, and, using a small telephone pole as a battering ram, smashed huge holes in the plaster walls. The senseless destruction led to the mansion's being officially condemned by county inspectors.

The final blow was dealt to the castle on March 21, 1973, when it burned to the ground. An alarm was sounded, but by the time firefighters arrived on the scene, only a tall chimney and burning embers remained. Today, only those who know the history of the estate would have any clue that the scattered ruins were once a part of a grand place.

There are those who maintain that the estate is still haunted by the Frenchman's wife, whose spectral form can be seen wandering through the remains of the castle, and that her voice can still be heard as she weeps for the life and the wonderful home that she lost. Others insist that old-time music can sometimes be heard floating through the trees and above the fields on summer nights when the crops are tall and when sound seems to carry for miles. Perhaps in another time and place, Lakeview still stands and the party continues, beckoning to all of us.

In its final years, after the last patients had departed, staff members started to report some odd occurrences in the now-empty wards and cells.

Bartonville State Asylum

If spirits truly are the personalities of those who once lived, then surely these spirits reflect whatever turmoil plagued them in life. As proof, you need look no further than the strange events at the old State Mental Hospital in Bartonville, a small town near Peoria.

In its final years, after the last patients had departed, staff members started to report some odd occurrences in the now-empty wards and cells. In more recent years, many vandals and trespassers claim to have had their own weird encounters in the place.

The first ghost story about the hospital came from its founder, Dr. George A. Zeller, who was one of the most influential mental health care providers in Illinois history. Shortly after the hospital opened in 1902, Dr. Zeller supervised the creation of cemeteries for the facility and a burial corps to deal with interment. Dr. Zeller's burial corps always consisted of a staff member and several patients competent enough to take part in the digging of graves. Of all the grave-diggers, the most unusual man was a fellow called A. Bookbinder. Old Book, as he was affectionately known, had come to the hospital from a county poorhouse. He had suffered a mental breakdown and lost the power of coherent speech while working in a printing house in Chicago. The officer who had taken him into custody had noted in his report that the man had been employed as a bookbinder, and a court clerk inadvertently listed this as the man's name. After Old Book was attached to the burial corps, attendants soon realized that he was especially suited

to the work. During Old Book's first interment, he removed his cap and began to weep loudly for the dead man.

"His emotion became contagious and there were many moist eyes at the graveside," Dr. Zeller wrote.

Old Book would do the same thing at each service. As his grief reached its peak, he would lean against an old elm tree in the center of the cemetery and sob loudly. Eventually Old Book died. More than one hundred nurses attended his funeral, along with male staff members and several hundred patients. As the last hymn was sung, four men grabbed the ropes holding the casket above the empty grave.

"At a given signal," Dr. Zeller wrote, "they heaved away the ropes and the next instant, all four lay on their backs. For the coffin, instead of offering resistance, bounded into the air like an eggshell, as if it were empty!"

"In the midst of the commotion," Dr. Zeller continued, "a wailing voice was heard and every eye turned toward the Graveyard Elm from whence it emanated. There stood Old Book, weeping and moaning with an earnestness that outrivaled anything he had ever shown before. . . . It was broad daylight and there could be no deception."

After a few moments, the doctor summoned some men to remove the lid of the coffin. As soon as the lid was lifted, the wailing sound came to an end. Inside the casket lay the body of Old Book, unquestionably dead. Everybody looked over to the elm tree. The specter had vanished!

"It was awful, but it was real," Dr. Zeller concluded. "I saw it, 100 nurses saw it and 300 spectators saw it." If it was anything other than the ghost of Old Book, Dr. Zeller had no idea what it could have been.

A few days after the funeral the Graveyard Elm began to wither, and within the year it died. Later, workmen tried to cut down the tree but stopped after the first cut of the axe caused the tree to emit what was said to be "an

agonized, despairing cry of pain." After that, Dr. Zeller suggested that the tree be burned, but as soon as the flames started around the tree's base, the workers, hearing a crying sound coming from it, quickly put out the flames.

The hospital was finally closed down in 1972 and remained empty for a number of years before being sold at auction in 1980.

Even though the site is private property and trespassing is forbidden, vandals and would-be ghost hunters still enter the place. Many claim to have encountered some pretty frightening things, from unexplained sounds to full-blown apparitions. Some might even say that many of the former patients are still around!

"The place is full of spirits" has been said on more than one occasion. I wouldn't be surprised if this proclamation is right.

The Gravedigger's Ghost

The Bartonville Asylum is haunted. There are four different buildings and a lot of hidden passageways. One part that is boarded up used to be the shower room and was thought to be a torture chamber. We went into one of the buildings last summer, and it was freaky. It was ninety-five degrees out, but as soon as I went in the building with my friends, the temperature dropped to below thirty. There was a downstairs, and we were going to go down into it, but we heard a lot of stuff, then left in a hurry.

I have been back since, but never went in. I just went to the graveyard. That place is very haunted. There is a ghost of a gravedigger that we have seen under a weeping willow.—*Chris B.*

Manteno State Hospital

Just south of Chicago, near a small town called Manteno, is a crumbling collection of buildings that once were part of the Manteno State Hospital. Although the hospital has been closed for nearly twenty years and many of the original buildings are gone, the place still manages to draw a steady stream of visitors.

The state of Illinois purchased one thousand acres of farmland in 1927 for the hospital, and construction began two years later. The design chosen was called the cottage plan, which was meant to give the inmates a homelike setting. Unfortunately, the cottages at Manteno were vast dormitories that were not homelike at all and afforded little privacy for the patients or staff. Most of the structures were of the Georgian Revival style, with circular windows, arched doorways and windows, low-pitched hipped roofs, rectangular windows, and occasional columns and cupolas.

The original twenty-four cottages at Manteno were actually large buildings with two main entrances, and included dining halls and dormitories. Eight additional two-story cottages were used as alcoholic wards in the 1950s and 1960s and were then closed down in the 1970s—some say because it was too easy for suicidal patients to jump from the upper story onto the inner staircases. The hospital was a city in itself. It had its own road system, kitchens, bakeries, general store, restaurant, security force, fire department, and a utilities system that was sufficient to run a moderate-sized town. A power plant produced steam that ran turbines to generate electricity and to heat the buildings. Heat, as well as hot water, was sent throughout the complex using underground tunnels that connected all of the buildings.

The tunnels could be reached from the basements of the various buildings and were most likely used not only to contain steam pipes, but also for staff access between the cottages.

In 1936, the hospital purchased an

Patients at Manteno suffered from many different illnesses . . . but the greatest percentage of the population was sent there for elder care, alcoholism, or schizophrenia.

Administration Building
Manteno Ill. State Hospital

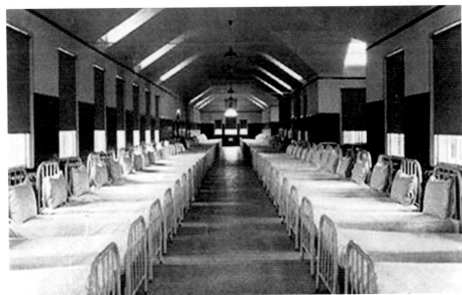

additional two hundred acres for a farm, which was to be managed by hospital employees, assisted by the patients, to grow grain and raise cattle and hogs to feed the inmates and staff. For years, the outdoor work was considered therapy for the patients, but the idea was eventually abandoned. All but four of the farm buildings were torn down in 1968 and the land was leased to local farmers to raise corn and soybeans.

Patients at Manteno suffered from many different illnesses, including depression, senility, and syphilitic disease, but the greatest percentage of the population was sent there for elder care, alcoholism, or schizophrenia. Physical restraints were not normally used, except in extremely violent cases, and while straitjackets were not often employed, patients suffering from outbursts or seizures were often placed in wrist or ankle cuffs. In addition, lobotomies and electroshock therapy were performed at Manteno from the 1940s to the 1960s.

Many of the inmates were not only mentally, but also physically, ill. There was a morgue on the premises, as well as a cemetery, which was shared with and cared for by the Veterans Administration. Patients were commonly buried on the grounds, because many of them did not have families or their families could not afford to bury them elsewhere. At the hospital, the state covered the cost of the burials.

Manteno State Hospital was closed down in 1985, and most of the inmates were transferred to other facilities. However, some that were deemed cured were released, and there are many stories about former patients who returned to the abandoned halls and buildings of Manteno—wandering about the only safe place they ever knew.

Some of the original hospital buildings remain today. A few have been renovated and are used by various companies, while others await new owners, funding, or destruction. The Illinois Veterans Home at Manteno occupies the northern portion of the campus, and a local bank occupies the former administration building. They have kept the building in its original condition, including the magnificent lobby and grand staircases. The cupola-topped tower can be seen from all over the grounds, and when illuminated at night, it is visible from more than a mile away.

Other buildings have been left abandoned, and there have been many incursions into them over the years. Each visitor has his or her own story to tell of dark tunnels, empty rooms, abandoned corridors, and spooky relics that have been left behind. Some people have entire collections of artifacts, including hospital robes, gowns, and even pieces of furniture. Scores of photographs taken by the curious will perhaps provide the best souvenirs in years to come, bearing witness to a place that is a rarely talked about part of Illinois history.

Nazi Prisoners in the Woods of Camp Pine

Deep in the Cook County Forest Preserve near Des Plaines are crumbling concrete foundations that once supported a collection of wooden barracks used to house 215 well-fed German prisoners of war. The old foundations and a rusted flagpole are all that remain today.

The encampment, once known as Camp Pine, was located about a half mile south of Lake Street and east of the River Road near the Des Plaines River. It was constructed in 1934 by the Civilian Conservation Corps (CCC) to provide employment for young men unable to find work during the Great Depression. For several years the men built various public works, and were employed in city and state parks and on constructing and repairing highways. But once the United States entered World War II, Camp Pine fell into disuse.

Rather than tear down the old barracks at this and other CCC camps across the country, Congress gave permission for them to be converted into housing for the tens of thousands of German soldiers captured in North Africa and Italy. The logistics of shipping food to Europe to feed captured prisoners figured into the decision to relocate them to the United States. Fort Sheridan was designated as the base camp for northeastern Illinois, but the overflow of prisoners forced the opening of other camps in Michigan, Wisconsin, and Illinois. All of the camps were in secluded areas, far removed from population centers.

When the prisoners arrived at Camp Pine, they were issued dark blue fatigues with the letters PW stenciled on the back of their shirts. Two American officers and thirty-eight enlisted men were assigned to guard the barracks. There was no central heating, and a separate building was provided for bathroom and bathing facilities. Church services were held for the men on Sundays, and the Red Cross made frequent deliveries of supplies.

The surroundings were rough, but morale remained high among the Germans; according to the recollections of most of the prisoners, the guards treated them well and were friendly. The boredom of captivity was alleviated by a daily regimen of sports and games, including soccer, Ping-Pong, and card games. The Pesche Greenhouse, which was located nearby and still operates today, hired several of the men to pick flowers. Fred Pesche spoke German and treated the prisoners just like his regular employees. Other inmates were hired to process food or to work on nearby farms for about eighty cents a day. The men were treated fairly and were well fed by their captors and by the families they worked for.

The internment of 375,000 German prisoners in the United States officially ended on July 23, 1946.

The most interesting story from those years involved a German infantry sergeant named Reinhold Pabel, who escaped from Camp Pine at the end of the war and jumped a train to Chicago, where he changed his name to Phillip Brick. He worked in a bookstore, filed an income tax return for 1946, married an American girl, and had a child with her in 1952—by which time he owned the bookstore. It wasn't until March 9, 1953, that the FBI learned his true identity and arrested him. Pabel was granted a "voluntary departure" by the government in 1953 but was allowed back into the country six months later after his story aroused sympathy among German Americans in Chicago. Reinhold Pabel remained in the country for another ten years before finally moving back to Germany.

McCormick Mansion

From its very beginnings, the Lake Forest estate of Edith and Harold McCormick was a magnificent curiosity. This Italianate villa on the shore of Lake Michigan, which was designed by architect Charles Adams Platt, cost $5 million to build. It was completed in 1912 and had extensive formal gardens, reflecting pools, and even a lawn bowling green. Elm trees lined a walkway that led to a stone tea pavilion, which was built at a cost of $600,000. The service area of the house had twenty-eight rooms just to house the garden staff. Despite all this grandeur, the McCormicks never stayed in this country retreat, and it would later be sold at auction for just pennies on the dollar.

Harold McCormick (the son of Cyrus McCormick, the inventor of the mechanical reaper and founder of the

International Harvester Company) married Edith Rockefeller (the daughter of John D. Rockefeller, founder of Standard Oil) on November 2, 1895. Tragically, in 1901, the McCormick's first child, John, died from scarlet fever. This, and the death of a nine-month-old daughter, left Edith in a state of shock from which she never recovered.

To help her heal from these losses, Harold decided to build her a country estate, and he hired Charles Adams Platt to create a dreamlike design. Using gardens, terraces, and fountains, Platt created the illusion of an Italian villa. Edith dubbed the place Villa Turicum, an ancient Celtic name meaning "settlement on the water." The house was brick covered with off-white stucco and trimmed with limestone; its roof was red tile. The main house had forty-four rooms, including thirteen bedrooms, each of which had its own bath and fireplace.

The mansion was situated on a seventy-five-foot bluff, at the base of which was a forty-foot oval swimming pool and bathhouse. A series of staircases led to the pool—or one could descend via elevator and tunnel.

As work on Villa Turicum was under way, Edith's mental state became erratic. Shortly after the house was completed, she abruptly left her family and entered a sanitarium in Switzerland, where she was treated for a nervous disorder by famed Swiss psychoanalyst Carl Jung. Haunted by the deaths of her children and rumors of her husband's infidelities, she would never completely return to her marriage—or her mansion.

Harold and Edith separated in 1921, and she chose to reside at her grand home on Lake Shore Drive. Even though she had acquired Villa Turicum in the divorce settlement, she refused to go there; it remained fully furnished and staffed, waiting in vain for Edith's return.

During this time, Edith got involved in a ruinous business venture with a protégé of Jung, Edward Krenn, and his partner, Edward Dato. The partnership, underwritten with Standard Oil securities, went bankrupt after the 1929 stock market crash.

Edith died in 1932, and the Rockefeller heiress went to her grave over $3 million in debt. Her belongings, as well as the valuable furnishings and artwork of Villa Turicum, were sold at public auction for next to nothing. And, at the height of the Depression, with no buyers in sight, the legendary house quietly faded into oblivion.

In 1948, the property was finally sold for $75,000 in back taxes, but development plans floundered and Villa Turicum was beginning to crumble. A newspaper account reported that "the grounds have gone to seed and the mansion itself is run down, its marble stairs chipped in spots, windows broken and boarded up, and bare spots on the walls where once murals and tapestries hung." The lawn had become overgrown, and the long walkway that led to the tea pavilion had come to look more like a tunnel than a path. Weeds and plants broke through the cracked driveway, and moss, grass, and eventually shrubs began to take hold on the stone stairway leading down to the beach.

The estate sat empty for years, as one development plan after another fell apart. Meanwhile, the legend of the empty house spread throughout the area. Curiosity-seekers came from all over to see the moldering mansion, and vandals and thieves plundered its marble and woodwork. During one terrible incident, a group of Boy Scouts who were camping nearby staged a mock battle in the mansion, using their hatchets to destroy doors, woodwork, and carvings.

In 1956, the estate was purchased by Robert Kendler of Community Builders, who tore down the house after finding it structurally unsound. The property was divided into lots and in 1972 was marketed as a housing development called Villa Turicum Estates.

Amazingly, portions of the original estate still existed a few years ago. *Weird Illinois* was lucky enough to see the broken stone steps and collapsed structures that continue to be watched over by statuary of broken sea creatures and headless goddesses. Most memorable was the once elaborate staircase that led up from the beach. Old photos show that the steps were once graced by three terraces, a series of fountains with water that cascaded from the mouths of stone dolphins, pelicans, and alligators. Although the teahouse with its cheerful red roof still remains, for the vast majority of this magnificent estate, photos are about all that we have left today.

A SUNDAY KISS. A red Austin-Healey, a gray Ferrari, and a blue Corvette line up for the gala opening of the $3,000,000 Meadowdale Raceway on Sunday. That's secretary Lee Brown giving the kiss to driver Ed Pazdur. (See Page 2)

Meadowdale International Raceway

Lost and forgotten in the woods of the Kane County Forest Preserve is the little known Meadowdale International Raceway. Built in 1958 as a way to promote growth in the Carpentersville area, the original track was a little over three miles long and boasted a number of turns and elevation changes. Its signature feature was the Monza Wall, a 180-degree, steeply banked turn that led into a four-thousand-foot main straightaway.

The inaugural event at Meadowdale turned out to be the beginning of the track's demise. Several major wrecks and a driver's death immediately gave the raceway a "killer" reputation that it was never able to shake. Patterned after European road-racing courses, the track was simply more challenging than many American amateur drivers were used to; it had none of the wide run-off

areas to which they were accustomed.

Moreover, the first several days of racing were plagued by high winds that churned dust into clouds, obscuring the drivers' vision and making the crowds dirty and miserable. Many spectators were so disenchanted that they never returned. Reports of massive traffic jams on local roads and a long walk from the parking area didn't help either.

And finally, the track itself had many flaws: The paving on the Monza Wall was rough, and what trackside run-off area there was ended abruptly at the bridges, which were only as wide as the paving. This created hard walls at severe angles to the track, which were just waiting to catch anyone unfortunate enough to lose control when approaching them.

Track management made many efforts to solve the problems, but as the years passed, there was not enough money to make all the changes that were needed. The only races that were somewhat profitable were rental events that attracted a modest number of spectators. But even these weren't enough to support the facility.

In July 1968, a last-ditch attempt was made to salvage the venue as a major professional racecourse. The Sports Car Club of America's Trans-Am race was held at Meadowdale. To prepare for the event, the Monza Wall was flattened and replaced with a blacktop path. However, the new paving was cheaply done and the surface broke up during the race, causing several accidents.

That season was the last gasp of Meadowdale. The raceway closed for good in 1969, and the track has since been swallowed up by the forest preserve called Raceway Woods. If you visit this lonely place, look down the old track, now broken and overgrown, and imagine what it must have been like in its heyday. Listen closely. Is that the roar of a race engine as it rounds a curve or simply the distant rumble of cars on the highway? Try to believe for just a moment that Meadowdale never closed down and the days of the track are not just a fading memory.

Vishnu Springs

Hidden away in a valley along the La Moine River in McDonough County is a place once considered magical by those who came here seeking peace, serenity, and healing waters. Today the site is just an abandoned village where a once stately hotel is all that remains as testimony to days gone by.

The special nature of the valley's healing waters was first discovered in the 1880s by residents of the nearby town of Colchester. Villagers soon realized that the spring water was different from the drinking water found elsewhere; it was said to have a peculiar salt content, seven medicinal properties, and an appealing taste. Men and women began coming from near and far to sample the spring water.

In an age when effective medicines were rare, the strange-tasting water offered hope to a great many people. People reportedly arrived on crutches and walked away without them. The owners of the land and the springs claimed that the water would "cure or benefit all kinds of debility, neuralgia, rheumatism, palpitation of the heart, dyspepsia, kidney trouble, worms" and even "female troubles, dislocated limbs, broken backs, deafness, blindness and laziness." And people believed the claims. They began buying the water for twenty-five cents a gallon and carried it home with them in jugs.

The owners of the spring were not immune to the magical charm of the area either. They named the place Vishnu after one of the owners, Darius Hicks, read about the 1861 discovery of Angkor Wat, in Cambodia, perfectly preserved for three hundred years by vegetation growing out of the Krishna River. Vishnu was a Hindu god, whose earthly incarnation was the Krishna River.

Deciding that Vishnu would become a health resort, Hicks began construction of a hotel, and in September 1889, the Capitol Hotel opened for business. As Hicks began publicizing the springs, the land in the valley went up for sale, and people quickly bought up lots selling for $30 apiece. By the following year, Vishnu had stores, a restaurant, a livery stable, a blacksmith, and a photo gallery. Hicks organized the Vishnu Transfer Line that made trips from Colchester to the new resort. For seventy-five cents, a passenger could be transported to Vishnu, have dinner, and then be transported back.

Hicks continued making improvements in the hotel. He bought an organ for the parlor and installed running water and an elevator. He added amusements, like a horse-powered carousel, and soon the lawn around the hotel was fitted with swings, hammocks, a croquet grounds, a picnic area, and a large pond that was dubbed Lake Vishnu and stocked with goldfish. He arranged activities such as dances, band concerts, and holiday celebrations, organized a literary society, and opened a schoolhouse.

The town itself, however, was not growing. Most of Hicks's efforts were being spent on a small number of full-time residents and the travelers who came to take the waters. There were never more than about thirty homes in the valley, and the hotel was not active in cold-weather months. For this reason, the village never really gained an economic base, even as a popular resort, since there was no railroad connection to it and it was far from any sizable town or city.

Meanwhile, Hicks's personal life was filled with problems. In 1889, he had married Hattie Rush, who had been married before and had children of her own, including a twelve-year-old daughter named Maud. Hattie suffered from a variety of illnesses and died in 1896. Scandalously, Hicks soon married his stepdaughter, Maud. Although the marriage was not actually incestuous, it was seen as improper, and Hicks was shunned by the more conservative members of the community.

In 1903, two events would take place that would lead

to the decline of Vishnu. On one warm summer day, the carousel was filled with children, carefully watched over by the supervisor, who made sure that the horse that turned the gears continued to walk at a steady pace.

Somehow, the supervisor's shirtsleeve became tangled in the gears of the carousel, and he was pulled into them. The children's cries of delight turned to screams of terror as the man was crushed to death. The carousel ground to

By the 1920s, Vishnu was nothing more than a ghost town, abandoned and nearly forgotten in the secluded valley.

a complete halt, and it never ran again.

Later that year Maud Hicks, who had borne Hicks a son earlier, gave birth to a daughter, but both mother and child died during the delivery. Maud's death was a tremendous shock to Darius Hicks. On the day following her funeral, he took his young son and left Vishnu, never to return. But his troubles were not yet over.

Hicks bought a farm a short distance north, near Blandinsville, and soon hired a housekeeper named Nellie Darrah. In the winter of 1908, Nellie became pregnant by Hicks, and when he refused to marry her, she had an abortion that resulted in her being hospitalized. When Nellie threatened to publicize their affair and her travails, Hicks wrote a letter that explained his entire situation, then shot himself in the head. Hicks was dead at the age of 58.

The death of Darius Hicks sounded a death knell for the community of Vishnu Springs. Even after moving away, Hicks had been the main promoter of the town. Now there was no one who was as invested, both financially and personally, in the village.

The hotel was sold and left to decay. By the 1920s, Vishnu was nothing more than a ghost town, abandoned and nearly forgotten in the secluded valley. Vandals stole valuable hotel furnishings while less destructive visitors filled the inside of the hotel with their signatures. The earliest names scrawled on the walls are those of Marie Feris and Lil Baker, who came to the Capitol in 1893, when it was still in business. The historic graffiti is still there, but the more recent marks and scrawls lack the charm and innocence of the signatures of the past.

In 1935, a man named Ira Post began a restoration

effort on the hotel. While he met with some success, after he died in 1951, the hotel struggled and was eventually abandoned. The grounds soon became overgrown and unkempt once more.

Other ventures, including a commune, all failed, and today Vishnu is little more than a crumbling shadow of its former self. Despite the interest of local societies and historic groups, the valley remained private property until the death of the last member of the Post family. Since then, the status of the land has remained in limbo, and the ultimate fate of Vishnu remains a mystery.

Vishnu today is a part of Illinois history that most have forgotten. To reach the site requires not only more than two miles of walking through dense forest but also a great sense of direction. If you should be lucky enough to find the place, however, you will feel as though you have stepped into another time. Little remains here except for the old hotel, but if you look closely, you are bound to stumble across other pieces of the past. Remnants of gardens remain among the undergrowth, along with forgotten souvenirs of the town that was once nestled under the trees. The stream that trickles into Darius Hicks's lake may still reveal a goldfish or two, descendants of those left here more than a century ago.

But be careful where you step in Vishnu and leave behind nothing that you bring with you. It is up to the caretakers of the past to preserve what the state of Illinois will not. Years ago Ira Post's niece and daughter erected a sign at the entrance to Vishnu. While the sign is gone, the sentiment behind it remains. It read in part: "Vishnu Springs was preserved as planned by Ira Post. The spring water of the wonderful world of nature is left to enjoy . . . the springs should be left as nature provided it. Take care of it all and then all will be benefited in the years to come. Ira Post died in 1951. The wishes expressed here were his. Help us to see that his wishes are carried out."

INDEX

Page numbers in **bold** refer to photos and illustrations.

WEIRD ILLINOIS

By
Troy Taylor

Edited by
Mark Moran and Mark Sceurman

ACKNOWLEDGMENTS

This has not been a solitary journey. There have been many who have helped and supported me along the way: Mark and Mark from *Weird N.J.*, John Winterbauer, Jim David, Jim Graczyk, Tom and Michelle Bonadurer, Jerome Pohlen, Stu Fliege, Bill Alsing, Brady Kesner, Len Adams, Bill Nunes, John Allen, Richard Lindberg, Jim Ross and Jerry McLanahan, my wife, Amy Taylor, and of course the dozens and dozens of people who provided great information and who contacted me about their weird stories, strange sites, and local legends. It's been a long, strange trip.

Publisher: Barbara J. Morgan
Assoc. Managing Editor: Emily Seese
Production: Della R. Mancuso
Mancuso Associates, Inc.,
North Salem, NY

SHOW US YOUR WEIRD!

Do you know of a weird site found somewhere in the United States, or can you tell us about a strange experience you've had? If so, we'd like to hear about it! We believe that every town has at least one great tale to tell, and we're listening. It could be a cursed road, haunted abandoned site, odd local character, or bizarre historic event. In most cases these tales are told only in the towns in which they originated. But why keep them to yourself when you could share them with all of America? So come on and fill us in on all the weirdness that's lurking in your backyard!

You can e-mail us at: Editor@WeirdUS.com,
or write to us at:
Weird U.S., P.O. Box 1346, Bloomfield, NJ 07003.

www.weirdus.com